RETHINKING
LIFE & DEATH

RETHINKING LIFE & DEATH

The Collapse of Our Traditional Ethics

PETER SINGER

St. Martin's Press
New York

ISBN 0-312-11880-5

First published in Australia by The Text Publishing Company

10 9 8 7 6 5 4 3 2

To Helga Kuhse, with thanks for fourteen years
as a friend and colleague in which we have
together rethought the ethics of life and death.

ACKNOWLEDGMENTS

For the past fourteen years Helga Kuhse and I have worked together in the general area covered by this book. We have learned from each other, and our thoughts have become intertwined to such an extent that it is now difficult to disentangle the ideas that were originally mine from those that were hers. Anyone who reads this book alongside her *The Sanctity of Life Doctrine in Medicine — A Critique* will see the extent of my debt to her. To mention just one instance, I have made good use of her perception that distinctions commonly used in medical ethics by those who wish to uphold the sanctity of human life — for example, the distinction between ordinary and extraordinary means of treatment — serve to disguise the quality of life judgments that are in fact being made. I have also drawn heavily, in Chapter 6, from our joint work, *Should the Baby Live?*, while Chapter 7 owes much to her detailed knowledge of the practice of euthanasia in the Netherlands. Beyond all that, however, without Helga's intellectual companionship and encouragement I would probably have stopped working in this field long ago, and this book would not have been written.

I am grateful to Michael Heyward and Di Gribble of Text Publishing for persuading me that this book needed to be written. Once the book was underway, both Michael Heyward and Bob Weil of St Martin's Press, New York, helped me shape it. Another debt is to my mother, Cora Singer, who has for many years maintained clippings files for the Centre for Human Bioethics. These were a valuable source of material for several chapters. Greg Pence generously made available to me the typescript of the second edition of his *Classic Cases in Medical Ethics*, a wonderful mine of information to be published by McGraw-Hill in 1995. Co-editing *The Great Ape Project* with Paola Cavalieri contributed substantially to my thinking in Chapter 8. Carole Outterson kindly provided me with unpublished data from her survey of the attitudes of senior English paediatricians. John Dwyer assisted with some legal materials. The task of improving a first draft was aided by detailed comments from Helga Kuhse, Paola Cavalieri, Greg Pence, Jeff McMahan and Bob Weil. Last and definitely least, but still worthy of thanks, was Esther Singer's research into the concept of death in *Monty Python's Flying Circus*.

CONTENTS

PROLOGUE

After ruling our thoughts and our decisions about life and death for nearly two thousand years, the traditional western ethic has collapsed. To mark the precise moment when the old ethic gave way, a future historian might choose 4 February 1993, when Britain's highest court ruled that the doctors attending a young man named Anthony Bland could lawfully act to end the life of their patient. A Dutch historian, however, might choose instead 30 November 1993, the date on which the Netherlands parliament finally put into law the guidelines under which Dutch doctors had for some years already been openly giving lethal injections to patients who were suffering unbearably without hope of improvement, and who asked to be helped to die. Americans have not witnessed such momentous judicial decisions or votes in Congress, but twelve Michigan jurors may have spoken for the nation when, on 2 May 1994, they acquitted Dr Jack Kevorkian of a charge of assisting a man named Thomas Hyde to commit suicide. Their refusal to convict Kevorkian was a major victory for the cause of physician-assisted suicide, for it is hard to imagine a clearer case than this one. Kevorkian freely admitted supplying the carbon monoxide gas, tubing and a mask to Hyde, who had then used them to end a life made unbearable by a rapidly progressing nerve disorder known as Lou Gehrig's disease, or ALS.

These are the surface tremors resulting from major shifts deep in the bedrock of western ethics. We are going through a period of transition in our attitude to the sanctity of human life. Such transitions cause confusion and division. That is why, for example, although the majority of people in most countries support laws allowing abortion, others sincerely believe that abortion is so great a wrong that they are prepared to block access to clinics that carry out abortions, to damage the clinics themselves and even to go to the paradoxical extreme of murdering doctors because they performed abortions. Other symptoms of our bewilderment can be found everywhere. Here are three examples:

• The American Medical Association has a policy that says a doctor can ethically withdraw all means of life-prolonging medical treatment, *including food and water*, from a patient in an irreversible coma. Yet the same policy insists that 'the physician should not intentionally cause death'.[1]

• Twenty years after the introduction of 'brain death' as a criterion of the death of a human being, one-third of doctors and nurses who work with brain-dead patients at hospitals in Cleveland, Ohio, thought that people whose brains had died could be classified as dead because they were 'irreversibly dying' or because they had an 'unacceptable quality of life'.[2] Organ transplantation is based on the idea that we die when our brain is dead—yet even the doctors and nurses most closely involved do not really accept this.

• A recent survey asked paediatricians in senior positions in the United Kingdom to say whether they agreed or disagreed with a number of different statements, among which were:

1. Abortion is morally permissible after twenty-four weeks if the fetus is abnormal;

2. There is no moral difference between the abortion of a fetus and the active termination of the life of a newborn infant when both have the same gestational age [that is, the same age dating from conception] and suffer from the same defects;

3. There are no circumstances in which it is morally permissible to take active steps to terminate the life of an infant with severe defects.

Nearly 40 per cent of the senior paediatricians responding indicated that they agreed with all three of these statements, even though you can't agree without contradicting yourself.

Each of these three examples is a snapshot that catches people halfway through a shift in their views. The American Medical Association has come to see the pointlessness of keeping people alive for ten, twenty or thirty years, if there is no hope they will ever recover consciousness—but it has not yet summoned the nerve to abandon the traditional doctrine that it is always wrong intentionally to end the life of an innocent human being. Health-care professionals who work with organ transplantation have been taught that patients whose hearts still beat are dead because their brains are dead, but have had difficulty reconciling this with their own feelings and way of thinking. Senior paediatricians have come to accept prenatal diagnosis and late termination of pregnancy if a serious abnormality is found. They also can see that there is no real difference between a late fetus and a newborn infant at the same gestational age. But active euthanasia for severely disabled infants remains illegal and is not sanctioned by medical codes of ethics, no matter how premature the infants may be, or how serious their defects.[3]

These are not academic problems found in the abstract theories of philosophers who remain remote from the real world, publishing papers in learned journals. These contradictions have direct consequences for human beings at the most deeply significant moments of their lives. The farce that the traditional ethic has become is also a tragedy that is endlessly repeated with minor variations in intensive care units all over the world. Since 1989, for me at least, the icon of this tragic farce has been the image of Rudy Linares, a twenty-three-year-old Chicago housepainter, standing in a hospital ward, keeping nurses at bay with a gun while he disconnects the respirator that for eight months has kept his comatose infant son Samuel alive. When Samuel is free of the respirator at last, Linares cradles him in his arms until, half an hour later, the child dies. Then Linares puts down the gun and, weeping, gives himself up. He acted against both the law and the traditional ethic that upholds the sanctity of human life; but his impulses were in accordance with an emerging ethical attitude that is more defensible than the old one, and will replace it.[4]

The traditional ethic is still defended by bishops and conservative bioethicists who speak in reverent tones about the intrinsic value of all human life, irrespective of its nature or quality. But, like the new clothes worn by the emperor, these solemn phrases seem true and substantial only while we are intimidated into uncritically accepting that all human life has some special dignity or worth. Once challenged, the traditional ethic crumples. Weakened by the decline in religious authority and the rise of a better understanding of the origins and nature of our species, that ethic is now being brought undone by changes in medical technology with which its inflexible strictures simply cannot cope.

This is not a cause for dismay or despair. A period of transition on so fundamental an issue is bound to be filled with uncertainty and confusion, especially among those who have been brought up to accept the traditional ethic as beyond question. But it is also a period of opportunity, in which we have an historic chance to shape something better, an ethic that does not need to be propped up by transparent fictions no-one can really believe, an ethic that is more compassionate and more responsive to what people decide for themselves, an ethic that avoids prolonging life when to do so is obviously pointless, and an ethic that is less arbitrary in its inclusions and exclusions than our traditional one. To achieve a better approach to life-and-death decision-making, however, we need to be open about the ways in which the traditional ethic has failed.

Readers will already know that I do not speak in hushed tones when I refer to the traditional ethic of the sanctity of human life. Nor do I try to disguise its failings by invoking sophisticated distinctions and complex doctrines. I am not interested in continuing to patch and adjust the traditional approach so that we can pretend that it works when it plainly does not. The failures of the traditional ethic have become so glaring that these strategies can only offer short-term solutions to its problems, solutions that, like the policy of the American Medical Association on patients in irreversible coma, need to be reformulated almost as soon as they are pronounced. To break with the traditional way of approaching these issues is inevitably to clash with our usual moral beliefs. Some find this shocking. In part, this has more to do with the directness with which I describe what we already do than with any radically new suggestions I make about what we should do. When sensitive practices have long been veiled, ripping the veils aside can be shocking enough. But I readily admit that that is not the only reason why this book will shock readers. Some of the conclusions that I draw are very different from the ethical views most people hold today. That, however, is not a ground for dismissing them. If every proposal for reform in ethics that differed from accepted moral views had been rejected for that reason alone, we would still be torturing heretics, enslaving members of conquered races, and treating women as the property of their husbands. The views I put forward should be judged not by the extent to which they clash with accepted moral views, but on the basis of the arguments by which they are defended.

Supporters of the traditional sanctity of life ethic who know my previous writings will not be surprised to find themselves under siege in this book. But the book may also make uneasy some who have more affinity with the position I defend. This will include some who believe that they can coherently defend liberal abortion laws by saying that they are 'pro-choice', without having to say when human life begins, or to show why the fetus should not count as a human being. Other natural allies of my position who may not like what I say here are those who have proposed changing the definition of brain death so that the death of the parts of the brain responsible for consciousness is sufficient for a patient to be declared dead. Even supporters of the present definition of brain death may be uncomfortable with the argument I put forward. These people may be disturbed because they have sought to present what they advocate in a form that leaves intact as much as possible of our traditional ethic. For those concerned with only one particular reform, that is a sensible political tactic—why take on the whole world when you can get by with only the anti-abortion movement against you?

We can try to deal one at a time with the problems of the sanctity of life ethic. But the overall result will be a jigsaw puzzle, the pieces of which have to be forced into place, until the whole picture is under so much pressure that it buckles and breaks apart. I think there is a better way. There is a larger picture, in which all the pieces fit together. Whatever issue of the moment may concern us, in the long run we all need to see this larger picture. It will offer practical solutions to problems we now find insoluble, and allow us to act compassionately and humanely, where our ethic now leads us to outcomes that nobody wants. I want to paint that larger picture.

PART I

Doubtful Endings

BIRTH AFTER DEATH

I don't know... I don't know how far we can go.
DR JAMES JACKSON, CHAIRMAN, MATERNAL AND CHILD
HEALTH SERVICES, HIGHLAND GENERAL HOSPITAL, CALIFORNIA

AN AMERICAN STORY

Brandishing a meat cleaver, Trisha Marshall burst into the apartment of a disabled man in his early sixties. She demanded money but the man, both of whose legs had been amputated, had been robbed before. Now he was prepared. He pulled out a gun and shot Marshall in the head. Then he called the police.

This incident took place on the night of 19 April 1993, in North Oakland, across the bay from San Francisco. Two days later, Marshall, now in the intensive care unit at Highland General Hospital, was declared brain dead. She was twenty-eight years old, and the mother of four children, all of them being cared for by other people. Berkeley police said that she was under investigation for several other robberies. She had cocaine and alcohol in her blood. She was also seventeen weeks pregnant.[1]

Although Marshall was brain dead, a respirator maintained her breathing, her heart was beating, her body was warm, and her bodily functions were continuing. Her parents and her boyfriend came to the hospital. Her boyfriend said he was the father of the child. Both he and Marshall's parents wanted the hospital to do everything possible to allow the baby to be born.

Ethical dilemmas in medicine have been widely discussed in

the United States since 1975, when the parents of Karen Ann Quinlan asked her doctors to turn off their comatose daughter's respirator. Most American hospitals now have ethics committees to consider cases that raise tricky problems. Trisha Marshall's treatment was discussed extensively by the ethics committee at Highland Hospital. The committee tried to establish what she would have wanted, and it also tried to do what it thought to be in the interests of the fetus. What it deliberately did not consider were the circumstances in which Marshall died, the fact that she had either not wanted to, or had not been able to, care for her existing children, and the cost of the intensive care required. The ethics committee agreed with the doctors that Marshall's bodily functions should be maintained as long as possible, so that the fetus could have a chance of developing to a stage at which it could be born.

When this decision became known, Highland General Hospital was criticised for what it was trying to do. The critics pointed out that, like most American public hospitals in run-down urban areas, Highland Hospital tries to care for the victims of crime, mental illness, AIDS, drug addiction and malnutrition, on a budget which is simply not adequate to the task. Maintaining Trisha Marshall's pregnancy was estimated to cost $200,000, with at least an additional $200,000 needed for the care of the baby, who would be born prematurely.[2] Dashka Slater, a journalist who covered the story, later wrote: 'Nearly every telephone receptionist, desk clerk, cop or librarian who learned what I was working on had an opinion about the Marshall case, and that opinion could usually be summed up in one blunt statement: "What a waste of money".'[3] George Wilson, chief of medical policy for Medical, the California state health insurer, said that Medical would not meet any costs incurred after Marshall's death: 'It's like the case of those Siamese twins who were just separated. The family has the right to ask for heroic measures, but does that family have the right to pull in society [to pay for it] while at the same time we have a perfectly miserable rate of immunizing kids at ten dollars each?'[4]

Dashka Slater reported that the doctors involved in the case 'admit to feeling as if they are being swept along by the rush of medical progress. There were times in my conversations with them when they almost seemed to be pleading for someone to slow them down, or at least for an ethical rudder to steer them through the rapids'. Slater's article contains this passage from an interview with Dr James Jackson who, as chairman of Maternal and Child Health Services at Highland Hospital, had overall responsibility for the attempt to save Marshall's child:

> Organ transplants are available, now we've just taken a brain-dead woman 105 days, maybe next time we'll start carrying them...' he breaks off, his mind boggling at the thought of what he and his colleagues might manage to do next. 'I don't know,' he finishes. 'I don't know how far we can go, but there must be some constraints. There's only so many medical resources on this planet.

For three and a half months Marshall's heart continued to beat while the respirator pushed air into her lungs, and nutrients were passed down a tube through her nose and into her stomach. Nurses moved her limbs to prevent them from stiffening, changed her position to stop bedsores, and kept her body clean. On 3 August, a baby boy was delivered by a caesarean birth, a little premature, but healthy. The media hailed the hospital's achievement as a medical miracle. A doctor from the hospital described the baby as 'cute'.

The story did not finish there. The baby, named Darious Marshall, spent three and a half weeks in an intensive care nursery, and then was declared fit to go home. But to whose home should he go? Marshall's family wanted to take Darious home. So did her former boyfriend. A custody dispute began. It was settled when a blood test showed that the boyfriend was not the father of the baby.

It is instructive to compare the story of Trisha Marshall with another case, in some ways similar and in others different. For this, we need to go halfway around the world, to Germany, and back six months before Marshall's attempted robbery went so badly wrong.

On 5 October 1992, Marion Ploch, an eighteen-year-old German dental assistant, left her place of work in southern Germany and set out to drive home. Between Feucht and Altdorf her car hit a tree. When the ambulance reached the scene of the accident, about a quarter of an hour later, she was unconscious and was found to have a fractured skull. A helicopter was called, and she was taken to a hospital in the quiet university town of Erlangen. Her parents, Gabriele and Hans Ploch, were called to the hospital, where they were told that their daughter was in intensive care, but could not survive. They were asked if they were prepared to allow her organs to be donated to others, but they refused.

Then came a startling piece of information. Their daughter, the Plochs were told, was pregnant. The pregnancy had begun about thirteen weeks before. Did they know who the father was? They did not. Marion Ploch was single and had not told her parents that she was expecting a baby, or that she had a special boyfriend. The doctors then told Marion's parents that although their daughter either was, or soon would be, brain dead, it might be possible to maintain her bodily functions until March— another five months—when the fetus could survive. Would Mr and Mrs Ploch agree to their daughter remaining on a respirator in order to make this possible? Under pressure, they gave their consent. Later they were to say that they had consented only after being threatened with the loss of custody of their daughter if they refused.[5]

Three days after the accident, medical tests showed that brain death had occurred. Soon after, Mr and Mrs Ploch reached breaking point. They tried to withdraw their consent to the continued maintenance of their daughter's bodily functions. The doctors, however, said that the life of the fetus was at stake, and they could not turn off the respirator. In desperation, the Plochs turned for help to the popular press. The 'Erlangen Baby' case, named after the town in which the hospital was situated, was soon in the headlines.

The doctors' decision to maintain Marion Ploch's bodily functions was attacked with a vehemence that makes the criticism of Highland General Hospital look like encouragement. No doubt because in Germany the shadow of Nazism hangs over every ethical issue, and also because German public hospitals are not under such severe financial pressure as American ones, the focus of the criticism was not on the cost of the procedure, but on the issue of human dignity. Hanna Wolf, a member of the German parliament, said that Marion Ploch had been 'degraded to a nutrient fluid, disposable after use'. Alice Schwarzer, editor of the German feminist magazine *Emma*, declared: 'The Pope will like it— women as incubators. I think it's perverse.' The hospital was flooded with abusive mail. Dr Johannes Scheele, professor of surgery at the hospital, and the doctor ultimately in charge of Marion Ploch's body, was likened to Josef Mengele, the chief doctor of Auschwitz. When a newspaper reported that Marion Ploch's body was given physical exercises—a normal procedure with patients in a coma, to prevent their limbs locking up— graffiti appeared prominently on the wall of the hospital, referring to its 'gymnastics for corpses'.

Another German doctor, Julius Hackethal, was not so sure that Marion Ploch really was a corpse. He attempted to lay a criminal charge against Scheele for causing 'bodily harm, poisoning and maltreatment of a patient in his care'. In defence of his view that Ploch was still a patient, he added: 'The expression "brain death" is a verbal construction that avoids the heart of the matter. In fact only the cerebrum of the patient does not function, but the rest of the brain works very well. She is alive.' But Hackethal found little support for this view, the general opinion being that 'all parts of the brain are dead...including the lower and older parts'. The public prosecutor before whom Hackethal had made his complaint refused to proceed with the charge.

While the storm of controversy raged around them, the doctors continued to do everything possible to keep the fetus alive. Scheele said: 'We don't see any ethical reason simply to let the embryo die'. The clinic's director, Dr Franz Paul Gall, agreed: 'The child's right to life requires the use of modern technological methods'. And in response to the wave of criticism that using Marion Ploch's body as an incubator showed a lack of respect to her, the clinic's legal adviser, Professor Hans-Bernhard Würmeling, said: 'Respect for the dead body is not an absolute ethical demand, as the right to life is'.

There was, however, some disagreement between the doctors and their legal adviser when they were asked what would happen if it became clear that the fetus had been damaged by the accident, or by its mother's subsequent treatment. Würmeling said that in this case it would be justifiable to turn off the machines. On the other hand Scheele said that such damage would not make a difference, because 'It is not up to us to decide when a life is valuable'. Although Würmeling is a highly respected legal scholar, in this situation he, like all other German lawyers, was guessing. German law had simply never faced the question of whether there is a legal obligation to support fetal life in a brain-dead woman.

Despite the abusive tone of many of the attacks on the doctors at the hospital in Erlangen, the German debate went more deeply into the fundamental questions of life and death than the American discussion. But it was also more confused. At least part of the unease caused by Marion Ploch's fate seems to have been due to resistance to the idea that she was really dead. Hackethal's dismissal of 'brain death' as a mere verbal formula gained no support among his medical colleagues, but it found a popular echo in the frequent comment that the machines should be switched off so that Marion Ploch 'could die with dignity'. Yet if brain death *is* death, she was already dead: how then could she be 'allowed to die', whether with dignity or without it?

Hackethal also had some religious support, right within the Erlangen hospital itself. Wilhelm Polster, the chaplain for the intensive care unit, was reported as saying: 'I don't accept the medical statements. For me a dead woman is someone who lies there white and stiff. In the end nobody knows when the soul leaves the body.' But the Catholic hospital chaplain Rainer Denkler claimed to know: 'The soul is the personality. As long as somebody is lying in a coma, there is still a capacity for a relationship. In her case the soul has departed.' He did not say how he knew this.

The law contributed to this confusion. German law, like the law in every developed nation (with the exception of Japan), accepts brain death as death for all legal purposes. Yet the judge of the local court appointed one of Marion Ploch's aunts as a guardian of her interests. Judge Gerold Wahl based this decision on the German Guardianship Law, which exists in order to allow the courts to appoint guardians for intellectually disabled people. But intellectually disabled people are alive, and have interests that may need to be protected. Dead people do not have interests in the same sense, and courts do not appoint guardians to look after their interests. What interests was Marion Ploch supposed to have? That question is not easy to answer. We could attempt to answer it by asking: what would she have wanted? But how could we answer such a question? Not surprisingly, Marion Ploch had never discussed such a bizarre end to her bodily existence. She might have wanted to be buried as soon as possible, or she might have preferred to give her fetus—the only child she could ever have—a chance of survival. No-one knew.

What of the interests of the fetus? Surprisingly, some of those whom one might have expected to be its strongest supporters were reluctant to defend its claims to life. The Roman Catholic chaplain Rainer Denkler said: 'I cannot share the decision to respirate and nourish a brain dead young woman for several months in order to make possible the birth of a 14-week-old embryo'. Johannes Gründel, a Catholic theologian at the University of Munich, suggested that to shut off intensive care would simply be 'to allow nature to take its course', and this would not be morally equivalent to an abortion. Dietrich Roessler, professor of theology at the University of Tübingen, maintained that 'the right of intact living and dying includes the right to a dignified burial, and it is to be accepted that it is the destiny of mother and child to die'. The mass-circulation tabloid *Bild-Zeitung* had little hesitation about speaking on behalf of the Creator. It had campaigned against the doctors' plan from the start. One of its stories carried the headline 'Whoever interferes with Creation will one day be punished'.

On 16 November 1992 the pregnancy spontaneously miscarried, and the fetus was born dead. The reason for the miscarriage will never be known, for Mr and Mrs Ploch—who had presumably had enough of modern medicine—refused permission for an autopsy of the mother or the fetus.

OUR CHOICE

'I don't know,' Dr Jackson of Highland General Hospital said to Dashka Slater, 'I don't know how far we can go, but there must be some constraints.' The cases of Trisha Marshall and Marion Ploch both raise the question of how far modern medicine can and should go. Jackson was unusually candid about one motivating factor that leads his colleagues to try to go one step further than others have gone:

> When I first came here I said, 'They do so much here with so little and they get so very little credit.'...So maybe we needed a Trisha Marshall. Maybe we needed a bridge over the River Kwai. Just as

they built that bridge for the morale of the men, it was a great morale-booster for our staff that they could do something like this and have it come out so well. People would expect us to make mistakes. But we built the bridge. We successfully bridged the river.

The metaphor is a revealing one. When the British prisoners of the Japanese built the bridge over the River Kwai, they may have boosted their own morale, but they were building a bridge that their captors wanted, and so contributing to the Japanese war effort. Their commitment to the success of the enterprise, understandable as it was in their harsh circumstances, showed that they had lost sight of the broader goals for which the war was being fought. Is Jackson admitting that his hospital team had also lost sight of the goals which medicine should strive to achieve? Are the bright lights of the television cameras pushing doctors to try to be the first in the world to achieve the next medical miracle?

There is a tendency for today's miracle to become tomorrow's routine procedure. Here is Jackson again:

I personally think that if you put another one of these cases in the literature, the next time this occurs it almost compels [doctors] to go full-blast, doing whatever they can do...the next hospital faced with this decision would probably end up doing just what we did. They would say, 'It's been done, we have the resources, and although we may be reluctant about committing them, we have no choice.'

A hospital, operating within a particular legal and ethical framework, may feel that it has no choice but to keep a brain-dead woman on a respirator for three months so that her fetus can survive. But we, as a community, do have a choice. Our difficulty is that the choice is an ethical one, and when it comes to questions about prolonging life or ending it, our ethics are in a confused, contradictory mess. How should we treat someone whose brain is dead, but whose body is still warm and breathing? Is a fetus the kind of being whose life we should make great efforts to preserve? If so, should these efforts be made irrespective of their cost? Shall we just ignore the other lives that might be saved with the medical resources required? Should efforts to preserve the fetus be made only when it is clear that the mother would have wanted this? Or when the (presumed?) father or other close relatives ask for the fetus to be saved? Or do we make these efforts because the fetus has a right to life which could only be overridden by the right of the pregnant woman to control her own body—and in this case there is no living pregnant woman whose rights override those of the fetus?

We need the answers to these questions before we can make a soundly based choice in situations like those that occurred in Oakland and Erlangen. If we cannot answer them, we will find ourselves confronted with more medical miracles, wondering if we would not prefer the genie who has produced them to go back into the bottle. But so far we have looked at only one corner of a much larger area that needs the same kind of hard ethical thought. Here, much more briefly, are a few events from the 1980s and 1990s that show the kind of questions we need to answer:

• If you are dead when your brain is dead, when do you die if you never had a proper brain in the first place? In both America and Italy, the parents of babies born with a brain stem but no other parts of the brain have asked that the baby's organs be donated to other babies who would die without them. But usually when organs are taken for transplantation, the patient is declared 'brain dead' when the brain has irreversibly ceased to function. (To wait for the heart to stop beating is to risk damaging the organs.) If a baby effectively does not have a brain, can it be considered brain dead? May the baby's organs be taken while its heart is still beating?

• In two famous cases, one in the United States and the other in England, Nancy Cruzan and Anthony Bland were not brain dead, but in what is called a 'persistent vegetative state'. Neither would ever recover consciousness. They did not need respirators, but they were being fed by a tube. In each case, their families wanted the tube withdrawn, and the highest courts of the countries in which they lived had to decide whether to allow this request to be acted upon.

• The ability to fertilise a human egg in a laboratory and transfer it to a woman's womb has helped thousands of infertile couples to have children, but it has also raised a host of new ethical dilemmas. Among them is the status of the newly fertilised embryos. Should we try to preserve their lives? If the embryo is not inside a pregnant woman, the woman's rights over her own body cannot settle the issue. We have to ask: when does a human life first have a claim to protection?

• In 1982 'Baby Doe' was born in Bloomington, Indiana, with Down syndrome and some additional problems that meant she could not digest food. Surgery could have overcome the problem, but the parents refused permission for an operation. Without it Baby Doe would die. The Indiana Supreme Court was asked to decide whether the operation should take place.

The advances of medical technology have forced us to think about issues that we previously had no need to face. When there was nothing we could do to preserve the lives of fetuses inside the bodies of pregnant women whose brains had died, we did not have to make up our minds about the status of a fetus whose mother had died months before it could be born. When infants born without brains never lived more than a few days, and organ transplantation did not exist, it was easy enough to say that *every* human being has a right to life. We did not have to ask whether some lives are more valuable than others. Now we cannot avoid that question, unless we are willing to be propelled along willy-nilly by the desires of doctors and scientists to be the first with the next medical miracle. Technology creates an imperative: 'If we can do it, we will do it'. Ethics asks: 'We can do it, but should we do it?' But the ethic within which we try to answer this question stands on shaky foundations that few of us now accept. Confused and contradictory judgments are the result.

HOW DEATH WAS REDEFINED

I'll be the judge, I'll be the jury,' said cunning old Fury;
'I'll try the whole cause, and condemn you to death.
LEWIS CARROLL, *ALICE'S ADVENTURES IN WONDERLAND*

PINK, SUPPLE... AND DEAD

Whatever happened to the old idea of death? By this I mean the idea so nicely summed up by the Erlangen Hospital chaplain, Wilhelm Polster: 'For me a dead woman is someone who lies there white and stiff.' When he said that, in the intensive care unit in which he worked Marion Ploch was a healthy pink colour. Her heart was beating. Blood was circulating through her body. She was not stiff. She was warm to the touch. And according to German law, she was dead. Trisha Marshall's body was similarly alive while her fetus developed inside her womb. Californian law said that at the time her son was born she had been a corpse for more than three months.

The idea that someone is dead when their brain is dead is, at best, rather odd. Human beings are not the only living things in the world. All living things eventually die, and we can generally tell when they are alive and when they are dead. Isn't the distinction between life and death so basic that what counts as dead for a human being also counts as dead for a dog, a parrot, a prawn, an oyster, an oak, or a cabbage? But what is the common element here? According to the classic account, death was 'the permanent cessation of the flow of vital bodily fluids'.[1] Living things, this account assumed, have vital bodily fluids. They may be blood, sap or something else, but when they stop flowing forever, all living things die.

Unfortunately, the classical definition of death is circular. How do we know whether a bodily fluid is a 'vital' one? By seeing if the being dies when it permanently stops flowing. But how do we know if the being has died? By seeing if its vital bodily fluids have stopped flowing. So we go around again. Still, for a long time the classical definition worked well enough. As recently as 1968, the fourth edition of *Black's Law Dictionary* carried the following version of the classical definition of death, which avoided the problem of circularity: 'DEATH. The cessation of life; the ceasing to exist; defined by physicians as a total stoppage of the circulation of the blood, and a cessation of the animal and vital functions consequent thereupon, such as respiration, pulsation, etc'.[2]

Using this definition, doctors knew that, if breathing and circulation had ceased, then after a decent interval you could be sure that the patient was dead. In much the same way, gardeners know that if the sap has permanently ceased to flow and the twigs are stiff and dry the tree is dead. Once those things have happened, others soon follow. The patient, or tree, begins to rot, or— depending on its nature and the climate—to dry out. Putrefaction and decay show that in the end the same grim reaper takes us all.

As a fan of the 1970s British television comedy series 'Monty Python's Flying Circus', I cannot now think of the question of defining death without recalling a sketch in which John Cleese complains to the owner of a pet shop about the condition of his recently purchased Norwegian Blue parrot. When the shopkeeper suggests that the bird may be keeping very still because it is pining for the fjords, Cleese explodes that the bird is 'stone dead...definitely deceased...bleeding demised...ceased to be...a stiff'.[3] Could anyone use such language about Trisha Marshall or Marion Ploch, as each lay, breathing, warm and supple, in the intensive care unit? Dead, *really dead*, seems to be the same for every living being. But to be 'brain dead' is something that can only happen to a being with a brain. It can't happen to a cabbage, nor to an oak, and not really to an oyster either. And though it would in theory be possible, no-one talks about 'brain death' in the case of dogs or parrots either. 'Brain death' is only for humans. Isn't it odd that for a human being to die requires a different concept of death from that which we apply to other living beings?

The question is a vital one, in every sense of the term. When warm, breathing, pulsating human beings are declared to be dead, they lose their basic human rights. They are not given life-support. If their relatives consent (or in some countries, as long as they have not registered a refusal of consent), their hearts and other organs can be cut out of their bodies and given to strangers. The change in our conception of death that excluded these human beings from the moral community was among the first in a series of dramatic changes in our view of life and death. Yet, in sharp contrast to other changes in this area, it met with virtually no opposition. How did this happen?

'THE BURDEN IS GREAT': THE HARVARD COMMITTEE ON THE DETERMINATION OF DEATH

In December 1967, in South Africa, Dr Christiaan Barnard transplanted a human heart into Louis Washkansky, a patient who was dying from heart failure. Louis Washkansky died anyway, eighteen days later, but soon everyone was doing heart transplants. Within a year, more than a hundred had been attempted. The new rage for heart transplants provided fresh impetus for attempts to solve a problem that had been slowly building up for more than a decade: when is it reasonable to stop treating a person on a respirator?

The respirator or, as it is also called, ventilator, is a relatively simple piece of machinery. It was developed during the polio epidemic that swept around the world in the 1950s. A Danish doctor, seeing how children stricken with polio were dying because they could not breathe, devised a means of using air bags to pump oxygen into the children's lungs. This staved off death—until the nurse stopped pumping. For a week, all the medical students and nurses of the Copenhagen medical school pumped air into the lungs of the polio victims. Some of them were saved. But, obviously, there had to be a better way of doing this. The answer was to attach a mechanical pump to the air bag instead of a nurse or student. That, essentially, is what a respirator is.

Soon respirators were to be found in every hospital. They saved the lives of many people. Some of these—accident victims, people who had taken drug overdoses, and diabetics who had gone into a coma—needed only temporary help with their breathing, and were soon returned to normal health. For other patients, however, the respirator brought a much more dubious benefit: they remained alive, their hearts continued to beat, but they were unconscious, and looked as if they would stay that way. For how long could this continue? Weeks, months, years? With the new machines able to keep pushing air into their lungs indefinitely, there seemed to be no limit.

For the patients it didn't really matter, because they were apparently not experiencing anything at all. For the family, however, the respirators prolonged their agony. If the person they loved could never recover consciousness, she was gone forever. Yet she was not dead, and so their grief could not be resolved by the usual rituals of death, burial and mourning. The use of respirators on irreversibly unconscious patients was also becoming a problem for the directors of intensive care units. They began to have nightmares about wards filled with permanently unconscious patients, each one needing not only a respirator and a bed, but also skilled nursing care.

It was into this situation that news of Christiaan Barnard's dramatic operation broke. Although kidney transplants had been possible for some time, they posed no special problems about death, because kidneys can be taken from the body of a donor whose heart has stopped beating. When the heart itself stops, however, it is liable to be damaged. To maximise the chances of a successful transplant, the heart must be removed as soon as possible after the donor has died. With the possibility of heart transplants, therefore, the thousands of permanently unconscious patients filling hospital wards around the world suddenly appeared in a new light. Instead of being an increasingly intolerable burden on a hospital's resources, they could become a means of saving the lives of other patients.

There was, however, a seemingly insuperable barrier to doing this: to remove the heart of a living patient would be murder.

Even before Barnard's sensational operation, Henry Beecher, chairman of a Harvard University committee that oversaw the ethics of experimentation on human beings, had written to Robert Ebert, Dean of the Harvard Medical School, suggesting that the committee should consider some new questions. He had, he told the dean, been speaking with Dr Joseph Murray, a surgeon at Massachusetts General Hospital and a pioneer in kidney transplantation. 'Both Dr Murray and I,' Beecher wrote, 'think the time has come for a further consideration of the definition of death. Every major hospital has patients stacked up waiting for suitable donors.'[4]

Ebert did not respond immediately; but within a month of the news of the South African heart transplant, he set up, under Beecher's chairmanship, 'The Ad Hoc Committee of the Harvard Medical School to Examine the Definition of Brain Death', a group of people who were to become better known as the Harvard Brain Death Committee.

The Harvard Brain Death Committee was made up mostly of members of the medical profession—ten of them, supplemented by a lawyer, an historian, and a theologian. It did its work rapidly, and published its report in the *Journal of the American Medical Association* in August 1968. It began with a remarkably clear statement of what the committee was doing and why it needed to be done:

Our primary purpose is to define irreversible coma as a new criterion for death. There are two reasons why there is a need for a definition: (1) Improvements in resuscitative and supportive measures have led to increased efforts to save those who are desperately injured. Sometimes these efforts have only a partial success so that the result is an individual whose heart continues to beat but whose brain is irreversibly damaged. The burden is great on patients who suffer permanent loss of intellect, on their families, on the hospitals, and on those in need of hospital beds already occupied by these comatose patients. (2) Obsolete criteria for the definition of death can lead to controversy in obtaining organs for transplantation.

To a reader familiar with bioethics in the 1990s, there are two remarkable aspects to this opening paragraph. The first is that the Harvard committee does not even attempt to argue that there is a need for a new definition of death because hospitals have a lot of patients in their wards who are really dead, but are being kept attached to respirators because the law does not recognise them as dead.

Instead, with unusual frankness, the committee said that a new definition was needed because irreversibly comatose patients were a great burden, not only on themselves (why to be in an irreversible coma is a burden on the patient, the committee did not say), but also on their families, hospitals, and patients waiting for beds. And then there was the problem of 'controversy' about obtaining organs for transplantation.

In fact, frank as the statement seems, in presenting its concern about this controversy, the committee was still not being entirely candid. An earlier draft of this second reason for a new definition of death was more explicit:

An issue of secondary but by no means minor importance is that with increased experience and knowledge and development in transplantation there is great need for tissues and organs of, among others, the patient whose cerebrum has been hopelessly destroyed, in order to restore those who are salvageable.

This draft was sent to Robert Ebert, the Dean who had appointed the committee. He advised Beecher to change it:

> The connotation of this statement is unfortunate, for it suggests that you wish to redefine death in order to make viable organs more readily available to persons requiring transplants...Would it not be better to state the problem, and indicate that obsolete criteria for the definition of death can lead to controversy in obtaining organs for transplantation?[5]

The Harvard Brain Death Committee took Ebert's advice: it was doubtless more politic to put things that way. The first draft, however, may give a more honest indication of their real motivation. Henry Beecher himself was later to say, in an address to the American Association for the Advancement of Science:

> There is indeed a life-saving potential in the new definition, for, when accepted, it will lead to greater availability than formerly of essential organs in viable condition, for transplantation, and thus countless lives now inevitably lost will be saved...At whatever level we choose to call death, it is an arbitrary decision. Death of the heart? The hair still grows. Death of the brain? The heart may still beat. The need is to choose an irreversible state where the brain no longer functions. It is best to choose a level where, although the brain is dead, usefulness of other organs is still present. This we have tried to make clear in what we have called the new definition of death.[6]

The second remarkable aspect of the Harvard committee's report is that it keeps referring to 'irreversible coma' as the condition that it wishes to define as death. The committee also speaks of 'permanent loss of intellect' and even says 'we suggest that responsible medical opinion is ready to adopt new criteria for pronouncing death to have occurred in an individual sustaining irreversible coma as a result of permanent brain damage'. Now 'irreversible coma as a result of permanent brain damage' is by no means identical with the death of the whole brain. Permanent damage to the parts of the brain responsible for consciousness can lead to a condition known as a 'persistent vegetative state'. In these people, the brain stem and the central nervous system continue to function, but consciousness has been irreversibly lost. Even today, no legal system regards those in a persistent vegetative state as dead. Admittedly, the Harvard committee report does go on to say, immediately following the paragraph quoted above: *'we are concerned here only with those comatose individuals who have no discernible central nervous system activity'*. But the reasons given by the committee for redefining death—the great burden on the patients, their families, the hospitals and the community, as well as the waste of organs needed for transplantation—apply in every respect to *all* those who are irreversibly comatose, not only to those whose entire brain is dead. So it is worth asking: why did the committee limit its concern to those with no brain activity at all?

One reason could be that there was at the time no reliable way of telling whether a coma was irreversible, unless the brain damage was so severe that there was no brain activity at all. Another could be that people whose whole brain is dead will stop breathing after they are taken off a respirator, and so will soon be dead by anyone's standard. People in a persistent vegetative state, on the other hand, may continue to breathe without mechanical assistance. To call for the undertakers to bury a 'dead' patient who is still breathing would be a bit too much for anyone to swallow.

The redefinition of death proposed by the Harvard Brain Death Committee triumphed. By 1981, when the United States President's Commission for the Study of Ethical Problems in Medicine examined the issue, it could write of 'the emergence of a medical consensus' around criteria very like those proposed by the Harvard committee. The criteria had proved to be reliable, in the sense that, as the commission reported, 'no case has yet been found that met these criteria and regained any brain functions'.[7] Already, people whose brains had irreversibly ceased to function were considered legally dead in at least fifteen countries, and in more than half of the states of the United States. In some countries, including Britain, parliament had not even been involved in the change: the medical profession had simply adopted a new set of criteria on the basis of which doctors certified a patient dead.[8] The President's Commission completed the work of the Harvard Brain Death Committee. In its authoritative report, entitled *Defining Death*, the commission proposed a 'Uniform Determination of Death Act' so that every state of the Union could have the same legal definition of death, based on the irreversible loss of all brain function. Subsequently most developed nations redefined death in similar terms.

A REVOLUTION WITHOUT OPPOSITION

The success of the new definition was undoubtedly due largely to the fact that the Harvard Brain Death Committee was right when it said that maintaining people in an 'irreversible coma' was a great burden on their families and on hospitals; and if the committee was on more dubious ground in saying that it was a burden on the patients themselves, at least it was clear that it was of no obvious benefit to the patients. Very few people would positively want to be maintained on a respirator if it was certain that they would never recover consciousness. In addition to the very reasonable desire to avoid the ghastly prospect of hospital wards filling with people whose brains had ceased to function, the final impetus for change came, as we have seen, from the highly publicised progress of organ transplantation. Everyone is a potential patient dying for want of an organ; and in that context the 'great need for tissues and organs', to which the Harvard committee referred in its draft report, was a powerful factor in winning support for the change. But the most extraordinary aspect of the process was the lack of opposition from the groups that could be expected to protest vigorously against any attempt to deny the sanctity of life of any member of our species, from the moment of conception onwards. Where was the pro-life movement? Where was the Roman Catholic Church?

For a group proposing so momentous a change in a matter of life and death, the Harvard committee was remarkably fortunate: it was able to quote the Pope in support of its view that the determination of death is a matter for doctors to decide. A decade earlier Dr Bruno Haid, chief of the anaesthesia section of the surgery clinic of the University of Innsbruck in Austria, had asked Pope Pius XII to advise doctors whether a patient 'plunged into unconsciousness through central paralysis, but whose life—that is to say, blood circulation—is maintained through artificial respiration, and in whom there is no improvement after several days' should be considered dead. The Pope had responded to the question in a speech to an International Congress of Anaesthesiologists held in November 1957. In replying, Pius XII had reiterated the church's concept of death as the complete and final separation of the soul from the body, but he also said, 'It remains for the doctor, and especially the anaesthesiologist, to give a clear and precise definition of "death" and the "moment of death" of a patient who passes away in a state of unconsciousness.'[9]

This statement must have made it very difficult for those within the Roman Catholic Church to mount any opposition to the Harvard committee's proposal. But there was also another reason why the pro-life lobby did not stand up against the move to declare that people whose brains had ceased to function were dead. They were worried that the wave of support for the idea of turning off the respirators on those whose brains had stopped working would sweep over into other areas and, in particular, euthanasia. Dennis J. Horan, President of American Citizens United for Life, wrote that total-brain-death legislation enhances the values of the pro-life movement 'by prohibiting euthanasia and allowing only those to be declared dead who are really dead'.[10] Germain Grisez and Joseph Boyle, two leading American Roman Catholic pro-life philosophers, were even more explicit:

> a correct definition of death, if it would eliminate some false classifications of dead individuals among the living, could relieve some of the pressure for legalizing euthanasia—in this case, pressure arising from a right attitude toward individuals really dead and only considered alive due to conceptual confusion.[11]

So for pro-life groups, the decision not to oppose the redefinition of death was made easier still by the fact that it made good sense as a tactical retreat, a withdrawal to a position that was easier to defend against the pressure for a change in the laws prohibiting euthanasia.

Still, the pro-life groups and Catholic philosophers like Grisez and Boyle needed some grounding for their view that a person whose brain has irreversibly ceased to function is dead. They could scarcely agree with Beecher that it was all a matter of arbitrary choice. If human life is sacrosanct from conception to death, its boundaries cannot be arbitrary! Arguing that an organism is 'a co-ordinated system', Grisez and Boyle concluded: 'Death is the irreversible loss of integrated organic functioning'. They then proposed that because the brain is the organ that maintains the 'dynamic equilibrium' of the system, death occurs when the functioning of the entire brain is completely and irreversibly lost. This is, they argue, a correct definition of death 'in factual terms... without any radical shifts in meaning, arbitrary stipulations, or subjective evaluations'.[12]

Thus Grisez and Boyle attempted to defend a definition of death in terms of the death of the brain without admitting that there is an element of evaluation in the definition. This attempt is unconvincing. Just as we can replace the role of the kidney in cleansing the blood, or transplant a failing heart in order to maintain the circulation of the blood, so we can replace the function of the brain in maintaining integrated bodily function. Now that there has been extensive publicity about cases like those of Trisha Marshall and Marion Ploch, in which the bodily functions of pregnant women have been sustained for long periods, this fact has become well known. When Grisez and Boyle wrote, however, it was widely believed that, no matter what medical care was given, one could not sustain the body of a brain-dead person for more than a few days. Even the President's Commission report echoes this view.[13] Naturally, when no-one tried to prolong the lives of people whose brains had ceased to function, those people died quickly. But the situation began to change in the mid 1980s. In 1986 the journal *Neurosurgery* published the results of a study from Japan, where the death of the brain is not accepted as the death of the human being. The Japanese doctors noticed that people whose brains have died lack an antidiuretic hormone normally made by the brain (an antidiuretic hormone is a hormone that constricts blood vessels). They decided to try giving an antidiuretic hormone to their brain-dead patients, by means of a drip. When they took this quite simple step, brain-dead patients who would otherwise have also been dead in the classic sense within a day or two instead lived an average time of twenty-three days after brain death.[14]

This study suggested that if other techniques could be used as well, brain-dead patients might be maintained indefinitely. That is just what the doctors in Erlangen and Highland General Hospital showed when they maintained the bodies of Marion Ploch and Trisha Marshall. Without 'integrated organic functioning', a pregnancy could not continue for more than three months and yield a healthy baby at the end. Other studies have shown that the bodily functions of brain-dead patients can be maintained for periods as long as 201 days.[15] The co-ordinated forces of modern intensive care medicine have replaced the role of the brain in regulating the body.

Why then should we choose the death of the brain as the uniquely determining feature of death, rather than the death of the kidneys or the heart, when the function of each of them can be replaced? The answer is that it is not really the 'integrative' or 'co-ordinating' functions of the brain that make its death the end of everything we value, but rather its association with our consciousness and our personality. That is why if our kidneys are destroyed, and we continue to survive as an integrated organism only because we are put on a machine that replaces the functions of our kidneys, we would never consider that our life is over. But if our brain is destroyed, and we continue to survive as an integrated system only because we are put on a machine that replaces the functions of our brain (but does not restore our consciousness) we would consider our life to be over. There is no 'fact of the matter' here. If we choose to mark death at any moment before the body goes stiff and cold (or to really be on the safe side, before it begins to rot) we are making an ethical judgment.

In summary, the redefinition of death in terms of brain death went through so smoothly because it did not harm the brain-dead patients and it benefited everyone else: the families of brain-dead patients, the hospitals, the transplant surgeons, people needing transplants, people who worried that they might one day need a transplant, people who feared that they might one day be kept on a respirator after their brain had died, taxpayers and the government. The general public understood that if the brain has been destroyed, there can be no recovery of consciousness, and so there is no point in maintaining the body. Defining such people as dead was a convenient way around the problems of withdrawing treatment from them. Even Roman Catholics and the pro-life movement saw some advantages in this redefinition of death. There was no-one to rock the boat.

BRAIN DEATH: WHO BELIEVES IT?

In the early 1980s, when the President's Commission issued its report, the definition of death in terms of death of the brain seemed to be one of the most solid achievements in bioethics. Among so many hotly contested issues in the area of life-and-death decision-making, this seemed one with such broad support that it would become a permanent achievement. By the end of the decade, as Sweden and Denmark, the last European nations to cling to the traditional standard, adopted brain-death definitions of death, this verdict appeared to be confirmed. Among developed nations, only Japan was still holding out.

But do people really think of the brain-dead as *dead*? The evidence suggests that they do not. Journalists frequently write stories such as this one, from the *Detroit Free Press*:

> A 17-year-old was pronounced brain dead after being accidentally shot in the head...John Ziemnick of Hubbell was being kept alive on life-support systems in Marquette General Hospital, nursing supervisor Pat Liana said. He was to be pronounced officially dead after doctors removed organs for donation to others, Liana said.[16]

The Harvard Brain Death Committee itself couldn't quite swallow the implications of what it was recommending. As we have seen, it described patients whose brains have ceased to function as in an 'irreversible coma' and said that being kept on a respirator was a burden to them. Dead people are not in a coma, they are dead, and nothing can be a burden to them any more.

Perhaps the lapses in the thinking of the Harvard committee can be pardoned because the concept of brain death was then so new. Today, doctors and nurses who work with brain-dead patients have no such excuses. It is apparent, however, that at some deep level even they do not think of being brain dead as being really dead. Donald Denny, director of organ procurement for the Pittsburgh Transplant Foundation, has reported that health-care professionals asking families for permission to take an organ from a brain-dead person often use language like: 'There's nothing more that we can do—we're just keeping him alive so you can consider organ donation'.[17] Stuart Youngner and colleagues at Case Western Reserve University surveyed doctors and nurses who worked with brain-dead patients at four university-affiliated hospitals with organ-transplant programs in Cleveland, Ohio. They found that the majority did not use a coherent concept of death in a consistent way. A significant minority, 19 per cent, regarded a patient in a persistent vegetative state as dead. When asked to give reasons for classifying a hypothetical patient as dead, one-third said either that the patient was 'irreversibly dying' or made a reference to the patient's 'unacceptable quality of life'.[18] Tom Tomlinson of the Centre for Ethics and Humanities in the Life Sciences at Michigan State University interviewed thirteen nurses and seven physicians to see how they naturally and habitually spoke and thought about brain-dead patients. The nurses worked in intensive care units, and the physicians were neurologists or neurosurgeons. All had extensive experience with brain-dead patients. When asked what they would say to the family of a patient who had been determined to be brain-dead, nine of the subjects made replies that suggested they did not think of the patient as really dead. The replies included:

> 'At this point in time, it doesn't look like the patient is going to survive.'
> 'The machine is the way he would have to live the rest of his life.'
> 'The machine is basically what's keeping him alive.'
> 'I'd ask what the patient's own desires would be. Would he want the respirator?'
> 'If kept on the respirator, the patient will die of sepsis.'[19]

The doctors and nurses who maintained the bodily functions of Trisha Marshall during her pregnancy also found it virtually impossible to think of her as really dead. As Dashka Slater reported:

> The doctors and nurses who tended to Marshall's body were educated people, and most would probably say that they agree with the way the California legislature has resolved the mind-body problem.

Still, it was difficult not to think of Marshall as a living woman. 'It was strange,' Jackson says of the experience. 'The nurses talked to her, and they played music to the baby. It was the greatest nursing performance I've ever seen. They treated her as if she were terminally ill. Not a dead person. Not a corpse.'[20]

Not surprisingly, the press presented a confusing picture of Trisha Marshall's state. The *San Francisco Chronicle* headlined one of its stories 'Brain-Dead Woman Gives Birth, then Dies' while the *Miami Herald* preferred 'Brain-Dead Woman Kept Alive in Hopes She'll Bear Child'. The *Toronto Star* even found a love angle to its story about the thoughts of David Smith, Marshall's boyfriend: 'Man Dreads Birth that Will Kill Lover'. The article quoted Smith as saying: 'It seems strange knowing that when the baby comes, she's gone'.[21]

Why do people refuse to accept that brain death is really death? One possible explanation is that even though people know that the brain dead are dead, it is just too difficult for them to abandon obsolete ways of thinking about death. Another possible explanation is that no-one believes in brain death because they can see that the brain dead are not really dead.

AN UNSTABLE COMPROMISE

The picture I have been presenting of brain death up to now suggests that it is a convenient fiction. It was proposed and accepted because it makes it possible for us to salvage organs that would otherwise be wasted, and to withdraw medical treatment when it is doing no good. On this basis, it might seem that, despite some fundamental weaknesses, the survival prospects of the concept of brain death are good. But there are two reasons why our present understanding of brain death is not stable. Again, advances in medical knowledge and technology are the driving forces.

To understand the first problem, we have to recall that brain death is generally defined as the irreversible cessation of all functions of the brain.[22] In accordance with this definition, a standard set of tests is used by doctors to establish that all functions of the brain have irreversibly ceased. These tests are broadly in line with those recommended in 1968 by the Harvard Brain Death Committee, but they have been further refined and updated over the years in various countries. For example, in the United States, the President's Commission appointed a panel of medical consultants who agreed on the tests that should be conducted. In the past ten years, however, as doctors have sought ways of managing brain-dead patients, so that their organs (or, in some cases, their pregnancies) could be sustained for a longer time, it has become apparent that even when the usual tests show that brain death has occurred, some brain functions continue. We think of the brain primarily as concerned with processing information through the senses and the nervous system, but the brain has other functions as well. One of these is to supply various hormones that help to regulate several bodily functions (for example, the antidiuretic hormone that the Japanese doctors were able to replace by a drip). We now know that some of these hormones continue to be supplied by the brains of most patients who, by the standard tests, are brain dead. Moreover, when brain-dead patients are cut open, in order to remove organs, their blood pressure may rise and their heartbeat quicken. These reactions mean that the brain is still carrying out some of its functions, regulating the responses of the body in various ways. As a result, the legal definition of brain death, and current medical practice in certifying brain-dead people as dead, have come apart.[23]

It would be possible to bring medical practice into line with the definition of brain death. Doctors would then have to test for all brain functions, including hormonal functions, before declaring someone dead. This would mean that some people who are now declared brain dead would be considered alive, and therefore would have to continue to be supported on a respirator, at significant cost, both financially and in terms of the extended distress of the family. Since the tests are expensive to carry out and time-consuming in themselves, continued support would be necessary during the period in which they are carried out, even if in the end the results showed that the person had no brain function at all. In addition, during this period, the person's organs would deteriorate, and may therefore not be usable for transplantation. There would be no gains to balance against these serious disadvantages. Not a single person who was kept longer on a respirator because of the need to test for hormonal brain functioning would ever return to consciousness.

So bringing medical practice into line with the definition of death does not seem a good idea. It would be better to bring the definition of brain death into line with current medical practice. But once we move away from the idea of brain death as the irreversible cessation of all brain functioning, what are we to put in its place? Which functions of the brain will we take as marking the difference between life and death, and why?

DR SHANN'S DILEMMA

'There's no use trying,' she said, 'one can't believe impossible things.'
'I daresay you haven't had much practice,' said the Queen.
'When I was your age, I always did it for half-an-hour a day.
Why, sometimes I've believed as many as six impossible
things before breakfast.'

LEWIS CARROLL, *THROUGH THE LOOKING-GLASS*

TWO BABIES

In February 1991, Melbourne's Royal Children's Hospital hosted a conference entitled 'Anencephalics, Infants and Brain Death: Treatment Options and the Issue of Organ Donation'. Normally I'd prefer to spend a fine late summer day outside, or at least in a room with a window, but the interest of this conference outweighed such thoughts. I had been invited to be a member of a special 'consensus development panel' asked to consider a series of extraordinary questions. Along with another philosopher, two lawyers, one of Australia's leading authors, a paediatrician, an intensive care specialist, and others in the health-care field, we were to see if it was possible to find some common ground about the moral status of two special categories of babies who are sometimes patients at the Royal Children's Hospital.

Some babies are born with most of their brains missing. They have only a brain stem. This condition is known as anencephaly, a term of Greek origin that translates as 'no brain'. In babies with this condition, the top of the skull may be missing, above the eyebrows. In its place there is merely a layer of skin. In other cases the skull is malformed, and filled with fluid. If a torch is held to one side of the skull, the light can be seen on the other.

Anencephaly is obvious as soon as the baby is born, and affects about one fetus in every two thousand. It used to be one of the more common forms of major birth defect. Today, however, it is often diagnosed before birth, by ultrasound. Since almost every pregnant woman receiving modern medical care has an ultrasound, and most women who are told they are carrying an anencephalic baby opt for abortion, the birth of an infant with this condition is becoming a rare event. Nevertheless, according to one estimate, about 300 anencephalic babies are born every year in the United States.[1]

Other babies are formed normally but suffer brain damage so catastrophic that they can never regain consciousness. This is most likely to occur as a result of extremely premature birth, or when there is a mishap during or shortly after birth. For those unfamiliar with the structure of the human brain, a very brief account may make the condition of these infants easier to understand. The human brain can be divided into 'higher' and 'lower' parts. The higher brain consists of the cerebral hemispheres, including the cerebral cortex. This is the seat of consciousness. Without a functioning higher brain we can neither see, hear nor feel anything. We can have no experience of pleasure or pain, and we can have no intentions, goals, or desires. The lower brain consists of the brain stem. It controls the things that we do unconsciously, like breathing, heartbeat, and reflex actions. So if the higher brain is destroyed, but the brain stem remains intact, there can be breathing, heartbeat and reflex actions, in the absence of any consciousness at all. A person in this condition may be described as being in an irreversible coma or a persistent vegetative state. They may also be said to be in a state of 'cortical death', because their cerebral cortex is dead.

Neither the anencephalic infant, nor the cortically dead infant, will ever become conscious. Both of them can, however, be kept alive for a long time—months or years—if given intensive care. The cortically dead infant is not brain dead, because the legal definition of brain death requires that the whole brain has ceased to function, and for these babies the brain stem continues to function. Nor is the anencephalic infant 'brain dead'—the condition might be better described as 'brain absent'. Anencephalics have a brain stem. It is often malformed and does not work properly, but sometimes it works well enough for the baby to breathe without any mechanical assistance. Both anencephalics and cortically dead infants may move their limbs, cough, sneeze, cry, and even appear to smile—all, however, without having any consciousness.[2]

Anencephalics usually die within a few hours of birth, and only 1 per cent survive for three months or more, but this is because no efforts are made to keep them alive.[3] In some instances, especially where the brain stem is working normally, they can survive for a long time. Baby K, an anencephalic born in October 1992 in Falls Church, Virginia, is still alive as this book goes to press because her mother has insisted that everything should be done to keep the baby alive. The hospital physicians regarded treatment, which included the occasional use of a respirator, as inappropriate. The hospital ethics committee agreed that medical treatment was futile and should be terminated. The mother, however, who has been described as acting on the basis of 'a firm Christian faith that all life should be protected', refused to give her consent to the withdrawal of treatment. In view of the mother's opposition the hospital decided that it need a court's permission to withdraw treatment. But the District Court ordered that treatment must continue and, when the hospital appealed, the United States Court of Appeals again ruled that treatment must continue.[4]

Despite the hopeless prognosis for the anencephalic and cortically dead infant, for one of Australia's leading children's hospitals to promote a discussion of a possible change in their moral status was a sign of the spread of open doubts about the traditional sanctity of life ethic. Furthermore, the hospital had been joined in its sponsorship of the conference by the Law Reform Commission of Victoria and the Australian Association of Paediatric Teaching

Centres. Jim Kennan, attorney-general and deputy premier of Victoria, gave added weight to the meeting by delivering an opening address in which he applauded the sponsors of the conference for taking on such tough questions. The significance of the occasion did not escape the attention of Right to Life Australia, an organisation founded to campaign against abortion. Entering the hospital that February morning, I passed through a line of demonstrators carrying placards and handing out leaflets opposing the conference. Australia is, however, a relatively tolerant country, and the meeting went ahead without disturbance.

The practical issue that had led the Royal Children's Hospital to support the conference was dramatically presented to us by Dr Frank Shann, director of the hospital's intensive care unit. He began by describing how, a couple of years previously, a baby boy had been brought into the hospital with severe heart disease. After suffering repeated heart attacks, he needed to be put on a ventilator and given drugs continuously in order to keep him alive. Apart from his heart disease, the baby was quite normal; but because the disease itself was so serious, the outlook was, Shann said, 'hopeless'. Tragic as this situation is, it is not a rare occurrence in a major children's hospital. But what was to come was more unusual. I shall let Shann continue the story:

> At the same time, in the adjacent bed in the Intensive Care Unit, was another baby who had been well until a sudden and catastrophic collapse occurred. He had some abnormal blood vessels in his brain and these suddenly burst; there was massive bleeding into his brain causing destruction of the whole of his cerebral cortex. However, his brain stem was partially functioning, and he made irregular gasping movements. These were not enough to enable him to survive off the ventilator but they were evidence that he did not have death of his whole brain, so he was not legally dead.
> There was therefore one child who was completely normal except for a dying heart in one bed, and in the next bed, a child with a dead brain cortex but a normal heart. As it happened, the two

children had the same blood group, so the heart of the child with no cerebral cortex could have been transplanted into the child with cardiomyopathy [heart disease].[5]

Under Australian law—and the legal situation would have been the same everywhere in the world—there was nothing that Shann could do. The child whose cortex had been destroyed was not legally brain dead, so he could not be considered as a heart donor. No other heart could be found for the child with heart disease. Within a short time, both children were dead.

BREATHING BUT DEAD?

Dr Shann was understandably distressed about the dilemma he had faced, and his inability to resolve it. He finished his presentation with a bold suggestion for remedying the situation:

> I suggest that the organ that really matters is the cerebral cortex. If the cortex is dead, there is permanent loss of consciousness and there can be no person, no personality, even though the organism may still be alive (with a beating heart, and even breathing movements). If the cortex of the brain is dead, the person is dead. I suggest that it should be legal to use the organs from the body of the dead person for transplantation.

The conference heard an array of other papers. The keynote address was given by an American, Dr Robert Truog, director of the multidisciplinary intensive care unit at Harvard Medical School. Truog supported Shann's view, arguing that death is a process, and the moment at which death is said to occur cannot be *discovered* by medical science, but rather must be *chosen*. So what point should we choose? Truog's choice was that 'death is the irreversible loss of the capacity for consciousness'.

If the definition of death in terms of the death of the whole brain was a significant step away from tradition, Truog and Shann were urging us to take another step again. If we took that step, then provided Shann was able to be quite sure that the infant with the bleeding in his brain had irreversibly lost the capacity for consciousness, he could have regarded the infant as dead, and used its heart to save the life of the other baby.

But was it possible, in these cases, to be completely sure that the capacity for consciousness had been entirely lost and could never be restored? Wasn't it still true that, in many cases of infants with severely damaged brains, we have little idea how much of the brain has been damaged? It was, we knew, possible to establish the death of the entire brain, including the brain stem. That is the standard concept of brain death. But it is a different matter to tell whether there is any prospect of a patient recovering consciousness if some parts of the brain are still functioning.

Here, however, a crucial piece in the argument was slotted into place by Dr Margaret de Campo, a radiologist at the Royal Children's Hospital. As de Campo explained, new ways of 'imaging', or obtaining a picture of the brain, are changing the situation. The names of these techniques—Three Vessel Angiography, Digital Subtraction Angiography, Dynamic Computed Tomography and Emission Tomography—did not mean much to me, but the upshot was clear enough: we can tell in which sections of the brain that blood is still flowing, and in which it is not flowing. If blood is not flowing to the cortex, then—even though the brain stem might still be functioning and so the patient would not be brain dead—the patient would be 'cortically dead' and would never recover consciousness. A powerful reason for continuing to treat patients in a persistent vegetative state—the desperate hope that maybe they will 'wake up'—was being pushed aside by the hard reality of more precise medical knowledge. There are still some cases in which the capacity for consciousness has been lost, but we cannot know why (because sometimes even when blood is flowing to the cortex, the patient will never recover). But we can be confident that we are not making mistakes in the other, and more important, direction: when there is no blood flow to the cortex, we can be sure that the capacity for consciousness has been irreversibly lost.

Not all the conference presentations were technical or philosophical. The most moving presentations came from three women who had all been mothers of babies who were patients of the Royal Children's Hospital. Two of them had had anencephalic babies. For Margaret Pearce, this happened ten years earlier, when parents were not encouraged to see their anencephalic child. Pearce had a difficult time grieving for the loss of a baby she had never been able to cuddle. Judy Silver, whose anencephalic baby—one of twins—had been born more recently, had held her child, had bathed her, and the baby had died peacefully in her arms. 'It was nice,' Silver said, and if that sounds banal when written down, no-one who heard her say it thought so at the time. For these two mothers, an anencephalic baby was still their baby, and some kind of person, whatever the doctors or philosophers might say about its lack of capacity for consciousness.

The third mother, Annie Gellert, gave us the other side of the story. Soon after giving birth to a daughter she called Heidi, Annie and her husband were told that their child had a terminal heart condition, and would not live to grow up. When Heidi was thirteen months old, however, a heart became available for transplantation. Despite some medical complications, Heidi did well, and her mother spoke of the joy she was bringing to the family. The gift of an organ from the family of the donor was, she said, 'incredibly brave' and something that provided 'hope and an opportunity that otherwise would not have been'.

At the end of the day, the arguments for and against the use of anencephalic and cortically dead infants as organ donors were summarised by two intensive paediatric care specialists. Dr Neil Campbell of the Royal Children's Hospital presented a coolly logical case in favour. His central point was highly persuasive: what we really care about—and ought to care about—is *the person* rather than the body. We may respect a dead body, but our concern should be for a conscious being. Because the anencephalic or cortically dead infant has no consciousness, no awareness, no past and no future, Campbell concluded that 'there is no meaningful sense in which it can be claimed that decisions about life support or organ removal matter to him or her'.[6]

Dr Steve Keeley, of Adelaide Children's Hospital, was much more heated than Campbell had been. The proposal that we regard anencephalic and cortically dead infants as dead would, he suggested, create 'an ethical fiction'. These children can breathe for an indefinite time without mechanical support. We were discussing, Keeley said, 'an intolerable proposition' that was 'against common sense', because we could not possibly choose to bury a spontaneously breathing, persistently vegetative child. Reminding us of the demonstrators outside, Keeley warned the consensus development panel that if, in attempting to increase the availability of organs, a group of 'experts' was to provoke uncertainty in the community and in parents about the criteria used to determine death, then the result could be the very opposite of the effect intended. Keeley did not argue against Campbell's view that anencephalic and cortically dead children can have no interest in their own continued existence; but he pointed to the 'grieving, weeping mother who sits there soothing, crooning to, and rocking her brain injured child' and insisted that 'the capacity for thought—though it may be the most singular characteristic of a human being—cannot alone define the essence of that child'.[7]

During the dinner break, Dr Campbell invited members of the consensus development panel upstairs to the neonatal intensive care unit he directed. There, in clear plastic cots, surrounded by humming machinery, lay several small babies. Campbell took us to one, a particularly tiny boy, breathing on a respirator and with several other tubes and wires connected to his body. He was warm, and pink, and looked like other babies. When Campbell picked him up and held him, he even seemed to smile. That was, Campbell told us, almost certainly some kind of automatic response, for the baby had been born too prematurely, and had suffered a massive bleeding in the brain. He was an example of the kind of baby we were discussing: cortically dead, he could have no future. There was no hope, and no real point in further treatment, but the doctors were giving the parents time to adjust and grieve before taking the baby off the respirator. Yet, even knowing this, we could not help responding to him as we would to any other living baby. Could we really think of him as *dead*?

THE CASE FOR A HIGHER BRAIN
DEFINITION OF DEATH

When the panel met after dinner we were in no doubt about the difficulty of our deliberations. It soon became clear that consensus on all the issues before us would be difficult to reach, and so we proceeded in a step-by-step fashion. First we agreed on a description of the present situation: the fact that death in the intensive care unit is a process and not an instantaneous event, that the acceptance of brain death has itself meant a shift from the traditional concept of death, and that the focus on the death of one organ, the brain, has naturally led to the question of whether it is the death of the whole brain or of the cortex only that ought to be regarded as crucial to a declaration that death has occurred. We also agreed that a shortage of organs often made it impossible to save the lives of infants with malformed or malfunctioning organs such as hearts and kidneys.

Next we considered what constitutes appropriate medical care in the case of anencephalic infants and infants whose cortex had been completely and irreparably damaged. Here too we were able to agree that attempts to sustain life were not obligatory. We supported what we understood to be the current medical practice in Australia, namely that parents and care-givers could decide together to turn off the respirator and give the baby no more treatment. Mindful of Margaret Pearce's distress at not being able to cuddle her anencephalic child, we suggested that parents should be supported in holding and cherishing their infant.

So we had found consensus on the acceptability of not prolonging the lives of these infants. When we turned to the ethical acceptability of removing organs, however, the consensus stopped. Some members of the panel thought that neither anencephalic infants nor cortically dead infants should be considered as potential organ donors. I was not among this group, basically because I agreed with Frank Shann that (as long as the parents were willing for organs to be donated) there was no point in allowing two babies to die when one could be saved. Several members of the panel shared my view that anencephalics and cortically dead infants could be considered as potential organ donors. But among those of us who thought this way, another important difference of opinion emerged.

One view was that we should change the definition of death along the lines that Shann and Truog had suggested, so that anencephalics and cortically dead infants would be legally dead, and therefore could be used as organ donors, much as those who are now 'brain dead' can be used. This was a tempting position because it was, in procedural and political terms, the simplest way of achieving the desirable end of allowing organs to be taken from these infants. It was just another shift in the definition of death, of the sort that society had already accepted when we moved to the notion of brain death. So why not take that extra step, to a concept of death as the death of the higher brain, or the cortex?

Several reasons could be offered to justify this step. The Harvard Brain Death Committee, on whose report the current definition of brain death is largely based, specified that its recommendations applied only to those who have 'no discernible central nervous system activity', but the arguments it put forward applied in every respect to patients who are permanently without any awareness, whether or not they have some brain stem function. This seems to have been no accident, for it reflected the view of the committee's chairman, Henry Beecher, who in his address to the American Association for the Advancement of Science, said that what is essential to human nature is 'the individual's personality, his conscious life, his uniqueness, his capacity for remembering, judging, reasoning, acting, enjoying, worrying, and so on'.[8]

The United States President's Commission for the Study of Ethical Problems in Medicine, in its report recommending uniform legislation establishing a whole-brain criterion of death, also put forward ethical arguments for brain death that apply equally to those who have suffered an irreversible loss of the capacity for consciousness, or who have never had this capacity:

> A patient correctly diagnosed as having lost brain functions permanently and totally will never regain consciousness. He or she will experience no pleasure or pain, enjoy no social interaction, and be unable to pursue or complete his or her life's projects. Why, then, is there an ethical issue over discontinuing medical interventions?[9]

So why *did* the Harvard committee and the President's Commission settle for the whole-brain criterion of death rather than a higher brain criterion? One plausible reason is that in 1968, when the Harvard committee issued its report, the irreversible destruction of the parts of the brain associated with consciousness could not reliably be diagnosed if the brain stem was alive. Thirteen years later the President's Commission was still faced with a situation in which there was no certain way of establishing the impossibility of any recovery of consciousness unless the entire brain, including the brain stem, had ceased to function.[10] As Margaret de Campo had told us, however, since that time the technology for obtaining images of soft tissues within the body has made enormous progress. Hence a major stumbling block to the acceptance of a higher brain definition of death has already been greatly diminished in its scope, and will soon disappear altogether.

Now that medical certainty on the irreversible loss of higher brain functions can be established in at least some cases, the inherent logic of pushing the definition of death one step further has already led, in the United States, to one Supreme Court judge suggesting that the law could consider a person who has irreversibly lost consciousness to be no longer alive. Here is Mr Justice Stevens, giving his judgment in the case of Nancy Cruzan, a woman who had been unconscious for eight years and whose guardians sought court permission to withdraw tube feeding of food and fluids so that she could die:

> But for patients like Nancy Cruzan, who have no consciousness and no chance of recovery, there is a serious question as to whether the mere persistence of their bodies is 'life', as that word is commonly understood...The State's unflagging determination to perpetuate Nancy Cruzan's physical existence is comprehensible only as an effort to define life's meaning, not as an attempt to preserve its sanctity...In any event, absent some theological abstraction, the idea of life is not conceived separately from the idea of a living person.[11]

Admittedly, this was a dissenting judgment. The majority decided the case on narrow constitutional grounds that are not relevant to our concerns here, and what Stevens said has not become part of the law of the United States. Nevertheless, dissenting judgments are often a way of floating an idea that is 'in the air' and may become part of the majority view in a later decision.

Another important impetus for moving to a higher brain definition of death comes from the weakness of the scientific and ethical foundations of the current whole-brain definition of death. We now know that the tests currently carried out as part of the accepted medical practice for establishing brain death do not really establish that *all* brain functions have ceased. Instead they allow a declaration of death to be made on the basis of the irreversible cessation of some brain functions while others continue. This suggests that some brain functions are important in deciding whether someone is alive or dead, while others (for example the hormonal functions) are unimportant. If this is the case, however, we need to begin discussing which brain functions are important, and why. Once such a discussion begins, there will obviously be a strong case for saying (using the very arguments that the Harvard committee used at the beginning of the whole debate) that what really matters is the irreversible loss of consciousness. Then, as soon as medical opinion accepts that we can reliably establish when consciousness has been irreversibly lost, the pressure will become intense for medical practice to move to a definition of death based on the death of the higher brain.

AGAINST BRAIN DEATH

Plausible as a change to a higher brain definition of death might be, I could not accept the proposal when it was put forward to the consensus development panel at the Royal Children's Hospital conference. This put me in unusual company—on the same side of this issue as those who were steadfastly opposed to taking organs from anencephalic or cortically dead infants. But the philosopher in me was in conflict with the practical reformer, and the philosopher came out on top. The notion of whole-brain death, I felt, was already something of a deception, an ethical choice masquerading as a medical fact. To move to a higher brain definition of death would stretch an already dubious deception too far. As Steve Keeley had said, it would not work—who was going to bury a 'corpse' that was still breathing while the lid of the coffin was nailed down?

My dilemma was a reflection of something larger that had gone wrong. But what? There has been a remarkable degree of international acceptance of the death of the whole brain as amounting, legally, to the death of the human being. And the higher brain criterion of death is, now that we have reliable means of diagnosing it, *more* logical than the whole-brain criterion. How can the higher brain criterion be both more logical than something we all accept, and at the same time, quite absurd?

The panel's deliberations made me think harder about brain death. I was beginning to see where the trouble began. The Harvard Brain Death Committee was faced with two serious problems. Patients in an utterly hopeless condition were attached to respirators, and no-one dared to turn them off. Organs that could be used to save lives were rendered useless by waiting for the circulation of the blood in potential donors to stop. The committee tried to solve both these problems by the bold expedient of classifying as dead those whose brains had ceased to have any discernible activity. The consequences of the redefinition of death were so evidently desirable that it met with scarcely any opposition, and was accepted almost universally. Nevertheless, it was unsound from the start. Solving problems by redefinition rarely works, and this case was no exception.

There was never a really good reason for considering the death of the whole brain—and only of the whole brain—as an indication of death. But this has only become clear now, when we know that doctors are, on a daily basis in every major hospital, classifying people whose brains have not entirely ceased to function as dead. If we were truly convinced that people are not dead until all their brain functions have ceased, we would have to take this as meaning that doctors are, on a daily basis, cutting the hearts, livers and kidneys out of living patients so that they can be donated to other patients. The facts about continuing brain function in patients declared to be dead have been published in reputable medical journals and, as far as I know, have not been disputed. Where, then, are the newspaper headlines, and the horrified public reactions? There are none. Why not? My guess is that we are not fundamentalists about the whole-brain criterion of death. We are just not interested in going back to a stricter interpretation of brain death, because that will mean that we have not, after all, solved the problems with which the Harvard committee began. When pressed, we don't really think it important whether *all* brain functions have ceased, or some have continued, as long as the fact that some have continued is not an indication that the patient might have recovered consciousness.

What, then, is the alternative? Shall we go forward to declaring dead those who are not only warm, pink and supple, but remain like this—*and breathing*—for a long time, even when they are just lying in a bed with no machines around them? If, like the Red Queen in *Through the Looking-Glass*, we practise believing impossible things for half an hour every morning, we might manage to swallow this. But if we cannot, we find ourselves in an untenable situation. We need to begin again, with a different approach to the original problems.

The suggestion I made to the panel was that instead of changing the definition of death so as to declare legally dead anencephalic infants and infants whose cortexes had been destroyed, it would be better to make it lawful to remove organs from living, precisely defined and indubitably diagnosed, anencephalic infants or infants whose cortexes have been destroyed. This suggestion was supported by one or two members of the panel, but it troubled most of the others. They wanted to think of human beings as either alive or dead. You could take a dead person's organs, under appropriate conditions, but as long as a human being was alive, these members of the panel thought, he or she was entitled to exactly the same protection as every other human being.

So the panel was split three ways: there were those who thought that anencephalics and cortically dead infants should be declared legally dead; those who thought that these infants were not dead, and therefore could not become organ donors; and those, including myself, who thought that these infants were not dead, but nevertheless could become organ donors. Given the strength of feelings on the issue, there was clearly no prospect of obtaining general consensus for any view. We took the easy way out. We agreed that all of the positions put forward were 'arguable', and should be widely discussed in the general community. The panel also recommended that the Victorian Law

Reform Commission would be an appropriate body to undertake such a community consultation.

That community consultation never happened. Perhaps the issue was not a high priority for the Victorian Law Reform Commission. When, if ever, it might have taken steps towards consulting the community we shall never know, because in 1992 the Labor government of Victoria was defeated at an election dominated by the state's financial difficulties. One of the first cost-cutting steps taken by the new Liberal government was to abolish the Law Reform Commission. Thus the use of anencephalic and cortically dead infants as organ donors remains impossible in Victoria, as it is elsewhere in the world.

While law reform bodies can be abolished, the issue raised by the Royal Children's Hospital cannot be. A year after the conference, it was again in the news in two countries. Laura Campo, a woman living in Florida who had no health insurance to cover prenatal care, went to a doctor only during the eighth month of her pregnancy. She was told that the fetus was anencephalic, but it was too late for an abortion. After listening to a talk show on organ donation, she decided to have the birth by caesarean section in order to increase the chance that her child would be born alive and could be useful as an organ donor. Baby Theresa was born on 21 March 1992. But the doctor in charge said that since Theresa had some brain stem function, she was not brain dead and he could not remove her organs. Together with Justin Pearson, the baby's father, Campo went to court to try to get a declaration that organs could be removed, but Judge Estella Moriaty refused, saying that 'death is a fact, not an opinion', and that she could not authorise anyone to take Baby Theresa's life to save another child, 'no matter how short or unsatisfactory the life of Baby Theresa might be'. After nine days, Baby Theresa began to deteriorate, and the respirator was removed. She died the next day—a day that also saw Campo and Pearson on 'The Donahue Show', pleading for a change in Florida's laws regarding brain death.[12] Only two weeks later, in Sicily, the Italian courts refused the parents of the anencephalic Baby Valentina permission to make her organs available for donation. Like Theresa, Valentina died soon after the court's decision.[13]

A WAY FORWARD?

The larger question still remains: what should we do with our concept of the death of the entire brain as equivalent to death—a concept so desirable in its consequences that it is unthinkable to give up, and so shaky on its foundations that it can scarcely be supported? The most clear-sighted proposal yet to be put forward comes from the Danish Council of Ethics. The council was established by the Danish parliament in 1987 to advise the minister for health on various ethical aspects of health care. At that time Denmark was the only country in western Europe that had no brain-based criterion of death. The council was therefore asked to report on this issue. After extensive community consultation, it recommended that the standard of death should continue to require the total and irreversible cessation of respiration and circulation. The cessation of all brain functions was not to count as death. It was, however, to mark a special stage, which the council called 'the irreversible process of dying'. When a patient was declared to be in the irreversible process of dying, all artificial measures to keep the patient alive were to be removed immediately, as the dying person could not benefit by them. But the use of artificial means of postponing the conclusion of the death process should, the council recommended, be permissible for a period of up to forty-eight hours, in order to allow transplantable organs to be removed, if the dying person had previously registered as an organ donor.[14]

The great merit of the Danish Council of Ethics proposal is that it separates, and thus allows us to think clearly about, three questions that have often been assumed, in the discussion of brain death, to be the same question. These questions are:

When does a human being die?
When is it permissible to stop trying to keep a human being alive?
When is it permissible to remove organs from a human being for the purpose of transplantation to another human being?

My own proposal to the panel at the Royal Children's Hospital was intended to avoid a similar confusion of the question of whether anencephalic and cortically dead infants are dead with the question of whether their organs may be taken from them. Unfortunately, the Danish Council of Ethics was no more successful with its proposal than I was with mine. The idea that we should be able to take the heart out of a human being who has not been declared dead was too radical for the Danish government. In 1990 it passed a law bringing Denmark into line with other European countries by making brain death a criterion of death.

We need to find another way of responding to human beings who can never be conscious. While the Royal Children's Hospital panel was unable to reach consensus on taking organs from infants with no prospect of ever gaining consciousness, this highly diverse group of people did agree that we need not keep such babies alive. This suggests that it may be easier to reach agreement about the second of the three questions listed above than about the first. If it is not possible to find a tenable basis for declaring people to be dead who have irreversibly lost—or never had—consciousness, we may still be able to find a justification for ending their lives. One reason why the Harvard Brain Death Committee advocated the new definition of death was, as we saw, to avoid the nightmarish prospect of filling our hospitals and nursing homes with living but permanently unconscious human beings. The definition of death in terms of the death of the whole brain has, however, been only a partial success in this respect, because it does not apply to patients in a persistent vegetative state. In 1993, in perhaps the most important decision of the twentieth century on the law relating to the sanctity of human life, Britain's highest court turned its attention to a patient in that condition.

TONY BLAND & THE
SANCTITY OF HUMAN LIFE

Traditional medical ethics…never asks whether the patient's life is worthwhile, for the notion of a worthless life is as alien to the Hippocratic tradition as it is to English criminal law, both of which subscribe to the principle of the sanctity of human life which holds that, because all lives are intrinsically valuable, it is always wrong intentionally to kill an innocent human being.

JOHN KEOWN, 1993

FINE PHRASES

We all like the notion of the intrinsic worth of human life. We accept such a noble idea without much critical scrutiny, as long as it does not restrict us from doing what we really think is important. Then one day we find it is making us do things that are manifestly pointless, or likely to lead to disaster. So we take a better look at the fine phrases we so readily accepted. And start to wonder why we ever believed them in the first place. Then we drop them.

This chapter describes a recent case concerning a young man named Anthony Bland, in which Britain's most eminent judges were forced to re-examine the fine sentiments summarised by John Keown. Nine judges had to ask themselves: could they really believe that every human life is intrinsically valuable? Could they really believe that it is always wrong intentionally to end the life of an innocent human being?

TONY BLAND'S TRAGEDY

In 1989 Tony Bland was seventeen years old and an avid football fan. On 15 April he went to Hillsborough Football Stadium in

Sheffield, to see his team, Liverpool, play Nottingham Forest in an FA Cup semi-final. As the match started, thousands of supporters were still trying to get into the ground. A fatal crush occurred, pushing hundreds of fans against some fencing that had been erected to stop them getting onto the playing field. Before order could be restored and the pressure relieved, ninety-five people had died in the worst disaster in British sporting history. Tony Bland was not killed, but his lungs were crushed by the pressure of the crowd around him, and his brain was deprived of oxygen. Later, in hospital, it was found that only his brain stem had survived. His cortex had been destroyed. Here is how Lord Justice Hoffmann was to describe his condition:

> Since April 15 1989 Anthony Bland has been in persistent vegetative state. He lies in Airedale General Hospital in Keighley, fed liquid food by a pump through a tube passing through his nose and down the back of his throat into the stomach. His bladder is emptied through a catheter inserted through his penis, which from time to time has caused infections requiring dressing and antibiotic treatment. His stiffened joints have caused his limbs to be rigidly contracted so that his arms are tightly flexed across his chest and his legs unnaturally contorted. Reflex movements in the throat cause him to vomit and dribble. Of all this, and the presence of members of his family who take turns to visit him, Anthony Bland has no consciousness at all. The parts of his brain which provided him with consciousness have turned to fluid. The darkness and oblivion which descended at Hillsborough will never depart. His body is alive, but he has no life in the sense that even the most pitifully handicapped but conscious human being has a life. But the advances of modern medicine permit him to be kept in this state for years, even perhaps for decades.[1]

Whatever the advances of modern medicine might permit, neither Tony Bland's family, nor Dr J. G. Howe, the doctor in charge of his care, nor Dr Michael Johnson, a specialist whose opinion Dr Howe had sought, nor the Airedale General Hospital in which he was a patient, could see any benefit to him, or to anyone else, in keeping him alive for decades. In Britain, as in many other countries, when everyone is in agreement in these situations it is quite common for the doctors simply to withdraw artificial feeding. The patient then dies within a week or two. In this case, however, the coroner in Sheffield was inquiring into the deaths caused by the Hillsborough disaster, and Dr Howe decided that he should notify the coroner of what he was intending to do. The coroner, while agreeing that Bland's continued existence could well be seen as entirely pointless, warned Dr Howe that he was running the risk of criminal charges—possibly even a charge of murder—if he intentionally ended Bland's life.

Lord Browne-Wilkinson, one of the judges who was finally to decide the case, later referred to the coroner's advice to Dr Howe, and made it plain why Howe would have been on dangerous ground if he had ignored it. In the past, Lord Browne-Wilkinson said, doctors had 'exercised their own discretion, in accordance with medical ethics', in cases such as this one, and had taken responsibility for deciding 'whether the perpetuation of life was pointless'. But Lord Browne-Wilkinson went on to refer to some doctors and nurses whose belief in the sanctity of all human life, no matter what the quality of that life, leads them to go to the police when a doctor decides not to prolong a life he or she believes to be pointless.

In Britain there are probably between 1000 and 1500 people in a persistent vegetative state in hospitals and nursing homes. In America, where doctors have been much more reluctant to use their discretion to withdraw life-support, and the courts have, at least in some states, been more eager to preserve life, a thorough study published in 1994 estimated that there were between 10,000 and 25,000 adults in a persistent vegetative state, as well as between 4000 and 10,000 children.[2] Although the coroner's warning must have been distressing to Bland's family and to Dr Howe, it provided an opportunity to settle in court, at least for the

British legal system (which is highly influential in many Commonwealth countries, among them Australia, Canada and New Zealand), the awkward question of whether life-support needs to be provided to people in this condition. After the coroner's warning, the administrator of the hospital in which Bland was a patient applied to the Family Division of the High Court for declarations that the hospital might lawfully discontinue all life-sustaining treatment, including ventilation, and the provision of food and water by artificial means, and discontinue all medical treatment to Bland 'except for the sole purpose of enabling Anthony Bland to end his life and to die peacefully with the greatest dignity and the least distress'.

At the Family Division hearing a public law officer called the Official Solicitor was appointed guardian for Bland for the purposes of the hearing. The Official Solicitor did not deny that Bland had no awareness at all, and could never recover, but he nevertheless opposed what Dr Howe was planning to do, arguing that, legally, it was murder. Sir Stephen Brown, President of the Family Division, did not accept this view, and he made the requested declarations to the effect that all treatment might lawfully be stopped. The Official Solicitor appealed, but Brown's decision was upheld by the Court of Appeal. The Official Solicitor then appealed again, thus bringing the case before the House of Lords (which is, in this context, not the upper house of the British parliament, but the highest court in the British judicial system).

We can best appreciate the significance of what the House of Lords did in the case of Tony Bland by looking at what the United States Supreme Court would not do in the similar case of Nancy Cruzan. Like Marion Ploch, Nancy Cruzan ceased to be an ordinary young woman and became a celebrated 'case' when she lost control of her car on a country road. Cruzan's accident happened in Missouri, in January 1983, when she was twenty-five. She was thrown out, and landed face down in a ditch filled with water. By the time help arrived, her brain had been without oxygen for several minutes. As a result, she was in a persistent vegetative state, and she remained that way for the next eight years. Her brain stem remained sufficiently intact to keep her body breathing without a respirator, but she had no swallowing reflex, and so she was given food and water by a tube passed down her nasal passage and into her stomach. Gradually her body became rigid and her hands curled up.

Nancy's parents, Joe and Joyce Cruzan, did not think that their daughter should be kept alive in this way, and so they went to court to get permission to remove her feeding tube. The Missouri Supreme Court refused, saying that since Nancy Cruzan was not competent to refuse life-sustaining treatment herself, and the state has an interest in preserving life, the court could only give permission for the withdrawal of life-sustaining treatment if there were clear and convincing evidence that this was what Cruzan would have wanted. No such evidence had been presented to the court.

The Cruzans appealed to the United States Supreme Court, arguing that their daughter had a constitutional right to be allowed to die. This was the first time this issue had been argued before the Supreme Court. (The earlier case of Karen Quinlan, about which I shall say more shortly, did not go beyond the New Jersey court system; and, in any case, Quinlan's parents applied only for permission to turn off her respirator, not to remove her feeding tube.) The Supreme Court was prepared to make the assumption, for the purposes of the case before it, that 'a competent person does have a constitutionally protected right to refuse lifesaving hydration and nutrition'. But the situation is different when patients are not competent to express their own wishes. Then, the court held, each state of the union can make its own decision as to what should happen. In particular, a state may, if it so wishes, refuse to allow treatment to be withdrawn unless there is clear evidence that the patient would have wished the

life-sustaining medical treatment to be withdrawn. As Justice Sandra Day O'Connor put it: 'Today we decide only that one state's
practice does not violate the constitution. The more challenging
task of crafting appropriate procedures for safeguarding incompe-
tents' liberty interests is entrusted to the "laboratory" of the states.'

Thus the Supreme Court did not decide whether it was permissible to withdraw Nancy Cruzan's feeding tube. It accepted
the right of the state of Missouri to demand, before permitting
this to occur, clear and convincing evidence that it was what
Cruzan would have wanted. Then, by a curious coincidence,
shortly after the Supreme Court issued this judgment, former
friends recalled that she had said things to them indicating that she
would wish to die, if she were ever in such a situation. This time
the state of Missouri did not oppose the Cruzans' application. The
lower court accepted that there was now 'clear and convincing'
evidence of their daughter's desire not to have her life sustained in
this situation, and it allowed the feeding tube to be withdrawn. So
Cruzan died a few months after the Supreme Court's judgment
was handed down. By this time she had been supported for nearly
eight years and, for at least seven of them, it had been clear that
she would never regain consciousness. Apart from the strain this
caused her family, it also cost the state of Missouri $130,000 a
year.[3] Nancy Cruzan's family obviously thought they had lost her
long before. On her tombstone they had engraved:

NANCY BETH CRUZAN

MOST LOVED

DAUGHTER–SISTER–AUNT

BORN JULY 20, 1957

DEPARTED JAN 11, 1983

AT PEACE DEC 26, 1990

As a matter of constitutional interpretation, the United States
Supreme Court may have been right to refrain from telling the
individual states of the union when they should allow a patient in
a persistent vegetative state to die. On the other hand, Britain

does not have a written constitution or a federal system of government, so the highest court in Britain could not avoid dealing with the central issue when the Bland case came before it. But American courts have up to now insisted that there should be evidence indicating that a patient in a persistent vegetative state would not have wished to be kept alive in the circumstances in which she now was. Without such evidence, they take it for granted that treatment must continue indefinitely.

Such indefinite prolongation of life has, so far, been the fate of Joey Fiori. In 1971 he was twenty-one years old, had served in the Vietnam war, and was about to marry his childhood sweetheart. Ten days before the wedding, a motorcycle accident left him severely brain damaged. He made slow progress in rehabilitation, but was still in a Philadelphia hospital for war veterans in 1976. Then, as a result of an apparent medical error, he suffered a seizure and went into a persistent vegetative state. Now forty-four years old, he lives in a nursing home, his condition unchanged. His care costs the federal government, which has acknowledged its responsibility for the medical malpractice, $150,000 a year. His mother, Rosemarie Sherman, visits him every day, but prays every night 'that God will take him'. Nor does she rely on prayer alone. She asked the nursing home to remove her son's feeding tube. The nursing home said that it required a court order to do so. At the first trial, the court granted the order, but the Pennsylvania Attorney General's Office appealed. A three-member panel of the State Superior Court upheld the appeal, saying that in the absence of any 'clear and convincing evidence' of Fiori's preferences, he must be kept alive. Given the length of time that Fiori has now been incapable of expressing any preference about such a matter, it seems improbable that such evidence will be forthcoming. As this book goes to press Joey Fiori is still alive, and the case is continuing its way through the courts.[4]

The main legal issue debated by the American judges in the Cruzan and Fiori cases was: how strong does the evidence about the patient's wishes have to be? In contrast to the characteristic American emphasis on personal autonomy, the British courts were not much interested in what Tony Bland's wishes might have been. As Sir Thomas Bingham, Master of the Rolls of the Court of Appeal, said in delivering his judgment: 'At no time before the disaster did Mr Bland give any indication of his wishes should he find himself in such a condition. It is not a topic most adolescents address.'[5]

But the British courts did not therefore conclude that Bland must be treated until he died (which might mean for half a century or more). Instead, the British judges asked a different question: what is in the best interests of the patient?[6] In answer, they referred to the unanimous medical opinion that Bland was not aware of anything, and that there was no prospect of any improvement in his condition. Hence the treatment that was sustaining Bland's life brought him, as Sir Stephen Brown put it in the initial judgment in the case, 'no therapeutical, medical, or other benefit'.[7] In essence, the British courts held that when a patient is incapable of consenting to medical treatment, doctors are under no legal duty to continue treatment that does not benefit a patient. In addition, the judges agreed that the mere continuation of biological life is not, in the absence of any awareness or any hope of ever again becoming aware, a benefit to the patient.

On one level, the British approach is straightforward common sense. As Lord Mustill said in the House of Lords, 'the pitiful state of Anthony Bland and the suffering of his devoted family must attract the sympathy of all'.[8] No doubt this sympathy was a powerful factor in leading all of the judges, in each of the three courts that considered Bland's case, to the same conclusion: that Bland's treatment could be discontinued. No-one who reads these judgments can be in any doubt about the fact that all the judges are searching for a solution that brings an end to a tragedy that is already terrible, and threatens to be drawn out, in the most grotesque way, over decades. Nevertheless, when we recall the pronouncements of judges in earlier cases about life and death, the judgments in the Bland case do break new ground, in two crucial respects. They allow considerations of the quality of life to enter into a decision whether life should be prolonged. And they accept as lawful a course of conduct that has as its aim and object the death of an innocent human being. Putting these two points together, it is no exaggeration to say that the Bland case marks the moment at which the British courts ceased to give effect to the traditional principle of the sanctity of human life. Let us look at each of these two points in turn.

DECIDING ON THE BASIS OF QUALITY OF LIFE

The standard view of the law, and of the traditional doctrine of the sanctity of human life in the Judeo-Christian tradition, was that every human life is of equal value. As Sanford Kadish, describing the view of human life taken by Anglo-American law, put it: 'all human lives must be regarded as having an equal claim to preservation simply because life is an irreducible value. Therefore the value of a particular life, over and above the value of life itself, may not be taken into account.'[9]

This position was restated quite categorically as recently as 1986 by Mr Justice Vincent, a judge of the Supreme Court of Victoria, Australia, when he ordered life-sustaining treatment to be provided for a baby born with a severe disability: 'the law does not permit decisions to be made concerning the quality of life nor any assessment of the value of any human being'.[10]

This seems very clear-cut. Faced with the prospect of a life like that of Tony Bland, however, the British judges shifted ground. Altogether, nine judges pronounced on the case, one in the Family Division of the High Court, three in the Court of Appeal, and five in the House of Lords. In slightly different words, each one made it clear that he did not value life that is human only in a biological sense. Since this is a fundamental point, it is worth looking at what each of them said. In the Family Division of the High Court, Sir Stephen Brown said:

> Anthony Bland...has no feelings, no awareness, nor can he experience anything relating to his surroundings. To his parents and family he is 'dead'. His spirit has left him and all that remains is the shell of his body...I am satisfied that there is no therapeutic, medical or other benefit to Anthony Bland in continuing to maintain his ventilation, nutrition and hydration by artificial means.[11]

In the Court of Appeal, Sir Thomas Bingham said: 'Looking at the matter as objectively as I can, and doing my best to look at the matter through Mr Bland's eyes and not my own, I cannot conceive what benefit his continued existence could be thought to give him'.[12]

Lord Justice Butler-Sloss weighed the principle of the sanctity of life against the quality of life, and found it wanting:

> The considerations as to the quality of life of Mr Bland now and in the future in his extreme situation are in my opinion rightly to be placed on the other side of the critical equation from the general principle of the sanctity and inviolability of life. In this appeal those factors which include the reality of Mr Bland's existence outweigh the abstract requirement to preserve life.[13]

Lord Justice Hoffmann attempted to argue that he was not making a quality of life decision. To the Official Solicitor's claim that a decision allowing Bland to die would be a decision that his life is not worth living, Hoffmann responded:

> There is no question of his life being worth living or not worth living because the stark reality is that Anthony Bland is not living a life at all. None of the things that one says about the way people live their lives—well or ill, with courage or fortitude, happily or sadly—have any meaning in relation to him.[14]

Here Hoffmann is playing with words. That Bland was legally alive was not in dispute. To decide, as Hoffmann did, that 'it would be right to allow Anthony Bland to die', makes sense only if one judges that Bland's mere biological life was not worth living. This, presumably, is how Hoffmann did judge Bland's mere biological life, and the fact that Bland was not, in some other (perhaps biographical rather than biological)[15] sense, 'living a life at all', was presumably why Hoffmann felt able to reach this judgment.

When the case came before the House of Lords, their lordships took the same view. Lord Keith of Kinkel discussed the difficulties of making a value judgment about the life of a 'permanently insensate' being, and concluded cautiously that, 'It is, however, perhaps permissible to say that to an individual with no cognitive capacity whatever, and no prospect of ever recovering any such capacity in this world, it must be a matter of complete indifference whether he lives or dies'.[16]

Lord Goff of Chieveley described medical treatment 'simply to prolong a patient's life' as 'futile' if the patient is unconscious and there is no prospect of an improvement in his condition.[17] Lord Lowry gave a brief judgment in which he agreed with Lord Goff, and said that 'it is not in the interests of an insentient patient to continue the life-supporting care and treatment'.[18] Lord Browne-Wilkinson thought that the decision whether continued treatment was a benefit to the patient was not one for the court to make, but for the doctor; all that the court had to decide is whether the responsible doctor has reached a reasonable and bona fide belief that continued treatment is not a benefit to the patient. In Bland's case, he had no doubt that it was 'perfectly reasonable' for the responsible doctors to conclude that sustaining Bland's life brought him 'no affirmative benefit'.[19] Finally, Lord Mustill concluded that to withdraw life-support was not only legally, but also ethically justified, 'since the continued treatment of Anthony Bland can no longer serve to maintain that combination of manifold characteristics which we call a personality'.[20]

There can therefore be no doubt that, with the decision in the

Bland case, British law abandoned the idea that life itself is a benefit to the person living it, irrespective of its quality. If Lord Goff thought life itself was always of value, he would not have been able to say that treatment that prolongs human life can be futile, and the other judges would not have been able to maintain that the care given to Anthony Bland was not benefiting him. The conclusion we can draw is that British law now holds that for life to be a benefit to the person living it, that person must, at a minimum, have some capacity for awareness or conscious experience.

LAWFULLY INTENDING TO END INNOCENT HUMAN LIFE

The second novel aspect of the decision in the case of Tony Bland is that it was as plain as anything can be that the proposal to discontinue tube feeding was intended to bring about Bland's death. This fact could hardly have been overlooked, since, as we have seen, one of the declarations sought by the administrator of the Airedale Hospital was that treatment could lawfully be discontinued 'except for the sole purpose of enabling Anthony Bland to end his life and to die peacefully with the greatest dignity and the least distress'. (How Bland, who could feel nothing, could have suffered distress was not explained; perhaps the administrator was making an oblique reference to the distress of Bland's family or of the hospital staff.)

A majority of the judges in the House of Lords referred to the administrator's intention in very direct terms. Lord Browne-Wilkinson noted that 'the whole purpose of stopping artificial feeding is to bring about the death of Anthony Bland'.[21] Lord Mustill was equally explicit: 'the proposed conduct has the aim for...humane reasons of terminating the life of Anthony Bland by withholding from him the basic necessities of life'.[22] Lord Lowry also accepted that 'the intention to bring about the patient's death is there'.[23]

This marks a sharp contrast to what for many years was considered the definitive view of what a doctor may permissibly intend. That view comes from the sensational British trial of Dr John Bodkin Adams in 1957. The prosecution alleged that Dr Adams had persuaded Mrs Morrell, an elderly patient, to leave him money and items of value in her will, and then murdered her by giving her overdoses of morphine and other opiates. Dr Adams told police that Mrs Morrell was in agony, and he was merely 'easing the passing'. The trial judge, Justice (later Lord) Devlin, directed the jury that 'if the first purpose of medicine, the restoration of health, can no longer be achieved...a doctor...is entitled to do all that is proper and necessary to relieve pain and suffering, even if the measures he takes may incidentally shorten life'.

The basis for this oft-quoted direction is the claim that to foresee that an act may shorten someone's life is not the same as to intend to shorten that person's life. If Dr Adams gave Mrs Morrell an injection with the intention of relieving her suffering, then even though he may have foreseen that the injection would shorten her life, he was not guilty of murder. Justice Devlin then continued: 'But it remains the fact, and it remains the law, that no doctor, nor any man, no more in the case of the dying than of the healthy, has the right deliberately to cut the thread of human life'.[24]

Even definitions of murder enshrined in statutes—for example, the definition used in Crimes Acts in Australian states such as New South Wales—typically include not only acts, but also omissions, if done with the intent to end life.[25] In these statutes, as in Justice Devlin's view, it is the intention to end life that marks the crucial distinction between murder and sound medical practice. In the Bland decision, it is not. In rewriting the law of murder regarding the question of intention, the British law lords have shown a clarity and forthrightness that should serve as a model to many others who try to muddle through these difficult questions.

The idea that it is always wrong intentionally to end an innocent human life is often seen as the one moral commandment that we must never violate. In extreme situations, however, it has always been difficult to defend. Therefore, those who claim to uphold it resort to strange distinctions in order to reach a reasonable outcome without appearing to break the absolute commandment. In the famous case of Karen Quinlan, decided in 1976, seventeen years before Bland's case, the distinction between 'ordinary' and 'extraordinary' means of life-support was invoked. Like Bland, Quinlan was in a persistent vegetative state—although this term was not then in use, and she was described as being in a 'permanent coma'. Her doctors agreed that she was unconscious and would never recover from this state. She was placed on a respirator, and her doctors advised her parents that without the respirator she would die. (Although the court hearing was conducted on the assumption that Quinlan would die when the respirator was turned off, to everyone's surprise she survived for ten years after the respirator was removed.) Quinlan's parents were Roman Catholics and so would not have accepted any active termination of their daughter's life, but they were advised by their priest that it was not obligatory to use 'extraordinary means' to prolong life. The use of a respirator in a case like this was, they were told, an 'extraordinary means'. Accordingly they applied to have it turned off. The doctors refused. Hence the issue went to court.

At the initial hearing, a court-appointed guardian for Karen Quinlan stated clearly the way he saw the central issue in the case: 'One human being, by conduct, or lack of conduct, is going to cause the death of another human being'. Rather more dramatically, the attorney for one of the doctors said that turning off Quinlan's respirator was 'like turning on the gas chamber'.[26] But Bishop Lawrence Casey, the Roman Catholic bishop of New Jersey, saw it differently. He told the court that because the respirator was an 'extraordinary means of treatment', the request of Quinlan's parents that it should be withdrawn was 'morally correct'.[27]

There are several difficulties with the view taken by Bishop Casey in this case, and with the appeal to the distinction between ordinary and extraordinary means of treatment in general. The most obvious problem is that there has never been any agreement as to how this distinction should be drawn. Why is a respirator extraordinary, and a feeding tube ordinary? Nor is there any clear basis in ethics for holding that it is acceptable to withdraw 'extraordinary' but not 'ordinary' means of life-support. It has been argued that extraordinary treatment may be withdrawn because it is burdensome to the patient. The intention with which the treatment is withdrawn, according to this argument, is to spare the patient burdensome treatment, rather than to bring about the patient's death. On this view, even if it is foreseeable that withdrawing the extraordinary means of life-support will bring about the patient's death, this is an 'unwanted side-effect' and not the intended consequence of the withdrawal.

The case of Karen Quinlan reveals clearly enough that appealing to the distinction between 'ordinary' and 'extraordinary' means of treatment is no way of getting around the need to base our decisions on judgments about the quality of a human life. Firstly, the very description of the respirator as 'extraordinary' depends on a judgment already having been made to the effect that it is not worthwhile prolonging the life of a patient in Quinlan's condition. Indeed, Bishop Casey himself implicitly admitted this in court, when he prefaced his opinion that the use of a respirator was extraordinary by saying that Quinlan 'has no reasonable hope of recovery from her comatose state'. Obviously, if Karen were only in a temporary coma, and did have a reasonable hope of recovery, the bishop and everyone else would regard the use of a respirator as essential. Similarly, even if Karen's condition were incurable, if she had a reasonable quality of life—imagine that she needed a respirator to breathe, but was conscious and able to enjoy a variety of activities—the use of the respirator would not be considered extraordinary. Thus labelling a means of treatment as 'extraordinary' serves to disguise judgment about the quality of life of the patient on whom the means of treatment is being used.[28]

Secondly, in the Quinlan case, appealing to the distinction between 'ordinary' and 'extraordinary' means can disguise, but cannot ultimately conceal, the fact that Quinlan's parents acted with the intention to end their daughter's life because it was so lacking in any positive qualities or redeeming features. In the case of a patient who has some awareness, it might be possible to argue that the intention, in withdrawing 'extraordinary' means of treatment that may cause the patient pain or discomfort, is to avoid inflicting on the patient a burden that has no proportionate benefit. Roman Catholic ethicists typically argue in this way, although others think that even this kind of intention is best understood as acting on an overall judgment that it is better that the patient should die rather than continue to live with the discomfort or pain of the continuing treatment. But this debate is irrelevant to the Quinlan case, because Quinlan's parents were advised by her doctors that she had no awareness and could feel no pain or discomfort. Thus the use of the respirator could not be 'burdensome' to her. So what intention could Quinlan's parents possibly have had, in asking for the respirator to be turned off, other than that she should die?

At the first trial in the Quinlan case, the judge ruled that Karen should not die. When this decision was appealed though, the New Jersey Supreme Court held that there was a constitutional right to privacy which allowed the family of a dying incompetent patient to discontinue 'artificial life support systems'. Nevertheless, the court went out of its way to say that this did not amount to a right to suicide, nor to assist in a suicide. The court accepted the argument that to remove such means of life-support is not to intend death.[29]

No doubt the British judges considering the case of Anthony Bland could have held that the course of treatment proposed was not intended to bring about the death of Anthony Bland. His death, they might have said, would be a foreseen but unwanted side-effect of removing the feeding tube, which constituted 'extraordinary' or 'disproportionate' medical treatment. But this would have been a patently artificial strategy, because no-one would consider a feeding tube to be 'extraordinary' or 'disproportionate' unless they had already judged the life of the patient who was being fed by it to be of such poor quality that it was not worth prolonging. The refusal of the British judges to consider such a strategy meant that they were discarding the fig leaf that might have hidden the true nature of their decision: that it can be lawful intentionally to bring about the death of an innocent human being.

BEYOND THE SANCTITY OF HUMAN LIFE

In reaching the decisions that, for Anthony Bland, continued life brought no benefit, and that it can be lawful intentionally to cause the death of an innocent human being, the British courts were breaking with the traditional principle of the sanctity of human life. On the whole, they seem to have taken this momentous step with due regard for the significance of what they were doing. The nature of the step was strongly pointed out to the House of Lords by Mr James Munby, the Queen's Counsel who appeared on behalf of the Official Solicitor. In his judgment, Lord Mustill agreed with Munby that 'in this part of the law, the court has moved a long way in a short time'. Nevertheless, he was, he said, satisfied that what he and his fellow law lords were deciding was both right and in accordance with the law.[30]

Of course, the British judges did not simply dismiss the principle of the sanctity of human life. On the contrary, when they referred to it they did so respectfully, and stressed its importance.

But they then weighed it against other considerations—and found it outweighed. At the Court of Appeal, for instance, Lord Justice Butler-Sloss said, 'the case for the universal sanctity of life assumes a life in the abstract and allows nothing for the reality of Mr Bland's actual existence'.[31] In the House of Lords, Lord Keith of Kinkel asked:

> Given that existence in the persistent vegetative state is not a benefit to the patient, it remains to consider whether the principle of the sanctity of life, which it is the concern of the state, and the judiciary as one of the arms of the state, to maintain, requires this House to hold that the judgment of the Court of Appeal was incorrect. In my opinion it does not. The principle is not an absolute one.[32]

Now it may seem that this respectful treatment leaves the principle of the sanctity of human life substantially in place, even if, in extreme cases like that of Tony Bland, it may be outweighed. But to think this would be to misunderstand the nature of the traditional doctrine of the sanctity of human life. Simply stated, this doctrine holds that it is *never* right intentionally to take an innocent human life. More fully elaborated so as to make clear its application to the medical context, it has been put like this: 'It is absolutely prohibited to either intentionally kill a patient, or intentionally to let a patient die, and to base decisions relating to the prolongation or shortening of human life on considerations of its quality or kind'.[33]

For those who subscribe to the doctrine of the sanctity of human life, this is an absolute prohibition. It is not a principle to be balanced against conflicting considerations. When those who uphold the sanctity of human life say that it is never right intentionally to take an innocent human life, they really do mean never. That is why traditionally minded Christian bioethicists have been dismayed by the decision in the case of Anthony Bland. Shortly after the judgment was handed down, Dr John Keown, a legal scholar from Queen's College, Cambridge, wrote about the decision in *Ethics & Medicine*, a journal that describes itself as 'seeking to develop a Christian mind on the complex and fundamental challenges posed to society by technological advance in medical science'. Lawyers have a maxim, 'hard cases make bad law', which suggests that judges are tempted to depart from sound principles in cases where to follow those principles would bring hardship upon people who do not deserve it. Keown clearly thought that this was what had happened in the Bland case, for he summed up his verdict by saying that it was 'a hard case which made bad law, largely by approving a consequentialist ethic radically inconsistent with the principle of the sanctity of life'.[34] Keown is right to say that the decision in the Bland case is radically inconsistent with the principle of the sanctity of life—but this does not mean that it is bad law. Rather, the utter hopelessness of Anthony Bland's condition led the judges to see that technological advances in medicine have made it impossible to retain the principle of the sanctity of human life. Instead, they switched to an ethic that sensibly takes into account whether sustaining life will benefit or harm the human being whose life is to be sustained.

ACTS AND OMISSIONS

One final puzzle about the Bland case remains to be solved. Does the decision allow doctors to kill their patients? This is precisely what opponents of euthanasia have claimed. Luke Gormally, director of the Christian-based Linacre Centre for Health Care Ethics, in London, put it plainly: 'the Law Lords in the Bland case have in effect declared non-voluntary euthanasia lawful'.[35] Moreover, on the basis of what we have seen so far, this conclusion seems inescapable. The judges declared that Bland's doctors were entitled to take a course of action that had Bland's death as its 'whole purpose'. They made this declaration on the basis of a judgment that prolonging Bland's life did not benefit him (or in

Lord Browne-Wilkinson's judgment, that it was reasonable for Bland's doctors to make such a judgment). What else can this amount to, other than allowing doctors to kill certain patients—at the least, those in a persistent vegetative state. But why only those ones?

Their Lordships, however, did not think they were legalising euthanasia. The reason why was given by Lord Goff of Chievely:

> I must however stress, at this point, that the law draws a crucial distinction between cases in which a doctor decides not to provide, or to continue to provide, for his patient treatment or care which could or might prolong his life, and those in which he decides, for example by administering a lethal drug, actively to bring his patient's life to an end. As I have already indicated, the former may be lawful...but it is not lawful for a doctor to administer a drug to his patient to bring about his death, even though that course is prompted by a humanitarian desire to end his suffering, however great that suffering may be...So to act is to cross the Rubicon which runs between on the one hand the care of the living patient and on the other hand euthanasia—actively causing his death to avoid or to end his suffering.[36]

The crucial distinction, then, is between ending life by actively doing something, and ending life by not providing treatment needed to sustain life. That distinction has long been discussed by philosophers and bioethicists, who would say that Lord Goff is accepting passive euthanasia, while rejecting active euthanasia.

When bioethicists debate whether it can make good sense to accept passive euthanasia while rejecting active euthanasia, two issues invariably emerge: how the distinction is to be drawn, and whether, once drawn, it carries enough ethical significance to bear the moral weight placed upon it. On the first issue James Munby had argued, on behalf of the Official Solicitor, that the removal of Bland's feeding tube was a positive act, and not merely an omission; hence, according to Munby, to remove Bland's feeding tube was actively to cause his death. In replying to this point, Lord Browne-Wilkinson revealed just how difficult the distinction between acts and omissions can be. Removing the tube, he said:

> is undoubtedly a positive act, similar to switching off a ventilator in the case of a patient whose life is being sustained by artificial ventilation. But in my judgment in neither case should the act be classified as positive, since to do so would be to introduce intolerably fine distinctions. If, instead of removing the nasogastric tube, it was left in place but no further nutrients were provided for the tube to convey to the patient's stomach, that would not be an act of commission. Again...if the switching off of a ventilator were to be classified as a positive act, exactly the same result can be achieved by installing a time-clock which requires to be reset every twelve hours; the failure to reset the machine could not be classified as a positive act. In my judgment, essentially what is being done is to omit to feed or to ventilate; the removal of the nasogastric tube or the switching off of a ventilator are merely incidents of that omission.[37]

Drawing the distinction in this way invites the objection that if a patient with good prospects of recovery temporarily needs a respirator, it would be possible for an interloper who had his own reasons for wanting a patient to die to bring about the patient's death by turning off the respirator. This would be the perfect crime, because there would have been no positive act that could count as murdering the patient. Lord Goff dealt with this objection:

> although the interloper may perform exactly the same act as the doctor who discontinues life support, his doing so constitutes interference with the life-prolonging treatment then being administered by the doctor. Accordingly, whereas the doctor, in discontinuing life support, is simply allowing his patient to die of his pre-existing condition, the interloper is actively intervening to stop the doctor from prolonging the patient's life, and such conduct cannot possibly be categorised as an omission.[38]

Lord Mustill recognised that this distinction between acts and omissions is 'morally and intellectually dubious' and thought that it was 'unpromising' to apply it in 'a context where the ethical foundations of the law are already open to question'. Nevertheless, he said, he was forced to try to make it work, and so he too declares that the proposed conduct 'will fall into the category of omissions'.[39]

This 'Rubicon' to which Lord Goff earlier referred is clearly no broad river! It is at best a meandering creek, one that seems about to dry up into a series of waterholes. Whether in the end their lordships have succeeded in separating cases of actively causing death from cases in which a doctor 'simply' allows a patient to die of a pre-existing condition, is not easy to say. Fortunately it is not a question we need to pursue any further here, because for our inquiry the second, ethical issue is of greater importance: does the distinction between withdrawing life-sustaining treatment and actively causing death bear the ethical weight that must be placed upon it by those who want to say that the former is good medical practice, and the latter is murder?

Here the law lords, even while they insist that the law draws the distinction in the way they have described, recognise that at this point law and ethics have come apart, and something needs to be done about it. Lord Browne-Wilkinson expressed the hope that parliament would review the law. He then ended his judgment with a remarkable admission that he could not provide a moral basis for the legal decision he had reached:

> Finally, the conclusion I have reached will appear to some to be almost irrational. How can it be lawful to allow a patient to die slowly, though painlessly, over a period of weeks from lack of food but unlawful to produce his immediate death by a lethal injection, thereby saving his family from yet another ordeal to add to the tragedy that has already struck them? I find it difficult to find a moral answer to that question. But it is undoubtedly the law and nothing I have said casts doubt on the proposition that the doing of a positive

act with the intention of ending life is and remains murder.[40]

Lord Mustill was just as frank and even more uncomfortable about the state of the law:

> The conclusion that the declarations can be upheld depends crucially on a distinction drawn by the criminal law between acts and omissions, and carries with it inescapably a distinction between, on the one hand what is often called 'mercy killing', where active steps are taken in a medical context to terminate the life of a suffering patient, and a situation such as the present where the proposed conduct has the aim for equally humane reasons of terminating the life of Anthony Bland by withholding from him the basic necessities of life. The acute unease which I feel about adopting this way through the legal and ethical maze is I believe due in an important part to the sensation that however much the terminologies may differ the ethical status of the two courses of action is for all relevant purposes indistinguishable. By dismissing this appeal I fear that your Lordships' House may only emphasise the distortions of a legal structure which is already both morally and intellectually misshapen. Still, the law is there and we must take it as it stands.[41]

It was presumably these sentiments that Lord Lowry had in mind when, in concluding his own judgment, he referred to 'the possible gap which my noble and learned friend, Lord Mustill, sees between old law and new medicine and perhaps also, I might add, new ethics'. He ended by pointing to the need for fresh legislation:

> It is important, particularly in the area of criminal law which governs conduct, that society's notions of what is the law and what is right should coincide. One role of the legislators is to detect any disparity between these notions and to take appropriate action to close the gap.[42]

The case of Anthony Bland has, for the moment, settled the question of the state of the law in Britain regarding patients who can never regain consciousness. The lives of such patients are of no benefit to them, and so doctors may lawfully stop feeding them in order to end their lives. With this decision the law has ended its unthinking commitment to the preservation of human life that is a mere biological existence. The law lords have taken the brave step of recognising that, at a minimum, consciousness is essential if continued life is to be worth having. In doing so they have shifted the boundary between what is and what is not murder. Before they handed down their decision, to take a course of conduct intended to end the life of an innocent human being was to make oneself liable to a charge of murder. Now, when the prolongation of life is of no benefit to the patient, conduct intended to end life is lawful. What is not lawful is to undertake a positive act intended to end such a life: this marks the new boundary of murder. What, though, is a positive act? It seems that switching off a respirator or withdrawing a feeding tube is not a positive act, whereas giving a lethal injection is; but beyond that, it is difficult to predict what a court might hold to be a positive act, and what it would not. And in any case, what ethical basis does this distinction have? A majority of the law lords appear ready to admit that the answer is: none. In Lord Mustill's words, the law has become 'morally and intellectually misshapen'.

Their lordships had inherited a legal framework that allowed them some room to manoeuvre, but not a great deal. Within that framework, they did what they could to reach a sensible decision in the case of Anthony Bland, and to point the law in a new direction that other judges could follow. In doing so, they recognised the moral incoherence of the position they were taking, but found themselves unable to do anything about it, beyond drawing the problem to the attention of parliament. They could hardly have done more to show clearly the need for a new approach to life-and-death decisions.

PART II

⟶◆⟵

Crumbling at the Edges

UNCERTAIN BEGINNINGS

I will not give to a woman an abortive remedy.

THE HIPPOCRATIC OATH

If a person's right to life is violated at the moment in which he is first conceived in his mother's womb, an indirect blow is struck also at the whole of the moral order, which serves to ensure the inviolable goods of man. Among these goods, life occupies the first place.

POPE JOHN PAUL II, 1979

PEGGY STINSON'S PUZZLE

In December 1976 Peggy Stinson was twenty-four weeks pregnant, but the pregnancy was not going well. The placenta was in the wrong position, and threatening to detach altogether, causing a haemorrhage that would endanger her life and that of her child-to-be. There was also a possibility that the baby would survive, but be seriously damaged. Taking all these things into account, on 15 December Peggy and her husband Robert talked over whether to terminate the pregnancy. Although it would be a late abortion, in the United States, where the Stinsons lived, the abortion could be performed safely and legally. Afterwards, they could conceive another child, with a good chance of a normal pregnancy.

The next day, while Peggy and Robert were still trying to make up their minds, Peggy went into premature labour. The baby, a boy they called Andrew, was born alive, but so premature that his survival was doubtful—and if he survived, there was a high risk that his prematurity would result in brain damage and some form of disability. The Stinsons asked that no heroic measures be taken to save Andrew's life, but Andrew's doctors threatened to take them to court if they did not consent to the procedures they advised. Andrew was placed on a respirator, and continued to be treated even after it became clear that, if he survived at all, he would be brain-damaged. This led Peggy to speculate in her diary about the narrow line between life and death: 'A woman can terminate a perfectly healthy pregnancy by abortion at 24½ weeks and that is legal. Nature can terminate a problem pregnancy by miscarriage at 24½ weeks and the baby must be saved at all costs; anything less is illegal and immoral'.[1]

Peggy Stinson is not the only person to have been puzzled by the extraordinary difference that birth makes. Pro-life advocates, coming from a position diametrically opposed to that of the Stinsons, often make the same point. How, they ask, can a hospital have a neonatal intensive care unit in which dedicated doctors and nurses work around the clock to save the lives of extremely premature newborn infants, while down the corridor an obstetrics and gynaecology unit carries out abortions on fetuses more developed than the premature infants being saved?

Our uncertainty over what to think about maintaining pregnancies in brain-dead women like Trisha Marshall and Marion Ploch is another aspect of this puzzlement. What is the status of a fetus whose mother has died? Is it really worth maintaining a woman's bodily functions for three months to preserve the life of a fetus? Would it make any difference if the fetus was closer to birth? If not, why is a late fetus so different from a premature baby? But if we can justify going to so much trouble and expense to save a fetus, how can that judgment be reconciled with a woman's right to have an abortion for any reason that seems sufficient to her?

What coherent ethic can accommodate our different practices regarding the born and the unborn? Not, certainly, the sanctity of life ethic. Conservative moralists like Pope John Paul II are absolutely right to see the acceptance of abortion as a threat to a wider moral order. The extraordinary change in ethical, social and legal attitudes to abortion in the 1960s and 70s was the first of a series of major setbacks for the traditional view of the sanctity of human life. If we consider it justifiable for a woman to kill her fetus in the womb because she considers her family complete, or does not wish to interrupt her career, or because the fetus has been shown to have Down syndrome, this judgment must have some bearing on our views about human life immediately after birth, or when, as in the case of Tony Bland, all capacity for consciousness has been lost. Morality may not all be a seamless web, as some have claimed, but it is not a set of isolated units either. The acceptance of abortion is another source of pressure on the sanctity of life ethic, another paring away from the margins that can eventually put the entire structure in jeopardy. Of course, what Pope John Paul II was not ready to contemplate is that the traditional ethic is in any case untenable and in need of replacement.

THE UNAVOIDABLE ISSUE

Even among supporters of legal abortion, the view I have just sketched would not be widely accepted. The anti-abortion movement calls itself 'pro-life', but those who defend abortion on request do not describe themselves as 'anti-life', or even 'anti-fetal-rights-to-life'. They prefer the term 'pro-choice', thus presenting the issue as one about a woman's right to choose whether to remain pregnant or not. They try to avoid taking a position on when a developing human being first has a right to life. This may be good politics, but it is poor philosophy. To present the issue of abortion as a question of individual choice (like sexual behaviour between consenting adults) is already to presuppose that the fetus does not really count. No-one who thinks that a human fetus has the same right to life as other human beings could see the abortion question as a matter of choice, any more than they would see slavery as a matter of the free choice of slaveholders.

In discussions with students, when I have used the analogy between being 'pro-choice' about abortion and being 'pro-choice' about slave ownership, I often get the reply: 'Yes, but the slaves also have the capacity to choose and ought to be free to choose, as well as the slaveholders!' That is true, of course, but what does this answer show? It shows that some difference in the abilities or capacities of fetuses as compared with older humans is at work in leading us to think differently about the rights of fetuses and slaves. The ability to choose, this reply suggests, is what gives human beings basic rights, including a right to life. Whether or not this position is defensible, it clearly denies basic rights to fetuses, because they are incapable of choice, and to that extent it is not just 'pro-choice', but also 'anti-fetal-rights-to-life'.

In fairness I should add that to describe the anti-abortion movement as 'pro-life' is just as misleading as describing advocates of legal abortion as 'pro-choice'. There are few vegetarians among the pro-life movement. Most of its members draw a sharp line between human beings, whose lives they wish to protect, and nonhuman animals, whose killing they support every time they eat their dinner. For that reason, the movement ought to call itself 'pro-human-life'. But that would still not be quite right, because the movement is not against killing in war, or capital punishment. 'Pro-innocent-human-life' is therefore closer to the mark. Even this will not quite do because the movement does not do anything to save children from death by malnutrition or preventable disease in poorer regions of the world, although this is—compared to fighting abortion—a much more certain and effective way of saving the lives of innocent human beings.

Advocates of legal abortion cannot remain neutral about when the developing human being acquires a right to life. If they advocate abortion on request, they are implicitly valuing the claim to life of a fetus as less important than the claim of a pregnant woman to choose the size of her family, pursue an uninterrupted career, or avoid bringing up a disabled child. This may be justifiable, but it is a substantive moral position because it rejects the idea that all human life is equally sacrosanct.

Admittedly, the protection of human life from conception

onwards has not always been part of the traditional sanctity of life ethic. Judaism has never taught that abortion is equivalent to murder. According to the Gospel accounts, Jesus did not mention abortion. Liberal Catholics, trying to soften the teaching of their church, often point out that in the middle ages Christian philosophers like Thomas Aquinas held that the embryo or fetus was 'unformed' and inert until the soul entered it, at 'quickening', the time when the pregnant woman first feels the fetus moving within her. Aquinas believed this occurred forty days after conception in the case of a male fetus, and eighty days after conception for a female fetus. In the absence of any scientific knowledge of the development of the fetus prior to quickening, it was not unreasonable to take this as the beginning of life. To carry out an abortion before quickening was therefore not seen as homicide, but rather as birth control. Only in the nineteenth century did it begin to be widely held, in the Roman Catholic Church and in many legal systems that, from the moment of conception, abortion is a form of homicide.

It is true that the condemnation of abortion from the time of conception as a mortal sin is a relatively new doctrine for the church. But the reason for the church's change of view on the stage of pregnancy at which abortion becomes the killing of a human being was surely, within the terms of its own view of the sanctity of human life, a sound one. Once modern biology had shown the actual nature of early human development, the church had little choice but to abandon its support for the unscientific Aristotelian embryology of Thomas Aquinas. (Liberal Catholics will hardly want to condemn one of the few instances in which the church has been willing to modify its views in the light of new scientific knowledge, much as they may regret the selectivity with which the church uses such knowledge.) After quickening was rejected as the point from which human life is sacrosanct, to embrace any other point in the development of the fetus would have given rise to awkward questions about where to draw the line, questions impossible to answer satisfactorily within the church's overall view of the value of human life. Thus the prohibition on abortion at any stage of pregnancy became a necessary part of the church's teaching on the sanctity of human life. The church maintained this view even in the extreme case (which modern medicine has fortunately made rare) in which both the pregnant woman *and* her fetus will die unless the fetus is killed. Despite the fact that killing the fetus is then the only way of saving one of the two lives that will otherwise be lost, the church steadfastly maintained that to do so is a direct violation of the sanctity of human life, and can never be right.[2]

The history of abortion in the criminal law follows a similar pattern. In the traditional common law of England, and in other countries following the common law tradition, abortion was a crime only after the fetus had moved and shown itself to be alive. In the nineteenth century this was changed by legislation, first in England and then in the United States, making abortion a crime at any stage after conception. The new legislation was introduced for several reasons. In the United States it was strongly supported by 'regular' physicians, graduates from leading medical schools, who were seeking to distinguish themselves from a wide range of untrained and differently trained 'irregular' purveyors of remedies for all kinds of physical ailments. One distinguishing feature of the regular physicians was that they took the Hippocratic Oath, which was seen as providing an ethical basis for medical practice. In taking the oath, physicians undertook not to perform abortions. At the same time, since physicians were better trained scientifically than their competitors, they understood that quickening did not mark any special moment in the development of human life. They therefore found illogical and unscientific the prevailing laws which made quickening the point at which developing life was to be protected.

In the second half of the nineteenth century, the newly formed American Medical Association began a crusade against abortion.

At the AMA's national convention in Louisville in 1859, delegates voted unanimously to protest against the 'unwarrantable destruction of human life' that resulted from the importance erroneously attributed to quickening. The AMA began to lobby state legislatures for stricter laws against abortion. The lobbying met with little opposition. Nineteenth-century feminists accepted that what Matilda Gage called 'this crime of "child murder", "abortion", "infanticide"' should be suppressed. Their concern was only to shift the burden of blame for the crime from women to men who needed to 'learn to check their sensualism, and leave their wives free to choose their periods of maternity'.[3] Sexual abstinence, not legal abortion, was then the feminist solution to the problem of unwanted pregnancy.

Not surprisingly, given the total absence of public support for legal abortion, the crusade against it was entirely successful. By the turn of the century, every state in the United States had laws prohibiting abortion at any stage of pregnancy. This ushered in a period of consensus about abortion that lasted more than fifty years. The laws did not succeed in eliminating abortion, any more than laws against prostitution have succeeded in suppressing that profession, but as James Mohr has written in his classic historical account of abortion in America: 'By 1950 American public opinion considered abortion socially odious, and virtually no one in American society yet dared call openly for its relegalization as an appropriate national practice'.[4] On an international level, when the World Medical Association met in Geneva in 1948 to modernise the Hippocratic Oath, the new version of the oath contained the words 'I will maintain the utmost respect for human life, from the time of conception'.[5]

In summary, until the 1960s, Christian teachings, Anglo-American law, public opinion and medical ethics were in agreement that the deliberate killing of the unborn human being is wrong from the moment at which it begins to live. The changes in attitude to early abortions that occurred in the nineteenth century reflected a change in beliefs about when the life of the developing human being began, rather than about the fundamental view that, once alive, the innocent human being must not be killed. Only against this background can we grasp just how dramatic the change that has come about in the last thirty years really is.

The prohibition on the direct killing of the fetus was the first area in which the sanctity of life ethic was directly challenged by a quality of life ethic, and lost. Abortion foreshadowed what was about to become accepted practice in other areas, including the withdrawal of treatment from patients in a hopeless condition, and the selective non-treatment of disabled infants. While opponents of abortion have made this point repeatedly, those who support abortion prefer, as we have already seen, to see the issue as one of freedom of choice. This tendency was reinforced in the United States by the Supreme Court's 1973 decision in *Roe v. Wade*. That decision was based on a finding that a constitutional right to privacy includes a right to decide whether to have an abortion, at least up to the time at which the fetus is viable. While *Roe v. Wade* certainly transformed the abortion situation in the United States, it followed, rather than led, opposition to restrictive abortion laws. The Supreme Court's decision came at the end of a decade in which the movement for abortion law reform had grown from negligible proportions to a major political force.

In many western countries, that opposition was triggered by the drug thalidomide, a sedative widely taken by pregnant women. It led to a sudden outbreak of babies born with strange deformities, such as flaps of skin instead of arms. There were many such babies born before the connection with thalidomide was discovered. Once this link became known, many women who had taken thalidomide and were still pregnant sought abortions. The European abortion law reform movement was strengthened by the trial and acquittal of a Belgian woman who had killed her baby after it was born deformed as a result of thalidomide.[6]

In the United States, although thalidomide had not been widely used, one highly publicised case was influential in beginning the process of abortion law reform. Sherri Finkbane took thalidomide while pregnant, just before it was shown to cause birth defects. When the connection became known, Finkbane, who was married and already a mother, sought an abortion from a hospital in Phoenix, Arizona, where she lived. For legal reasons, the county medical society refused to approve the procedure. With sympathetic national media attention focused on her, Finkbane tried unsuccessfully to obtain an abortion in California and New Jersey. President Kennedy and a host of lesser officials and commentators discussed the thalidomide tragedy. Finkbane then flew to Sweden, where she finally obtained an abortion— which showed that the fetus was deformed. After this episode, as Mohr comments, 'abortion no longer seemed to involve a choice between absolutes—life or not life—but matters of degree—what kind of life under what kind of conditions'.[7]

The public sympathy for more liberal abortion laws awakened throughout the western world by the thalidomide tragedy was reinforced by figures about the number of women who were injured or died as a result of illegal abortion. A resurgent feminist movement began to gain political clout and, in contrast to the feminist movement of the previous century, it made legal abortion one of its priorities. In 1967 the British parliament passed a law allowing abortion to be performed by a medical practitioner to prevent 'risk of injury to the physical or mental health of the woman or of any of her existing children of the family greater than if the pregnancy were terminated'. Since the risk of the abortion procedure, when performed by a competent doctor, is vanishingly small, virtually any risk to the physical or mental health of the mother was sufficient to make the abortion legal. Another clause, obviously influenced by the thalidomide tragedy, allowed abortion if there were a substantial risk that the child would be seriously handicapped. In the United States, by the time *Roe v. Wade* was decided, eighteen states, including California and New York, had already reformed their laws to allow abortion in a variety of circumstances, usually related to the health of the woman, risk of abnormality, or the pregnancy being a result of rape or incest. Two-thirds of Americans lived in those states, or within 100 miles of them.[8] Effectively, those who took the view that human life is sacrosanct from conception onwards had already been defeated by the time *Roe v. Wade* was decided. That decision turned the defeat into a rout, and by entrenching a right to abortion in the constitution, ensured that future battles to change the law would be waged through the courts rather than the state legislatures.

From this period, although the laws of various countries differed in detail, safe and legal abortion was available on request to most women living in developed nations. Abortion became a routine procedure. In the United States, for example, about 1.5 million legal abortions are carried out each year. The majority of women having abortions are not desperate teenagers, but mature women in their twenties and thirties.[9] In some other countries, such as Russia, abortion is widely used by married women as an alternative to contraception, and the number of abortions carried out is much higher still.

The use we make of our increasing ability to detect abnormal fetuses during pregnancy is another indication of the way in which the legitimacy of abortion has become an assumption of medical practice. Some abnormalities can be detected by ultrasound screening, which almost all pregnant women in developed countries have. More complex tests are routinely offered to pregnant women, especially those who are thirty-five years of age or older, since it is these women who are more likely to have an abnormal child. Most women have an abortion if any of these tests shows that the child will be born with a serious problem. Abortion on these grounds is now common practice, either up to the time of viability or without any limit, throughout western Europe, and in countries as diverse as Australia, India, Israel, Japan, Turkey, and the United States. There is strong public support for this. In the United States, for instance, a national sample of adults has been asked on thirteen occasions between 1972 and 1987: 'Please tell me whether or not you think it should be possible for a pregnant woman to obtain a legal abortion if there is a strong chance of a serious defect in the baby?' The answer has been remarkably consistent, with between 75 and 78 per cent answering 'yes'.[10] Implicit in the acceptance of prenatal diagnosis and abortion is both a willingness to make quality of life judgments (that is, the judgment that life with a particular kind of disability is not as desirable as the life of a normal child) and an expression of the priority of quality of life over sanctity of life, at least as far as the fetus is concerned.

NEW REPRODUCTIVE TECHNOLOGY AND THE ABORTION DEBATE

At the beginning of life, as at the end of it, the advance of science and technology has sharpened some of the old issues, and forced us to face new ones. In 1978 the birth of Louise Brown, in England, proved that a human egg fertilised in vitro—in a glass dish— and transferred to a woman's womb could implant and develop into a normal baby. The birth of the first human being to result from in vitro fertilisation was hailed as a medical miracle, and brought hope to millions of infertile couples.

It also opened up a new area of scientific research: experimentation on the human embryo. With it came a host of new ethical questions. Considerations of 'a woman's right to control her own body' are powerless to resolve debate about the moral status of an embryo that is not in anyone's body. 'Pro-life' groups immediately insisted that the embryo is a living human being who ought to be protected. Even they, however, soon discovered that the possibility of embryo experimentation demanded a more precise discussion of when human life begins than had ever been needed before. Abortion does not destroy embryos that consist of only a few cells, because by the time a woman knows she is pregnant, the embryo has usually had at least two weeks to develop and implant in the lining of the uterus. It was not obvious, even to all Roman Catholic theologians, that the early embryo, before implantation, was a human individual. Father Norman Ford, Master of Melbourne's Catholic Theological College, was troubled by the fact that for some time after fertilisation, the embryo could split into identical twins. This suggested that during this early period the embryo was a cluster of cells, rather than an individual being. Ford has a point. If we think of the embryo as an individual from conception—let's call her Marion—then what happens to Marion if the embryo splits? Are the newly formed twins Marion and a new twin, say, Ruth? Or are they two new twins, say, Ruth and Esther?

Both answers give rise to paradoxes. If Marion still exists, which one of the twins is she? There is no basis for saying that one of them is more closely linked to the original Marion than the other. But if neither of the new twins is Marion, what has happened to her? Has she vanished? Should we regret the loss of a human individual, as I would regret the disappearance of one of my daughters, even if she were replaced by two others? Ford concluded that as long as twinning is still a possibility, the cluster of cells does not constitute an individual organism. Therefore the life of a human individual does not begin at conception, but about fourteen days later, when the possibility of twinning is lost. His view has not been endorsed by any official church body, but it has also not been condemned.[11]

Those who wish to stand by the moment of conception as the

beginning of an individual human life may imagine that they, at least, do not have any problems of boundary definition. But modern science has given us such a precise knowledge of what happens at conception, as well as the power to interfere with the fertilising egg, that these problems have become inescapable. There is no 'moment' of conception. Conception in human beings is a process that lasts about twenty-four hours. It begins when a sperm works its way through the outer layer of the egg. This outer layer then locks up, so that other sperm cannot enter. At this point, however, the genetic material of the egg and sperm is still separate. The woman's genetic material is not evenly distributed throughout the egg but concentrated in what is called a 'pronucleus', which is surrounded by a soupy material that fills the egg. After the sperm enters the egg, its tail disappears and its head forms another pronucleus. The two pronuclei, at first like two islands floating in the soupy fluid, gradually draw together, but the genetic material does not merge until about twenty-two hours after the sperm first came into the egg, at a stage known as syngamy. Since it is this merging of the genetic material that forms the genetic constitution of the new individual (or individuals, if identical twins will emerge), it seems reasonable to say that conception is a process that is not complete until syngamy has taken place.

To ask in which hour of this process a human life begins may seem as pointless an exercise as the proverbial scholastic debates about how many angels could fit on the head of a pin. But for anyone concerned about human life 'from conception' it has practical consequences scarcely less significant than the debate at the other end of life, about the precise moment of death.

Consider, for example, what happened in Victoria, Australia, in 1986–87. Monash University's in vitro fertilisation team, headed by Professor Carl Wood and Dr Alan Trounson, was an international leader in developing new techniques for overcoming infertility. The group now sought a way to help men who produced very few sperm. The team wanted to see if, under a microscope, they could inject a single sperm into an egg, and if the egg would then fertilise in a normal manner. But Victoria had a law that, while allowing experimentation on embryos that had become 'surplus' during the process of in vitro fertilisation, forbade the creation of new embryos specifically for the purposes of experimentation. Wood and Trounson were free to go ahead with their research if they transferred each embryo they created by micro-injection to a woman's womb, hoping that the embryos would develop into a child; but they were not free to create the embryos and observe them under a microscope to see whether the procedure produced normal embryos. (Once 'fixed' for examination under a microscope, the embryos could no longer develop into a child.)

Wood and Trounson, however, thought it unethical to go ahead with embryo transfers without first having examined the fertilising eggs for genetic and other abnormalities. To do so, they reasoned, would put their patients at risk of becoming pregnant with an abnormal embryo. So they applied to a government advisory committee for permission to micro-inject sperm into forty eggs and observe the process of fertilisation up to—but not including—the moment of syngamy, when the genetic material combines. The experiment would then be terminated. This meant that the committee had to decide whether an egg in the process of fertilisation is an embryo before syngamy. After first splitting 4-4 on the question of whether the experiment could be permitted under the existing law, a majority of the committee finally agreed to recommend to the Victorian government that the law should be amended to allow experimental procedures involving 'the fertilisation of the human ovum [egg] from the point of sperm penetration prior to but not including the point of syngamy'. This the government did, and the experiment went ahead. About forty human eggs were fertilised, and then fixed onto a glass slide for examination under a microscope. Was this the destruction of forty individual human lives? The answer depends on whether one accepts the moment the sperm enters the egg, or the moment at which the genetic material of the sperm and egg merge, as the beginning of a new human life.[12]

As well as blurring the line marked by conception, the revolution in reproductive medicine has made the embryo a product in a way that it never was before. Looking at embryos in glass dishes on laboratory benches makes it more difficult to cling to the belief that all human life is equally precious from the moment of conception. We can say: this embryo is precious for the couple from whom the egg and sperm came, because they have been trying for many years to have a child, and this could be the child they want so much. But if—as really happened in one case that also involved Wood and Trounson—the couple from whom the egg and sperm came are killed in a plane crash while their embryos remain frozen in a tank of liquid nitrogen in a laboratory, it is hard to see that the embryo is really precious in any sense.[13] True, given a woman willing to accept it into her womb, and a lot of luck, it could develop into a child. (It will need luck because even the most skilled in vitro fertilisation teams only succeed in getting about 10 per cent of their embryos to implant.) But does the potential of the embryo really make it inherently precious, rather than perhaps being precious for a particular couple who may want it?

There are two serious objections to regarding the fact that the embryo has the potential to become a human being as a sufficient reason for preserving its life. The fact that the embryo has a certain potential does not mean that we can really harm it, in the sense in which we can harm a being who has wants and desires or can suffer. What it means if the embryo does not realise its potential is really that a particular human being will not come into the world. But every decision to procreate or not is a decision about whether a particular being will or won't come into the world—even though the precise nature of that being may be undetermined at the time the decision is made.

Decisions not to procreate are not wrong, because the world already has enough human beings. As I write, the governments of 140 countries have agreed on a wide-ranging plan to slow the growth of the world's population, currently projected to reach eight billion by 2015.[14] Even though developed nations may have ample food supplies, our planet's ecological systems do not recognise national boundaries. The average resident of the United States, Australia or Germany uses several times as much of the world's fossil fuels, minerals, and even wood, as the average person in India or China; and those in developed countries make a far greater per capita contribution to global warming and the pollution of our atmosphere and oceans. Thus the need for a reduction in population growth is as great in the developed countries as it is in the developing world.

This consensus that the world has more people than are desirable from an environmental, economic and political point of view is a relatively new development. As recently as 1930, the world had only two billion people, and many nations thought population growth was the path to prosperity and a bigger role on the world stage. It is only to be expected that the changed attitude to bringing more people into the world should have an impact on our view of abortion. It does so by undercutting the claim that the potential of the embryo or unborn child is a reason for bringing it into the world.

Even if we put aside—as we should not—our concerns about global overpopulation, and return to focus on the specific embryo in front of us in a laboratory dish, there is a second reason why the potential of that embryo is not a reason for treating it as sacrosanct human life. We think that it is all right for laboratory technicians to dispose of surplus sperm and eggs, but not to discard embryos that have just fertilised. Yet that egg and sperm could also develop into a child, given roughly the same amount of luck that the embryo would need to develop. Getting the egg and sperm to form an embryo is the easiest part of the in vitro fertilisation process. If it is claimed that destroying an embryo does it harm because of the loss of its potential, why should we not say the same about the egg and sperm? The potential for new human life is there in both cases.

A few years ago John T. Noonan, an American Roman Catholic theologian, wrote an article, often quoted by opponents of abortion, entitled 'An Almost Absolute Value in History'. In this article he tried to counter arguments about the potential of the egg and sperm, when still separate. Noonan argued that the difference between destroying a single sperm and destroying a fetus is that the sperm has less than one chance in 200 million of becoming a reasoning, feeling being, whereas the fetus is already sensitive to pain and has an 80 per cent chance of developing into a baby outside the womb. The article contains this passage:

> As life itself is a matter of probabilities, as most moral reasoning is an estimate of probabilities, so it seems in accord with the structure of reality and the nature of moral thought to found a moral judgment on the change in probabilities [of a child resulting] at conception...Would the argument be different if only one out of ten children conceived came to term? Of course this argument would be different. This argument is an appeal to probabilities that actually exist, not to any and all states of affairs which may be imagined.[15]

Alas for Noonan's argument, recent advances allowing earlier diagnosis of pregnancy have shown that his estimate of the probabilities was seriously astray. Even when fertilisation occurs through sexual intercourse, Noonan's figure of 80 per cent for the chances of the fetus surviving does not apply to the early embryo. Before the embryo implants in the uterus, the probability of it surviving to birth is no more than 30 per cent. Immediately after implantation it is still less than 60 per cent. It reaches 80 per cent only about six weeks after conception.[16] Apart from these revised figures for natural conception, however, the success of the micro-injection technique for fertilising human eggs, described above, means that the chances of the sperm in the micro-injection needle becoming a child are far better than one in 200 million; they are, in fact, very similar to that of the embryo after fertilisation. New knowledge and new techniques thus turn Noonan's argument against abortion on its head. If the argument from potential is to be based on the probabilities that actually exist, then we can take a more permissive approach to the destruction of embryos in the laboratory, and to the use of early means of stopping a pregnancy, such as the 'morning after pill', because these early embryos have only a small chance of surviving anyway, not really significantly better than that of the sperm selected for micro-injection. Or are we seriously to believe that every sperm is sacred?

By now, I hope, most readers who have followed the convoluted arguments of this section will be feeling that there is something absurd about all these attempts to define a precise moment at which a new human being comes into existence. The absurdity lies in the attempt to force a precise dividing line on something that is a gradual process. Recognising this is a first step towards understanding—and moving beyond—the apparently insoluble dilemma of the abortion debate.

UNLOCKING THE ABORTION DEADLOCK

If we were to put the case against abortion as a formal argument, it would go like this:

First Premise: It is wrong to take innocent human life.

Second Premise: From conception onwards, the embryo or fetus is innocent, human and alive.

Conclusion: It is wrong to take the life of the embryo or fetus.

As a matter of formal logic, the argument is valid. If we accept the premises, we must accept the conclusion. Since abortion does take the life of the fetus, we would then have to agree that abortion is wrong. Conversely, if we want to reject the conclusion, we must reject at least one of the premises. (For simplicity, in what follows I shall use 'fetus' to refer to the embryo or fetus, and I shall leave out the word 'innocent', since there is no debate over the claim that the fetus is innocent in the required sense.)

Those who do not think abortion is wrong generally attack the second premise. They deny that a new human life comes into existence at conception, and suggest instead some other point, at or before birth, when a new human life comes into existence. But human development is a gradual process, and it is not easy to see why any particular moment should be *the* moment at which a human life begins.

Birth would be the best cut-off line for those who wish to defend a woman's right to an abortion at any stage of pregnancy. But can anyone really deny that the fetus, just before birth, is a living human being? It is certainly alive—doctors can tell when a fetus has died in the womb. And what else could it be but human? Moreover, as Peggy Stinson realised, reflecting on the way in which the unexpected birth of Andrew had changed everything, there is something arbitrary about making so much depend on birth. The tiny, very premature baby in the intensive care ward on the day after his birth was really not very different from the fetus that Peggy and Robert were considering aborting the day before the birth. Why should the location of the fetus/infant, inside or outside the womb, be so significant that it marks the beginning of a new human life?

Because defenders of abortion can give no clear answer to this last question, they often take not birth but viability—the stage at which the fetus could survive outside the body—as the beginning of the new human life. That was the view taken by the United States Supreme Court in *Roe v. Wade*. The court referred to the state's interest in potential life, and said that this becomes 'compelling' at viability. The court then said that viability is usually regarded as being seven months, or twenty-eight weeks, but may occur as early as twenty-four weeks. Striking a compromise between these two dates, the court divided the thirty-nine weeks of pregnancy into 'trimesters' and said that abortion could not be prohibited until the end of the second trimester—that is, after twenty-six weeks. There is, however, nothing fixed about the time of viability; it depends on the medical expertise and equipment available. Twenty years after *Roe v. Wade*, many premature infants born as early as twenty-four or twenty-five weeks are surviving, some of them without serious damage.[17] The World Health Organisation, which keeps statistics on infant mortality, now regards twenty-two weeks as the dividing line between spontaneous abortion and birth. No wonder that, as Justice Sandra Day O'Connor said in another Supreme Court decision on abortion, decided ten years after *Roe v. Wade*: 'The *Roe* framework, then, is clearly on a collision course with itself...As medical science becomes better able to provide for the separate existence of the fetus, the point of viability is moved further back towards conception.'[18]

Viability also depends on the pregnant woman's access to a modern medical centre. Suppose that a woman who is twenty-five weeks pregnant is living in Melbourne, a city with excellent intensive care units for premature babies, but she then travels to a remote part of the desert west of Alice Springs, three days from the nearest airstrip. Are we to believe that the fetus inside her was a living human being when she was in Melbourne, but not when she was in the desert? What happened to it, then? Did it die? Did it cease to be human? Merely asking these questions shows how untenable it is to make the start of a new human life dependent upon viability.

Even if defenders of abortion could accept such oddities, and acknowledge that recent advances in caring for premature infants mean that human life now begins two weeks earlier than it did when *Roe v. Wade* was decided, what will they say if it becomes possible to build an artificial womb and nurture an embryo from fertilisation to 'birth' without it ever being inside a woman? That possibility, known as ectogenesis, could easily be with us at some time during the next twenty years. It will in effect mean that every fetus is viable at any stage during pregnancy. If viability marks the start of human life and therefore the cut-off line at which abortion becomes wrong, life will begin at conception, and it will be wrong to kill the fetus at any time after conception. But the argument stated above might then no longer be relevant to abortion, which would become an 'evacuation procedure', in which the pregnancy ends but the fetus is preserved alive, and presumably given up for adoption. When I wrote about this topic a decade ago, at the beginning of the revolution in reproductive technology, I suggested that perhaps this would solve the entire abortion controversy. Women could have complete control over their bodies without killing fetuses. Leslie Cannold subsequently asked women from both sides of the abortion controversy what they thought of this proposed solution. She found that neither those who considered themselves 'pro-life', nor those who considered themselves 'pro-choice' liked it at all! Whatever their views on abortion, most of the women shared a notion of good motherhood that ruled out abandoning one's own child in this way.[19]

If neither birth nor viability offers a satisfactory way of marking the start of a human life, what other possibilities are there? No-one would today point to quickening as the moment at which human life begins, but some have suggested taking the start of brain functioning as a more scientific reinterpretation of what quickening was thought to signify. In a recent article the German bioethicist Hans-Martin Sass refers to this as a 'brain-life' criterion, to suggest a symmetry with brain death. His argument is that if we accept brain death as marking the end of life, we should also accept the first signs of brain life as marking its beginning. He therefore proposes setting up something analogous to the Harvard Brain Death Committee, to work out the details of the criteria and the methods of showing that the necessary kind of brain life is present. Sass himself suggests that the adoption of the brain life criterion would mean the protection of human life from the end of the tenth week after conception, since this is when there is 'neuro-neuronal integration in the cortical plate zone'.[20]

The idea of a human life stretching from the beginning of brain life to the irreversible loss of brain function is in many ways appealing, but its plausibility as a criterion of when a new human life begins assumes our acceptance of brain death as really marking the end of life. We have seen that the use of brain death as a criterion of death is an ethical decision, not a scientific one. The same would therefore be true for the use of a brain-life criterion. This is evident from the specifics of Sass's proposal, for he does not take as his marker the symmetrical equivalent of existing whole-brain definitions of death. If he were to do so, he would have to hold that human life must be protected from fifty-four days after conception, when the first brain-stem activity has been observed.[21] If, on the other hand, we are prepared to go beyond the point at which the brain begins to function, why go only as far as ten weeks? Others have suggested that we should wait for brain wave activity, as measured by an EEG. But then, do we date the beginning of life from the first signs of EEG activity, during the fourteenth week, or do we wait for this activity to become continuous, which does not happen until the thirty-second week?[22]

Since the choice between these different standards of brain life is clearly ethical rather than scientific, whatever criterion we choose could not honestly be said to mark the beginning of human life, although it might be regarded as a useful indicator of when the developing life first gains the kind of moral status that requires it to be protected in certain ways. Taken as an ethical proposal, the brain-life suggestion is not really a challenge to the second premise of the argument against abortion outlined above, but rather to the first premise. The position here is very similar to that which holds for the proposal that the irreversible loss of all capacity for consciousness should be a criterion for the death of the organism. In both this proposal and the brain-life proposal, what is being suggested is a resort to a convenient fiction that turns an evidently living being into one that legally is not alive. Instead of accepting such fictions, we should recognise that the fact that a being is human, and alive, does not in itself tell us whether it is wrong to take that being's life.

On the question of when a human life begins, Norman Ford may well have got it right. Certainly around fourteen days after conception, once the possibility of the embryo dividing into twins is passed, there exists an individual being who is alive and human. But while Ford may be right about this, that tells us nothing about the ethical significance of the existence of an individual human being, nor about the justifiability of abortion after that time. To unlock the abortion deadlock, we have to turn our attention to the first premise of the argument against abortion, and ask: why is it wrong to take human life? The key to a resolution of the whole abortion debate is the recognition that it is both possible and necessary to question this first premise. What, in the end, is so special about the fact that a life is human?

MAKING QUALITY OF LIFE
JUDGMENTS

Every legislator, every doctor, and every citizen needs to recognize that the real issue is whether to affirm and protect the sanctity of all human life, or to embrace a social ethic where some human lives are valued and others are not. As a nation, we must choose between the sanctity of life ethic and the 'quality of life' ethic.

RONALD REAGAN, 1983

HOW THE REAGAN ADMINISTRATION
CHOSE A QUALITY OF LIFE ETHIC

Ronald Reagan was elected president of the United States in 1980, with strong support from conservative Christians, pro-life groups, and the so-called 'Moral Majority' organised by the Reverend Jerry Falwell. In his first two years in office Reagan supported moves to overturn *Roe v. Wade*, but without success. The birth of an infant who became nationally known by his court-given pseudonym, 'Baby Doe', provided Reagan with an opportunity to do something concrete to repay the support given him by those who strongly believed in the sanctity of all human life. Baby Doe was born on 9 April 1982, in Bloomington Hospital, Indiana. As soon as Baby Doe was born, it was apparent that he had Down syndrome, a condition formerly known as 'mongolism', which involves some physical abnormalities, and intellectual disability. The nature of the intellectual disability varies from mild to moderate, with IQ levels usually between 35 and 70. People at the upper end of this range can live independently with little supervision. Others need help with managing their financial affairs, and need to be supervised when shopping, cooking or travelling outside the home.[1]

Baby Doe had an additional problem that is sometimes associated with Down syndrome: the passage from his mouth to his stomach, known as the oesophagus, was not properly formed. Food put in his mouth would not be able to reach his stomach. Without an operation, he would starve to death. In these circumstances an operation to restore the oesophagus is normal procedure. It is major surgery, but the chances of success are good.

Two paediatricians were consulted, and they recommended that Baby Doe be transferred to another hospital, where the surgery could be performed. Dr Walter Owens, the obstetrician who had delivered Baby Doe, was not sure about the wisdom of this recommendation, so he spoke to two other obstetricians. They supported Dr Owens' own inclination, which was to keep Baby Doe at Bloomington Hospital, and give him drugs to ensure that he was free from pain. Treated in this way, Baby Doe would die in a few days, or at most a week or two.

Dr Owens and the paediatricians discussed their conflicting opinions with Baby Doe's parents. The baby's father was a schoolteacher who had sometimes worked closely with Down syndrome children. The couple already had two children. They decided that it was in the best interests of their family as a whole to follow Dr Owens' recommendation.

The management of Bloomington Hospital reacted to this decision by asking Judge John Baker of the local Monroe County Court to give an emergency ruling on whether it could follow the course of treatment Dr Owens had recommended. Judge Baker said that the parents of a minor have a legal right to choose a medically recommended course of action for their child, and therefore directed the hospital to follow the treatment prescribed by Dr Owens. He also appointed the Monroe County department of public welfare as Baby Doe's guardian, to decide whether there should be an appeal to a higher court.

Three days passed. The department of public welfare decided not to appeal against Judge Baker's ruling. The case was by now in the news, however, and the Monroe County prosecutor's office appealed to the Indiana Supreme Court. That court rejected the appeal. With Baby Doe now five days old, and still not being fed, a Monroe County deputy prosecutor flew to Washington to ask the United States Supreme Court to intervene. But before he could begin proceedings, Baby Doe died.

The public reaction was immediate, and mostly hostile to Baby Doe's parents, and to the courts. Both the *Washington Post* and the *New York Times* published editorials against the decision to allow Baby Doe to die. Letters of protest poured in to Congress and the White House. The Reagan administration acted with remarkable promptness. Barely two weeks after the death of Baby Doe, President Reagan ordered that all providers of health care receiving federal funds should be notified that they must not discriminate against the handicapped. Subsequently 6800 American hospitals received new guidelines, telling them that in each delivery ward, maternity ward, paediatric ward, and intensive care nursery, they must display a poster indicating that 'DISCRIMINATORY FAILURE TO FEED AND CARE FOR HANDICAPPED INFANTS IN THIS FACILITY IS PROHIBITED BY FEDERAL LAW'. The poster then said that any person knowing of such discriminatory denial of food or customary medical care should immediately contact a 'Handicapped Infant Hotline', for which a toll-free twenty-four-hour telephone number was given. Confidentiality was assured.

During 1983, the hotline had 1633 calls. 'Baby Doe squads' were set up to respond to these calls. They consisted of lawyers, doctors and government officials, and they stood by, ready to leave at an hour's notice to investigate a complaint. They would arrive at a hospital without warning, sometimes in the middle of the night, seize records and take charts from attending doctors. At Vanderbilt University Hospital, a hotline call led to three investigators and a newborn-care specialist examining, after midnight, every infant in the facility, diverting the hard-pressed hospital staff from patient care for a total of fifty-four staff-hours. The specialist described the hospital's care as 'exemplary'. In none of their investigations did the Baby Doe squads find a provable violation of federal anti-discrimination laws. Their work did, however, mean that doctors gave life-prolonging treatment to some severely disabled infants who might not otherwise have been treated. In one case, this treatment cost $400,000 for a baby whose doctors were quoted as saying 'has zero chance for a normal life expectancy'. A New Mexico paediatrician reported spending an 'agonizing hour' trying to resuscitate an infant with multiple abnormalities that was 'in no way a viable child', simply because of his fear of being 'turned in' by someone in his hospital. In other cases, parents refused to permit surgery on their baby, and custody of the baby was taken from them.[2]

Most health-care professionals working in hospitals that cared for newborn babies thought the new 'Baby Doe guidelines' were unworkable; they were outraged by the Baby Doe squads, which they saw as an intrusion upon sensitive decisions that should be made by the parents and the health-care team. The American Academy of Pediatrics, the official body representing 24,000 paediatricians, joined with the National Association of Children's Hospitals and the Children's Hospital National Medical Center, in Washington, DC, to have the regulations struck down by a court. In support of their case, the academy said that some conditions were 'simply not treatable' and there was no point in prolonging the lives of infants with these conditions. The academy mentioned three examples: anencephaly; a brain haemorrhage leading to the destruction of the cortex; and the absence of a major part of the digestive tract, for example, the intestine and bowels. Babies with this condition cannot be fed by mouth, nor even by a tube into the stomach. They could be kept alive by a drip directly into the bloodstream, but the long-term prospects are poor.

At the court hearing, before Judge Gerhard Gesell, the Reagan administration was represented by the Surgeon General of the United States, Dr C. Everett Koop. Dr Koop was himself a paediatric surgeon, well known for his support for pro-life policies. President Reagan was warm in his praise:

This Administration has a Surgeon General, Dr C. Everett Koop, who has done perhaps more than any other American for handicapped children, by pioneering surgical techniques to help them, by speaking out on the value of their lives, and by working with them in the context of loving families. You will not find his former patients advocating the so-called 'quality of life' ethic.[3]

I have no idea what ethic Koop's former patients advocate, but we can discover Koop's own ethic by his responses to the cases put forward by the Academy as not suitable for treatment. When asked how he would treat a baby born without a brain, he replied: 'we should not attempt to interfere with anyone dealing with that child. We think it should be given loving attention and would expect it to expire in a short time'.

His answer was similar when he referred to a child born without an intestine:

we would consider customary care in the case of that child the provision of a bed, of food by mouth, knowing that it was not going to be nutritious, but not just shutting off the care of that child...nor do we intend to say that this child should be carried on intravenous fluids for the rest of its life.

Koop knew that a child without an intestine could survive on intravenous fluids 'for a year and half'. He told the court that he knew about this, because 'I was the first physician that ever did that'. Yet now, he was telling the court that the Baby Doe guidelines, which he had helped to formulate, were not intended to say that this should be done. Instead, he supported 'customary care' which would mean that, like Baby Doe, the infant would die from starvation within a short time.

Given this evidence, the difference of views between Walter Owens, who had recommended that Baby Doe be allowed to starve to death, and C. Everett Koop, who was prepared to recommend that a baby without an intestine should starve to death, was not a difference between one doctor who applies a quality of life ethic and another who applies a sanctity of life ethic. It was, rather, a difference between two doctors applying a quality of life ethic in different ways. Owens thought that the quality of life of someone with Down syndrome was below the standard at which medical treatment to sustain the life of an infant becomes obligatory. Koop thought that the quality of life of someone with Down syndrome was above that standard, but that the quality of life of someone without an intestine was below it. What other reason could he have for not advocating that babies without intestines be given the extra eighteen months, or perhaps more, that they could live?

Judge Gerhard Gesell struck down the Baby Doe guidelines, in part because there had been no consultation with those affected by them, as the Administrative Procedure Act required. In July 1983 the department of health and human services therefore issued for public comment a new proposed rule, which, among other changes, reduced the size of the poster that had to be displayed in hospitals. More significant, however, was a statement that the law 'does not require the imposition of futile therapies which merely temporarily prolong the process of dying of an infant born terminally ill, such as a child born with anencephaly or intra-cranial bleeding'.

The language used here is revealing. It carefully avoids any reference to quality of life. Instead, it talks of not requiring 'futile' treatment that can 'merely temporarily prolong the process of dying of an infant born terminally ill'. The latter phrase reminds me of the joke that life is a terminal disease, sexually transmitted. Why is an infant whose cortex has been destroyed by massive intra-cranial bleeding, or for that matter an anencephalic infant who retains some brain-stem function, 'terminally ill'? Like people in a persistent vegetative state, these infants could be supported on respirators indefinitely, for years or perhaps decades. They might even have a normal lifespan. It is true that they will always need medical treatment, but then, that is true of children with diabetes too, and we do not consider them 'terminally ill'. It is also true that, in contrast to children with diabetes, the anencephalic infant and the infant whose cortex has been destroyed will remain unconscious for their entire lives. But to see *that* fact as the basis for judging treatment to be 'futile' is to make the decision depend on an assessment of the quality of the child's life. Plainly, it is 'to embrace a social ethic where some human lives are valued and others are not'.

Here we have the major lesson to emerge from the Baby Doe case: for all President Reagan's brave words about the importance of maintaining the sanctity of life ethic, and for all C. Everett Koop's expertise in paediatrics and his commitment to a pro-life position, the Reagan administration could not avoid making quality of life judgments about how severely disabled newborn infants should be treated. But that was not the end of the story. After sending out its proposed rule in July 1983, the department of health and human services received 16,739 comments, 97 per cent in support of the rule, many written in identical terms as recommended by groups such as the Christian Action Council. One hundred and forty-one paediatricians or newborn-care specialists sent in comments and, of these, 72 per cent opposed the rule.

In January 1984 the department therefore issued its 'Final Rule' in which the size of the poster was reduced still further (by now it had shrunk from 17 x 14 inches to 7 x 5 inches) and said that only 'medically beneficial' treatment was required. (The term 'medically beneficial' serves, like the term 'futile', to disguise the fact that a quality of life judgment is being made when it is said, for instance, that it is not 'medically beneficial' to maintain on a respirator an infant who will never be conscious.)

The American Academy of Pediatrics apparently believed that this revised rule was as good as it was going to get, and did not oppose it; but the American Medical Association stepped into the gap. Together with the American Hospital Association, the American College of Obstetricians and Gynaecologists, and the American Academy of Family Physicians, the AMA argued that medical decisions should be left in the hands of parents, with the advice of the medical team. The AMA took the rule to court, and the 'Final Rule' suffered the fate of its predecessor. It was declared invalid. The Reagan administration appealed to the Supreme Court, but in 1986 the Supreme Court also struck down the regulations, holding that they were not validly based on anti-discrimination law, because no evidence had been offered to show that additional regulations were needed to protect handicapped newborns from discrimination. The court also said that the regulations ignored the accepted role of parental consent in medical care for infants, and it found that conditions like multiple handicaps or extreme prematurity might (unlike race, for example) legitimately be used as a grounds for non-treatment. In reaching this decision, the court referred with approval to earlier decisions in which lower courts had allowed parents to choose non-treatment where that decision had been an informed one, made in the best interests of the infant.[4]

Meanwhile, without waiting for the result of the appeal, supporters of the rule in Congress tried a new tack. They added new clauses to a bill reauthorising a federal government program against child abuse, which said that funds under this program would not be available to any state that did not put into place procedures to prevent the withholding of 'medically indicated treatment' to disabled infants with life-threatening conditions. The legislation did, however, specify conditions in which treatment was not required. This included treatment for infants in an irreversible coma, treatment that would 'merely prolong dying', and treatment that 'would be virtually futile in terms of the survival of the infant and the treatment itself under such circumstances would be inhumane'. That there are quality of life judgments lurking under all of these exceptions should need no further spelling out.

The amendments to the Child Abuse Prevention and Treatment Act came into effect late in 1984. A subsequent survey of American paediatricians specialising in the care of newborn infants showed that 76 per cent thought that the regulations were not necessary, 66 per cent considered the regulations interfered with parents' right to determine what course of action was in the best interests of their children, and 60 per cent believed that the regulations did not allow adequate consideration of infants' suffering.[5]

In 1989 the sad case of Samuel Linares gave Americans a glimpse into what a rigid commitment to preserving the lives of all babies may mean for the parents involved. Samuel was the third child of Rudy and Tamara Linares, a young couple who lived in a working-class suburb of Chicago. In August 1988, when Samuel was seven months old, he swallowed a balloon that stuck in his windpipe. He was taken to a Chicago hospital, but his brain had been without oxygen for too long, and he was in a coma. He was put on a respirator and for eight months his condition did not change. The family asked for the respirator to be turned off, but the hospital refused. In December Rudy Linares unhooked the respirator himself, but the hospital staff quickly reconnected it. In April 1989, the hospital decided to move him to a long-term care unit. Shortly before the move, Mr and Mrs Linares visited Samuel in hospital. Tamara Linares left. Rudy Linares then pulled out a .357 magnum and told the nurse to keep away, saying, 'I'm not here to hurt anyone, I'll only hurt you if you try to plug my baby back in'. He disconnected Samuel from the respirator, and cradled his baby. After about thirty minutes he felt for a heartbeat. When he found none, he asked a doctor for a stethoscope. The doctor slid the stethoscope across the floor to him. When Linares was sure Samuel was dead, he broke down, crying, and surrendered to the police, who were now waiting at the entrance to the unit.

Rudy Linares was charged with murder, but the grand jury refused to issue an indictment for homicide. The decision was greeted with general approbation. The next day Dr Robert Stein, the medical examiner for the county in which Samuel Linares died, ruled that the death was 'accidental' and, even more extraordinarily, that the child died at the time he swallowed the balloon, eight months before his father unhooked him from the respirator! Despite evidence from the medical staff that the boy was not brain dead, Stein disagreed, adding his own version of what constitutes death: 'The person was dead. The only thing you kept living was the organs'.

Rudy Linares was later charged with a misdemeanour relating to his unlawful use of a weapon. The judge wished him good luck, and gave him a suspended sentence.[6]

TREATING TO DIE

Despite the Reagan administration's fierce response to it, the only unusual thing about the Baby Doe case was the publicity it received. Very many severely disabled infants, especially those who are judged to have poor prospects of a life of reasonable quality, and who are unwanted by their parents, are deliberately treated in such a way that they die rapidly and without suffering. Perhaps the clearest illustration of the way in which doctors have found themselves unable to work within the framework of the traditional sanctity of life ethic comes from the treatment of babies born with spina bifida.

Spina bifida means, literally, a 'divided spine'. In serious cases, the baby is born with a part of its spine split and the spinal cord exposed. The nerves which run along the spine will then be damaged. The result is partial or complete paralysis of the legs, and no ability to control the bowel or bladder. The spine may also be deformed. Intellectual disability is often present in people seriously affected by spina bifida, but by no means always. Spina bifida is one of the more common birth defects. It used to be said to occur in about one birth in every thousand, but better nutrition, especially folic acid, has been shown to reduce its incidence. In addition, some cases are detected during pregnancy with the result that they do not come to birth.

Until the 1950s, almost all babies born with spina bifida died soon after birth. Sometimes this was because midwives and family doctors made sure that they did not live; but even if the doctors did their best, the open wound over the spine was sure to become infected, and in the days before antibiotics, this was likely to prove fatal. Operating on the baby to close the wound on the spine only meant that the cerebro-spinal fluid which would have leaked out of the wound now built up in the brain, where it caused the baby's head to swell, and often led to brain damage. In the 1950s, however, antibiotics became available, and a way was found to drain the cerebro-spinal fluid into the bloodstream. Suddenly it was possible to save the lives of thousands of children who would otherwise have died.

At this point Dr John Lorber enters the story. Lorber was a paediatrician in Sheffield, an industrial city in the north of England that had a high rate of spina bifida. Lorber was at first enthusiastic about the new mode of treating these babies. In 1963, together with two colleagues, he published an influential paper stating that every infant with spina bifida must be operated on as soon as possible since otherwise further nerve damage could occur. In Sheffield and in many other centres in Britain and America this was the way spina bifida was handled for the next few years. The parents were rarely consulted about this decision— they were simply told that their baby needed an operation, and given a form to sign. But the operation to close the wound at the back of the spine was only the beginning of the treatment. After that a tube with a one-way valve was installed to drain the excess cerebro-spinal fluid from the head into the bloodstream. Then orthopaedic operations were needed to correct deformities of the spine and hip. Some children needed thirty or forty orthopaedic operations before they had finished school.

After a decade of universal active treatment of all babies with spina bifida, Lorber began to have doubts about what he and his colleagues were doing. He analysed the records of the 848 children they had treated in Sheffield. Half had died, most of these during the first year of life. Of those who had survived, only six had no handicap, and seventy-three were only moderately handicapped. More than 80 per cent were severely handicapped: that is, they had at least two, but usually more, of the following conditions: no bowel and bladder control, or a urinary bypass with frequent kidney infections and progressive chronic kidney damage which sometimes led to kidney failure; paralysis to such a degree that they were unable to walk without caliper splints, crutches, or other appliances and had to rely on a wheelchair for part of the day; pressure sores on feet, knees, or buttocks; hydrocephalus which was treated by a drainage tube, requiring new operations to deal with frequent complications. In addition to these physical problems, approximately one-third of the surviving children were intellectually disabled.

In the light of these figures, Lorber decided that the initial enthusiasm for the new mode of treatment had led to its being used without sufficient reflection. He called for a reassessment of priorities 'to ensure that, with all the intensive effort and good will, we shall not do more harm than good'. He suggested a more selective policy. He went back through the records and found that the size and location of the opening over the spine were, along with other medical indications, good predictors of the severity of the disability that the child would have. He therefore proposed that infants with spina bifida should be examined for 'adverse criteria' that indicated the virtual certainty of severe disability. If the medical team had concentrated its efforts on treating only infants without any of these adverse criteria, all those who survived with nothing worse than a moderate handicap would have received treatment.

That left an obvious question: what should happen to the

others—the majority of babies with spina bifida—who would not be actively treated? Lorber's answer was clear. 'No treatment' meant that nothing should be done to prolong their lives. The wound should be left open. If an infection developed, no antibiotics should be given. If excess fluid accumulated in the head, this should not be drained. If the babies did not eat and lost weight, they should not be tube-fed. Instead they should be kept comfortable and free from pain. In these circumstances, Lorber felt able to predict, very few, if any, would live longer than six months.

Lorber presented his case for a selective approach in the *British Medical Journal* in 1971 and 1972. The pendulum of medical opinion then began to swing away from universal intervention. In a leading article, the *Medical Journal of Australia* endorsed selective treatment for spina bifida. Medical teams in Oxford, Edinburgh and Melbourne published details of their own selective treatment practices. In 1973 Drs Raymond Duff and A.G.M. Campbell, writing of the need to break down 'the public and professional silence on a major social taboo', published in the *New England Journal of Medicine* the details of 299 deaths of infants under their care in Yale-New Haven Hospital. Of these, forty-three, including seven cases of spina bifida, were the result of a decision to withhold medical treatments. The British government's department of health and social security endorsed selective treatment. It was also supported at meetings of spina bifida associations, consisting of parents of children with spina bifida, and social workers and others connected with the people with the condition.

Since that period, the selective treatment of spina bifida infants has been normal practice in many paediatric hospitals in most of the developed world. Some doctors continue to be opposed to it, and do not practise it. Others think that Lorber's criteria exclude too many children with good prospects of an acceptable quality of life. Undoubtedly, since Lorber published his proposals, new ways of treating spina bifida have made it easier for some people to cope with the condition. It would be surprising if any medical criteria for treatment or non-treatment remained unchanged for twenty years. The issue with which we are concerned, however, is not the details of the criteria for selection, but the principle of selective non-treatment itself. As long as we think that there are some cases in which it is acceptable, we are accepting a quality of life ethic.

Surveys of paediatricians and obstetricians have consistently shown that the doctors who treat newborn infants support selective non-treatment. In 1975 a questionnaire was sent to all 400 paediatric surgeons in the surgical section of the American Academy of Pediatrics, and 308 chairpersons of teaching departments of paediatrics. The response rate was nearly two-thirds. The first question was: 'Do you believe that the life of each and every newborn infant should be saved if it is within our ability to do so?' Only 18 percent of those responding answered in the affirmative, the remaining 82 per cent indicating that they did not believe that we should save every newborn infant. Other questions described various situations and asked the doctors what they would do. For instance, in the situation that was later to arise with Baby Doe—a Down syndrome infant with a blockage of the digestive system, and parents who refused permission for surgery—77 per cent of the surgeons and 50 per cent of the general paediatricians said that they would not oppose the parents' refusal. Moreover, even among those respondents who said that they would oppose the refusal, most would limit this opposition to attempts to persuade the parents to change their mind. Only 3 per cent of the surgeons and 16 per cent of the paediatricians said that they would go to the lengths of getting a court order to allow the operation to go ahead. In two other American surveys carried out in California and Massachusetts before the Baby Doe case, a majority of paediatricians said that they would not recommend surgery for a Down syndrome infant with a life-threatening blockage in its intestine. These views may not be very different from those of the American public as a whole. In a 1983 Gallup poll, Americans were asked what they would do if they had a badly deformed baby in need of treatment. Forty-three per cent said that they would ask the doctor not to keep the baby alive, and 40 per cent said they would want the baby kept alive.[7]

Together with my colleague Helga Kuhse, and with the assistance of my mother, Cora Singer, a retired medical practitioner, I surveyed paediatricians and obstetricians in my own state, Victoria, in 1983. We found that 90 per cent of obstetricians. and 83 per cent of paediatricians had, on at least one occasion, directed that less than maximum efforts should be made to preserve the life of a disabled infant. Almost all the doctors said that they consulted with the baby's parents before making such a decision.[8] Our survey was subsequently used as a model for similar surveys of paediatricians in Warsaw, Poland in 1987; in Calgary, Canada in 1990; and in the United Kingdom in 1992. These have shown that whereas Australian, Canadian and United Kingdom paediatricians have broadly similar views and practices, Polish paediatricians are significantly more conservative. Thus close to 98 per cent of respondents in each of the three English-speaking countries rejected the view that in all circumstances every possible effort should be made to sustain life; but Polish paediatricians split 50–50 on this question. Similarly, when decisions whether or not to continue treatment had to be made, approximately 90 per cent of the Australian, Canadian and United Kingdom doctors discussed the decision with the parents and with the nursing staff, but in Poland, only 8 per cent discussed the decision with parents, and 4 per cent with nursing staff. The close parallels between Australia, Canada and the United Kingdom suggest that the English-speaking medical community has shared attitudes and practices in this area. The divergent views of Polish doctors may be explained by the influence of the Roman Catholic Church, but in this instance Marxism—which had been the official ideology of Poland until shortly before the survey—reinforced the Catholic view of the fundamental value of all human life, irrespective of quality. The strength of medical paternalism in Poland is also clear from the very low proportion of Polish paediatricians who discussed such matters with the parents of the infant.[9]

What does the law say about this? The selective non-treatment of infants has been tested in four British court decisions since 1981—one a criminal trial, and the other three decisions of the Court of Appeal. The criminal trial was that of Dr Leonard Arthur, and it is extraordinary because it involved the medically induced death of a Down syndrome infant with no other abnormalities. John Pearson was born in Derby General Hospital on 28 June 1980. The midwife noticed the signs of a child with Down syndrome. When Molly Pearson, John's mother, was given the news she wept, and said to her husband: 'I don't want it, Duck'. Later that day the baby was examined by Dr Arthur, a senior and respected consultant paediatrician at the hospital. He confirmed the diagnosis of Down syndrome. In other respects the baby seemed healthy. The parents were present while Dr Arthur examined the child. Afterwards he noted in John Pearson's records: 'Parents do not wish baby to survive. Nursing care only.' Dr Arthur also prescribed a high dose of a pain-killing drug, DF 118, to be administered as required, at the discretion of the nurse in charge, but not more often than every four hours. By the evening of his first day, John Pearson was already 'going grey' and his breathing was becoming laboured. He appears to have been given water, but not food. Over the next two days his condition gradually worsened. He continued to be given water and DF 118, and on the morning of his fourth day, he died.

This was not the first time that Dr Arthur had made sure that a Down syndrome baby, rejected by its parents, did not survive. Previous cases had remained known only to the parents and the hospital staff. That did not happen this time, because a member of the hospital staff described John Pearson's treatment to an anti-abortion organisation called Life, which reported the death to the police. As a result, Arthur was charged with murder.

At the trial, in Leicester in 1981, the prosecution accused Arthur of prescribing DF 118 in order to cause the baby to die; and it also alleged that his direction for 'nursing care only' showed that he intended the baby to die. The prosecution introduced evidence from an autopsy that showed the level of DF 118 in John Pearson's blood to be ten times that of a therapeutic dose. Professor Alan Usher, an eminent pathologist who served as a consultant to the British government, said that the baby had died from pneumonia, caused by inactivity of the lungs, which was due to poisoning by DF 118. He added that uncomplicated Down syndrome is not a painful condition, and he could see no reason to administer a pain-killer. Another doctor also said that he found the level of DF 118 in John Pearson's body was consistent with fatal poisoning.

The prosecution's case looked overwhelming. The defence managed to shake it a little, however, by producing another senior pathologist, who said that the autopsy indicated that John Pearson may have had other abnormalities that caused him to develop pneumonia, and so may have died of natural causes. Recalled to the stand, Professor Usher admitted that the additional evidence presented by his colleague showed that John Pearson could have been more susceptible to pneumonia than an ordinary infant, but he concluded by saying: 'I don't wish to alter my opinion that this is a fatal poisoning'. Despite this statement, the judge, Mr Justice Farquharson, took the unusual course of refusing to allow the charge of murder to go to the jury. He ordered that the charge of murder could not be sustained, because the prosecution had not shown that John Pearson died as a result of what Arthur did. He withdrew it, substituting for it a charge of attempted murder.

The issue before the jury then became one of what Arthur was trying to do. In what must have been a calculated gamble by the defence, neither Arthur nor John Pearson's parents gave evidence at the trial. In a statement Arthur gave to the police, he had said that his 'sole intention' in prescribing DF 118 was 'to reduce any suffering on the part of the infant', but he did not say why he expected a healthy baby with Down syndrome to be suffering. This left the jury to reach its own conclusions about the aim of the course of treatment that Arthur had prescribed for the baby.

On the other hand, several distinguished medical practitioners testified that they regarded what their colleague had done as 'normal medical practice'. Alex Campbell, Professor of Child Health at the University of Aberdeen, said that he had on a number of occasions put an infant on 'nursing care only', with the intention that it would not survive. Another witness, Dr Peter Dunn, said that in cases like that of John Pearson, food would be withheld 'in the hope that complications would develop which would lead to death by natural causes'. The most eminent of all the medical practitioners in court, however, was Sir Douglas Black, President of the Royal College of Physicians, who told the jury he thought it 'would be ethical to put a rejected child upon a course of management that would end in its death . . . I say that it is ethical that a child suffering from Down's syndrome . . . should not survive.'

Mr Justice Farquharson considered the views of these medical practitioners to be highly significant. He told the jury that he imagined they would 'think long and hard before deciding that doctors of the eminence we have heard . . . have evolved standards which amount to committing crime'.

The jury did not have to think for very long. After only two hours, it found Arthur not guilty. There were scenes of public rejoicing in the courtroom. The Times headlined its coverage of the verdict 'Women Cry "Thank God" As Dr Arthur Is Cleared'. Dr John Havard, secretary of the British Medical Association, said that he hoped that the Director of Public Prosecutions 'will now realize that it is not appropriate to bring criminal proceedings against eminent and distinguished paediatricians'. Life, the group that reported the case to the police, must have been deeply disappointed with the verdict; and no doubt it was then even more dismayed to learn that the acquittal was popular with the public. An opinion poll conducted at the time of the trial asked 2000 adults if they thought a doctor should be found guilty of murder if, with the parents' agreement, 'he sees to it that a severely handicapped baby dies'. Only 7 per cent thought a doctor should be found guilty in such a case; 86 per cent thought he should not be.[10]

The Arthur trial was notable for what it tells us about the practice of medical infanticide—and the apparent widespread acceptance of this practice by the British public—but a jury's verdict does not establish any legal precedent. The three cases about severely disabled infants decided by the British Court of Appeal between 1981 and 1990 did. The first of these, known as Re B, was similar in its facts to the later American case of Baby Doe. The parents of a baby with Down syndrome and a blockage of the intestine refused consent to surgery to remove the blockage. (This operation is a simpler one than the operation that Baby Doe would have needed, but the effects of not operating were the same—death by starvation.) The High Court (which in Britain is rather low in the hierarchy of courts) ruled that the parents' decision should be respected. On appeal, the Court of Appeal reversed this ruling and ordered the operation performed, on the basis that it was in the baby's best interests. In doing so, however, the court suggested that there might be other circumstances in which 'the life of [the] child is demonstrably going to be so awful that in effect the child must be condemned to die'.[11]

Re C was a case closer to this criterion. Baby C was born prematurely on 23 December 1988, and was made a ward of the court because the local social services department viewed her parents as incapable of caring for her properly. She had an usually severe build-up of fluid on the brain, and the brain was malformed. At sixteen weeks of age she had a developmental age of four weeks, and her doctors believed that she was 'permanently unable to interact mentally, socially and physically'. The doctors also thought that her long-term survival was in any case unlikely. The social services department nevertheless thought that if she developed an infection or illness, she should be treated in the same way as a child without any disabilities. The hospital thought this inappropriate, and so the matter went to court to be resolved. Mr Justice Ward of the High Court ordered that the hospital should relieve the baby's distress, but otherwise was at liberty to 'treat the minor to die'. He later reworded this order, saying that the hospital was at liberty 'to treat the baby to allow her life to come to an end peacefully and with dignity'. This case also went to the Court of Appeal, which on this occasion left the paediatric team with discretion to treat Baby C as it saw fit.[12]

The subject of the third case, *Re J*, was another brain-damaged premature baby, and also a ward of the court. At five months of age, he still had difficulty in breathing without a ventilator, was paralysed, appeared to be blind and was likely to become deaf. Doctors said it was debatable whether he would ever be able to sit up or hold his head up. He was, however, capable of feeling pain. Doctors sought the guidance of the court about whether to keep the baby on a ventilator if he stopped breathing. In the High Court, Mr Justice Scott Baker ruled that it would not be in Baby J's best interests to put him back on a ventilator if he stopped breathing, unless the doctors caring for him thought it appropriate to do so. This ruling was upheld by the Court of Appeal, which explicitly rejected the absolutist view that life must be preserved, irrespective of its quality. Instead, Lord Justice Donaldson said that courts should carry out a 'balancing exercise' in assessing what course was in the best interests of the child. There were cases, he said, in which it was not in the child's best interests to have treatment that would cause it increased suffering without sufficient compensating benefit. Lord Justice Taylor agreed that the paramount consideration was what was in the child's best interests, and added: 'I consider the correct approach is for the court to judge the quality of life the child would have to endure if given the treatment and decide whether in all the circumstances such a life would be so afflicted as to be intolerable to that child'.[13]

The practice of withholding treatment from spina bifida babies was also tested in a very public way in Australia. Baby M was born on 14 July 1989, with a severe form of spina bifida and other malformations. She was likely to be paralysed in the lower legs, unable to walk, and incontinent. There was a significant risk of mental retardation and of epilepsy. Dr Peter Loughnan, Baby M's attending doctor at Melbourne's Royal Children's Hospital, consulted with her parents about how she should be treated. The parents, who were practising Roman Catholics, sought guidance from two parish priests, and from the Roman Catholic chaplain at the hospital. All three were advised by Loughnan about the course of treatment he would recommend. The parents then agreed to his recommendations, which were for conservative management without any attempt to prolong Baby M's life by aggressive surgery. Baby M was given paracetamol as a pain-killer, and phenobarbitone as a sedative. She was fed on demand, but not given tube feeding.

About five days after this plan of management was put into operation, Baby M's doctors were visited by the police, who had received a complaint from the Right to Life Association, an anti-abortion group, alleging that the doctors and parents had decided to allow Baby M to die because they thought her quality of life unacceptable. (The information was provided to the Right to Life Association by the baby's great-aunt.) The police surgeon examined Baby M. The treating doctors called in several other specialists, all of whom agreed that the treatment of Baby M was appropriate to her condition. The police also declared themselves satisfied. Ten days after birth, Baby M developed respiratory problems, and seemed to be dying. She was given morphine, and she died two days later. Because of the police involvement, the hospital reported the death to the coroner, a public official whose duty it is to investigate deaths that may be unnatural.

Two years later, an inquest was held before deputy state coroner Wendy Wilmoth. The Right to Life Association had its own expert witnesses, including a paediatric neurosurgeon from Los Angeles, who told the inquest that he would have operated to close the wound on the baby's back, as he did in virtually all cases of spina bifida. He also said he would not have given phenobarbitone, because it was a sedative that tended to depress the urge to feed, and he pointed out that the nursing notes showed that Baby M was getting far less food than she needed. If Baby M did not suckle well, he said, he would have given her food through a tube.

Baby M's own doctors made it clear that their decision not to operate was based on the 'gloomy' prognosis for the child. They gave evidence about her disabilities, both certain and probable. The inquest thus was the stage for a contest between the universal treatment policy of the Right to Life Association's witness, and the quality of life policy of the doctors at the Royal Children's Hospital.

The deputy state coroner found that the treatment the doctors had chosen for Baby M was 'legally, ethically and morally sound', and that the infant died 'from natural causes', although 'in the presence of phenobarbitone and morphine at toxic levels'.[14] Though somewhat confusing in its phrasing and its substance, this finding met with general approbation. Ms Wilmoth also said that she considered the intervention by the Right to Life Association in the private life of a family to be improper—a condemnation that was forcefully echoed in all the media coverage of the issue. The Roman Catholic Archbishop of Melbourne even wrote to Baby M's parents to tell them that he had spoken to the vice-president of the Right to Life Association, a Catholic priest who had been a central figure in the activities of the association in this case, 'seeking to ensure that he understood that excessive zeal can be harmful to people'.[15]

For the Right to Life Association, the inquest had backfired in the worst possible way. The association had shown that a doctor at one of Australia's leading children's hospitals had, on the basis of a quality of life judgment, selected a form of treatment that meant that few, if any, efforts were made to prolong this particular baby's life, and she did not get enough food to sustain her, but she did get toxic levels of drugs. What was the result? A resounding endorsement, from the coroner and the media, of what the doctor had done, and a scathing condemnation of the Right to Life Association for interfering in the case!

SELECTIVE NON-TREATMENT AND INFANTICIDE

We have now seen that when a baby is born with a sufficiently severe disability, selective non-treatment is an accepted part of modern medical practice—accepted by paediatricians, by the British department of health and social security, by the British Court of Appeal, by an Australian coroner, and apparently by a significant proportion of the public, probably a majority in countries like Britain and Australia. In fact, 'selective non-treatment' is something of a misnomer. The blunt expression used by Mr Justice Ward in his original order in the case of Baby C is more apt: 'treating to die'. For John Pearson drugs were used to make death swift and certain. John Lorber put spina bifida babies with adverse criteria on chloral hydrate, a sedative that made them sleepy, and he instructed the nurses to feed them only when they demanded it. 'No wonder,' wrote Dr Robert Zachary, one of Lorber's former colleagues at Sheffield who opposed the switch away from full treatment of all babies with spina bifida, 'these babies are sleepy and demand no feed, and with this regimen most of them will die within a few weeks, many within the first week'.[16]

Supporters of pro-life groups see all this as a shocking indictment of modern secular society. Commenting on the acquittal of Dr Leonard Arthur, Nuala Scarisbrick, a spokesperson for the anti-abortion group Life, said: 'Now to be unwanted is to be guilty of a capital offence'. That comment was a little loose, in two respects. First, there is no question of John Pearson having been guilty of anything. The acquittal perhaps tells us that the jury thought there are circumstances in which innocent human life may be taken. Second, the jury's verdict said nothing about how we may treat unwanted people as a whole; it only said something about how we may treat unwanted babies. With these important modifications, however, Nuala Scarisbrick was not so far off the mark. The jury's verdict suggests that the protection we give to the lives of older human beings does not apply to an unwanted baby. Obviously, Nuala Scarisbrick was shocked by this. Should we all be shocked by it?

Killing unwanted infants or allowing them to die has been a normal practice in most societies throughout human history and prehistory. We find it, for example, in ancient Greece, where disabled infants were exposed on the mountainside. We find it in nomadic tribes like the Kung of the Kalahari Desert, whose women will kill a baby born while an older child is still too young to walk. Infanticide was also common on Polynesian islands like Tikopia, where food supplies and population were kept in balance by smothering unwanted newborn infants. In Japan before westernisation, 'mabiki'—a word that has its origins in the thinning of rice seedlings so that there is room for each plant to flourish, but which came to be applied to infanticide too—was very widely practised, not only by peasants with limited amounts of land, but also by those who were quite well off. Even in nineteenth-century Europe, unwanted infants were given to foundling homes run by women known as 'angel makers' because of the very high death rates that occurred.[17]

The fact that infanticide was—and in many parts of the world, still is—widely practised does not, of course, mean that it is right. No argument from 'everyone does this' to 'this is right' can be valid. Even if infanticide could be shown to be the natural response of human beings to the birth of infants born in unfavourable circumstances, that would not make it right. Still, it is worth knowing that from a cross-cultural perspective it is *our* tradition, not that of the Kung or the Japanese, that is unusual in its official morality about infanticide. Recognising that fact puts the modern medical practice of infanticide in a broader perspective.

This broader perspective may also lead us to a different view of the abortion debate. We saw that the strength of the case against abortion lies in the gradual nature of human development, and the fact that birth does not mark any dramatic change in the nature of the being who is one day inside its mother's womb, and the next day outside it. The wide support for medical infanticide suggests that, instead of trying to find places to draw lines, we should accept that the development of the human being, from embryo to fetus, from fetus to newborn infant, and from newborn infant to older child, is a continuous process that does not offer us neat lines of demarcation between stages. But, we may then add, so too is the development of the moral status of the human being.

Birth is a significant point because the mother has a relationship to her baby that is different from the relationship she had with her fetus; and others can now relate to the baby too, in a way that they could not earlier. But it is not for that reason a point at which the fetus suddenly moves from having no right to life to having the same right to life as every other human being. On the contrary, the beliefs and practices I have described only make sense on the assumption that our attitude to the newborn infant is somewhere between what we think about a fetus in the womb, and an older child or adult. Pro-life groups such as Life in Britain and the Right to Life Association in Australia have failed to understand this; and so their attempts to advance their cause by instigating the prosecution of Dr Leonard Arthur and the investigation of the death of Baby M at the Royal Children's Hospital have merely confirmed the high degree of public, medical and judicial support for making life and death decisions for infants on the basis of quality of life judgements. Thousands of years of lip-service to the Christian ethic have not succeeded in suppressing entirely the earlier ethical attitude that newborn-infants, especially if unwanted, are not yet full members of the moral community.

Making selective medical infanticide more public has made it easier to see what is happening. As in the case of Tony Bland, there is less talk now of distinctions between ordinary and extra-ordinary means of treatment, and more open acknowledgment of what Lord Justice Taylor called the correct approach: 'to judge the quality of life the child would have to endure if given the treatment'. The Reagan administration's response to the Baby Doe case was the most concerted effort by any government in recent times to prevent the application to newborn infants of 'a social ethic where some human lives are valued and others are not'. The failure of that attempt therefore tells us much about the erosion of the sanctity of life ethic beyond the boundary of birth. When it came to the really tough cases, Reagan's own administration could not stick with a sanctity of life approach, no matter how hard it tried to disguise its departure from the line it had at first tried to draw. If, as President Reagan wrote, the choice was between the sanctity of life ethic and the quality of life ethic, the decision has been made unequivocally in favour of the latter.

ASKING FOR DEATH

I will neither give a deadly drug to anybody if asked for it,
nor will I make a suggestion to this effect.

THE HIPPOCRATIC OATH

THE PROBLEM

Questions about embryos and fetuses, infants, and patients with
no brain function, or only brain-stem function, are all questions
about human beings at the margins of the concept. That is why
these debates so often turn into questions about what it is to be a
human being. In contrast, to ask whether doctors may kill their
conscious, autonomous patients—if the patients request it—is a
direct challenge to what has often been seen as the core of the traditional Hippocratic ethic. Granted, the fact that a patient asks
repeatedly to be killed means that families, doctors and judges are
not forced to decide whether the quality of life of someone who
cannot decide for herself is so poor that it is better that her life not
continue. It is, after all, the patient's life, and as long as the patient
is capable of reaching an informed decision, then who better to
decide whether life is worth living? Doesn't the patient have a
right to ask for this help and, if a doctor is willing to give it, why
should the law stand in the way? Yet when a patient asks for assistance in dying, and the doctor then gives the patient a lethal
injection, there is no way of disguising what is happening. The
doctor's intention is clear, as it was in the case of Tony Bland, but
this is undoubtedly a killing, not an allowing to die. So this is

another area in which the traditional ethic is struggling to survive. Politically, it is here that the most vigorous battle against the sanctity of life ethic is now being fought. The stories that follow show some of the ways in which pressure is building for a change.

Michigan, USA

In 1989, Janet Adkins, a fifty-four-year-old Oregon woman, was in the early stages of Alzheimer's disease. She was still able to speak quite coherently, and to play tennis. But she could no longer read a book, or read music and, when playing tennis, she had difficulty in keeping score. She knew that she might live another ten years or more, but that in the final phase, which can last for several years, she would be unable to recognise or communicate with anyone, and would lie huddled in bed, her mind completely gone. She did not want to end her life that way.

Adkins tried an experimental treatment for Alzheimer's. It didn't work. She then decided that she wanted to die, while she was still capable of thinking coherently. She had heard of a Michigan pathologist, Dr Jack Kevorkian, who had developed a 'suicide machine' and offered to make it available to people who were incurably ill and wanted to die. (At that time Michigan had no law against assisting suicide.) She contacted Dr Kevorkian, who discussed her desire to die with her, and then asked her to get her doctor to send him her medical records. After he had studied them, Kevorkian agreed to help Adkins.

In June 1990, Janet Adkins came to Michigan with her husband Ron and her three sons. Her husband, thinking and perhaps hoping that she might still change her mind, bought them all return tickets. Kevorkian met them in a motel room, and videotaped a conversation with Janet and Ron Adkins. On the tape Janet Adkins smiles and chuckles from time to time. She speaks about the things she can no longer do, and her desire to 'get out with dignity'. Kevorkian asks her what she would say to people who said she was doing the wrong thing. She replies: 'I'm sorry. I just still want to get out'.

The Adkins family spent the night thinking things over one more time. Janet Adkins had not changed her mind, and the family were prepared to support her decision. The next afternoon, Janet met Kevorkian again and told him that she wanted to go ahead. He was willing to help her, but had been unable to find a place where she could die comfortably. Clinics, churches and funeral homes had all refused to provide a room when he told them what he wanted it for. He therefore had installed a bed in his 1968 Volkswagen van. Now he drove the van to a public park. Inside the van, Janet lay down on the bed, and Kevorkian put an intravenous line into her arm. A harmless mixture of salt and water was flowing down the line. Janet moved a switch that changed the fluid to a sedative, and also started a timing device that would soon allow potassium chloride to flow into the drip. As a result of the sedative, Janet Adkins fell into a deep sleep. Soon after, the potassium chloride took effect, and her heart stopped. Kevorkian then notified her family, and the police. The local district attorney attempted to prosecute him for murder, but the judge dismissed the charge as there was no evidence that Kevorkian had done anything other than assist Janet Adkins to commit suicide, and that was not against the law.

Kevorkian later helped twenty other people to commit suicide. In 1992 the Michigan legislature passed a law making assisted suicide an offence. Kevorkian continued to help terminally ill people commit suicide. After his public statement that he had assisted Thomas Hyde to commit suicide in August 1993, Kevorkian was charged with violating the new law. In December he was taken to Oakland County jail where he refused bail and went on a hunger strike. Meanwhile in neighbouring Wayne County, where Kevorkian also faced charges of assisting suicide, Judge Richard Kaufman declared the new law unconstitutional on the grounds that it was an unnecessary intrusion upon personal decisions based upon personal moral beliefs. The prosecutor announced that he would appeal against this decision. In an editorial, the *New York Times* supported Judge Kaufman's decision and said that Michigan legislators should devise a law that 'protects the desperately sick from ill-considered self-destruction while recognizing their right to decide rationally to die with dignity'.[1] After seventeen days without food, amidst national and often favourable publicity, Kevorkian was released on bail, and promptly helped another terminally ill man to die.

In April 1994, with the constitutionality of the law against assisting suicide still unresolved, Kevorkian went on trial in Oakland County on the charge of assisting Hyde to commit suicide. Kevorkian admitted supplying carbon monoxide gas, tubing and a mask, which Hyde then used to end his life. He said that he did so in an effort to end Hyde's suffering, not necessarily to cause his death. (The law against assisting suicide had an exemption for acts intended to end suffering, rather than to cause death.) The jury watched a home video of Hyde, taken about a month before he died. On the video Hyde, who was suffering from Lou Gehrig's disease, a debilitating nerve disorder also known as ALS or amyotrophic lateral sclerosis, described how much he wanted to end his suffering, and to die. The jury acquitted Kevorkian. Five of its members worked in medically related jobs. One, a nurse, said after the trial, 'I don't feel it's our obligation to choose for someone else how much pain and suffering they can go through'. Another, a nurse's assistant, said, 'I do believe an individual has a right to decide what happens to their own lives and bodies and not the Government or the legislature'.[2]

Rochester, New York, USA

At the age of forty-five, Diane had already survived vaginal cancer and overcome a problem with alcohol. In 1990, when she had been a patient of Dr Timothy Quill for eight years, she developed a severe form of leukaemia. Without treatment, the disease would kill her within a few months. The only treatment available was an intensive form of chemotherapy, followed by bone-marrow trans-plantation, which involved radiation treatment over her whole body. The probability that she would survive all this treatment, and recover from the leukaemia, was no better than 25 per cent.

Diane thought about the treatment, and then decided not to take it. The chances of survival, she considered, were not worth enduring so severe a course of therapy. Though disturbed by this decision, Quill recognised that Diane was an intelligent woman who understood what she was doing, and she unquestionably had the right to do what she was choosing to do.

Some days later Diane told Quill that she was worried about the prospect of dying slowly, and asked for enough sleeping tablets to kill herself when the time came. Quill probed to make sure that she was not irrationally depressed, and then came to the conclu-sion that, if he did not help her, she would become preoccupied with how she might die, and would not be able to make the most of the time she had left. He wrote out a prescription for barbitur-ates, and told her how to use them as sleeping tablets, and how to use them to kill herself.

Diane lived another three months, with her family close around her, until she began to decline rapidly. She saw Quill one last time. In Quill's words: 'When we met, it was clear that she knew what she was doing, that she was sad and frightened to be leaving, but that she would be even more terrified to stay and suffer'.[3]

Two days later, Diane's husband called to say that she had said her goodbyes to him and her son that morning, and asked them to leave her alone for an hour. When they returned, she had died, apparently peacefully.

Quill published an account of Diane's death in the *New England Journal of Medicine*. He said that he did so partly in order to show that there was an alternative to the approach being taken by Dr Jack Kevorkian. In New York state, assisting suicide is a crime punishable by up to fifteen years' imprisonment. A district attorney attempted to prosecute Quill but, after hearing the evidence, a grand jury decided not to indict him.[4]

Sydney, Australia

For a man of fifty-three Rex Mortimer had had a varied life. He had been a dock worker, a lawyer, a newspaper editor, and an associate professor of government at Sydney University. In 1979 he learned that he had a brain tumour. He and his wife Mary began to discuss how he might end his life with dignity. They looked for, and eventually found, a doctor who would prescribe them sleeping pills they could use. But by then Rex was in hospital. Mary went to the hospital and helped her husband take the pills. Then she went home, believing he would die, and waiting for the phone to ring. By 8.00 am she could stand the suspense no longer, and rang the hospital, 'trying to sound normal', to inquire how he was. She was told that he had had a good night's sleep and was sitting up eating his breakfast. Mary later said: 'I was devastated. This was something we had planned. Responsible adults had done this together, we had as much assistance from a doctor as we could get, given that what we were doing was quite illegal. So there we were.'

When she went to see Rex later that day, he repeated that he wanted to die. Mary became increasingly concerned that, as a result of the brain tumour, he was losing his mental faculties. She was also terrified of being discovered, and of the hospital staff resuscitating her husband. Nevertheless, she once again helped Rex to take sleeping pills. This time, he died soon afterwards. For some time, however, Mary 'lay awake at night waiting for the police to knock on my door and arrest me'. Thirteen years after Rex's death she decided to speak out about what she had done, in order to support a proposal to legalise medical assistance for the terminally ill who wish to take their own lives.[5]

British Columbia, Canada

Like Thomas Hyde, whom Kevorkian helped to die, Sue Rodriguez suffered from Lou Gehrig's disease. In 1993, when she was forty-two years old, her life expectancy was estimated to be between two and fourteen months. She knew that, during those months that remained to her, she would lose the ability to swallow, speak, walk and move her body without assistance. In the final stage of her illness she would be unable to leave her bed, would need a respirator to breathe, and would be able to obtain nourishment only through a tube.

Rodriguez knew all of this, and wanted control over when and how she would die. She could have killed herself while still able to move around, but she did not want to end her life while she could still enjoy it. Her problem was that, by the time she was no longer able to enjoy life, she would be physically unable to kill herself. She would need the assistance of someone else. But to assist suicide is a crime in British Columbia, where she lived, as it is throughout Canada. Sue Rodriguez saw this as contrary to the Canadian Charter of Rights, which has in it a clause guaranteeing equal protection and benefit of the law to all, and ruling out discrimination on a variety of grounds, among them disability. After all, she argued, suicide itself is not a crime, and able-bodied people can commit suicide without assistance. The law that stops anyone from aiding suicide therefore particularly discriminates against those with disabilities that make it impossible for them to take their own lives.

Rodriguez took her case to court, applying for an order declaring that the section of the criminal code that makes assisted suicide a crime is invalid, to the extent that it prohibits a terminally ill person from being assisted by a physician to commit suicide. When her application was denied, she appealed to the British Columbia Court of Appeal; when this appeal was dismissed, she appealed to the Supreme Court of Canada. Here too she lost, but this time very narrowly. Four of the nine judges, among them the chief justice, accepted her argument that the prohibition of assisted suicide discriminated against people who wish to commit suicide but cannot do so by reason of physical disability. Five judges, however, held that nothing in the Canadian Charter of Rights required the court to hold that there was a constitutional right to assisted suicide. In reaching this decision, they noted that the first section of the charter qualifies the rights and freedoms set out in the following sections, by making them 'subject to such reasonable limits prescribed by law as can be demonstrably justified in a free and democratic society'. In their view, a prohibition on assisted suicide was reasonable and justified by the need to protect life, and particularly the lives of vulnerable members of society.[6]

A few months after the verdict, Sue Rodriguez died. Svend Robinson, a member of parliament who had supported her cause, said he was at her home when a doctor helped her to die, but he refused to identify the doctor. Canadian police announced that they would investigate. In a statement released after her death, Rodriguez expressed the hope that there would soon be new legislation so that terminally ill people could have another option available.[7]

Winchester, England

In August 1991 Lillian Boyes was dying in the Royal Hampshire County Hospital, in Winchester. For twenty years she had suffered from an extremely painful form of rheumatoid arthritis. Now, at seventy, she had developed ulcers and abscesses on her arms and legs, fractured vertebrae, internal bleeding, deformed hands and feet, swollen joints, and gangrene from steroid treatments. Simply to be touched caused her great pain. She had, she told her family and Dr Nigel Cox, her consultant rheumatologist for the previous thirteen years, reached the point at which she wanted to be helped to die. Dr Cox was sympathetic but said that he could not do this. Mrs Boyes then said that she wanted her treatment stopped. Dr Cox agreed to this, but it made the pain worse. Her body could no longer absorb the quantities of opiod pain-killers, including heroin, that Dr Cox was giving her. A nurse was later to say 'she howled and screamed like a dog' when anybody touched her. A hospital chaplain said that he had seen IRA bomb victims, but had never seen anyone 'so much eaten by pain' as Mrs Boyes.

By 16 August, it seemed that Mrs Boyes had hours, rather than days, to live. She was still crying out with pain, and again told Dr Cox that she wanted to die. Her two sons, who were with her, supported her request. After a further injection of heroin failed to stop the pain, Dr Cox injected two ampoules of potassium chloride—a double dose of a lethal drug that has no curative or pain-killing properties. Mrs Boyes relaxed, and for the first time for months her son could clasp her hand. Then she died.

Dr Cox entered in the medical notes the details of the injections he gave. No-one raised any complaint at the time, but some days later a Roman Catholic nurse who did not usually work on that ward read the notes and reported it to the management, who called the police. Mrs Boyes' body had by then been cremated, so it was not possible to prove that the potassium chloride had caused her death. Dr Cox was therefore charged with attempted murder. He was found guilty. The judge told him that he had 'betrayed his unequivocal duty as a physician', and gave him a twelve-month suspended prison sentence. The General Medical Council also reviewed his case. A doctor convicted of a serious crime is normally struck off the medical register, which means that he or she cannot work as a doctor. In Dr Cox's case, the council said that while a doctor could ease pain and suffering, it is 'wholly outside that duty to shorten life in order to relieve suffering'. Nevertheless, the council added, it had decided 'to temper justice with mercy' and impose no penalty.[8]

THE SOLUTION?

Here is an account of the medical care a Dutch woman received during her last illness.

In 1988 Carla was forty-seven years old, married, and had four teenage children. She developed a painful swelling in her lower abdomen, and went to see her doctor about it. He sent her to a large general hospital in Delft. She was operated on, and found to have cancer. It was not possible to remove the cancer entirely. After the operation Carla had chemotherapy, and she felt reasonably well until March 1990, when it was found that the cancer had returned. This time chemotherapy did not help, and her pain increased. She was readmitted to the hospital in Delft. Here she was seen by Dr Pieter Admiraal, who is a member of the hospital's terminal-care team.

Admiraal was able to stop Carla's pain by a continuous infusion of morphine, delivered through a needle placed under her skin. Although relieved by the fact that she was no longer in pain, she worried that in the end her condition might get worse. During one of Admiraal's regular visits, she asked him if she would be able to have help in dying when the stage had been reached at which she found her condition unbearable. Carla's husband, Henk, was present, and was visibly upset by the request—even though he knew that his wife was going to die from her illness, he seemed unprepared to lose her so soon. Admiraal was willing to listen to Carla's request. Euthanasia, he told her, was not a taboo subject. But he said that the final decision was not his, nor hers, alone. At this hospital, it had to be agreed to by a team of two doctors, a nurse, and one of the three pastoral care-givers at the hospital— either the Roman Catholic chaplain, the Protestant chaplain, or the Humanist counsellor. Carla was a Roman Catholic, and so she raised the issue of euthanasia with the hospital's Roman Catholic chaplain. He did not reject the idea—on the contrary, he was sympathetic to it.

Carla now began to deteriorate more rapidly. If she drank anything, she would almost immediately vomit. She was given fluids through a tube, and was offered food through a tube as well. But she did not accept the offer of a feeding tube, saying that she did not wish to prolong her life. She lost weight, and became very weak. She could not move around in her bed, and became sore; her tumour was still growing, and it began to block the flow of blood to her legs. Her legs became swollen and painful.

Carla's family was with her much of the time, and her husband and one of the children often slept in the same room. Her family doctor also visited her frequently. She remained alert, and was sustained by her Catholic faith. The time came at which she asked for her suffering to be ended. The family discussed the request. Her husband now accepted her desire to die. At first her eldest son did not—he still had hopes that she might get better. But after Carla talked to him further, he also agreed with her decision. Then the hospital staff was consulted: the nurses who had cared for her every day, the gynaecologist, and the Roman Catholic chaplain. They all thought that Carla's wish should be respected. The medical staff agreed that nothing more could be done to relieve her suffering, other than to help her to die.

Carla, Admiraal, and the family met, and agreed that euthanasia would be carried out on the following day. Carla signed a form to indicate her desire for this. Carla's family doctor—and his wife—came to say farewell to her. The Catholic chaplain had already performed the final sacraments. When the time came, Carla confirmed that she still wished to die. Her husband, two of her sisters, her parish priest, and two of her children were with her when Dr Admiraal gave her an injection. She went to sleep. A few minutes later she was dead.[9]

There have long been advocates of voluntary euthanasia. Until recently, no matter how strong the arguments of the advocates of voluntary euthanasia might seem, they could always be met with the cold political realism of the fact that no country, anywhere in the world, allowed doctors or anyone else to kill people who asked to be killed. There were, of course, some exotic examples, from ancient times or far-flung tribes, where euthanasia, voluntary or not so voluntary, had been openly practised. But what twentieth-century nation would be prepared to take the lead into territory where no modern legal system had ever gone before? And if doctors were to carry out voluntary euthanasia, what national medical association would be prepared to accept that to kill the patient was good medical practice?

We now know the answer. Carla's death is not an isolated example of how death comes to those who are very ill in the Netherlands. According to a study carried out for a government-appointed committee of inquiry, about one in fifty deaths in the Netherlands is the result of voluntary euthanasia. The total number is approximately 2300 cases each year. In addition, there are about 400 cases per year in which doctors do not provide euthanasia, but instead help their patients to commit suicide.[10] How is it that the land of tulips, windmills and peasants in wooden clogs has also become the land in which doctors can carry out voluntary euthanasia without fear of prosecution?

The story of the open practice of euthanasia in the Netherlands began with a familiar situation: an incapacitated, elderly woman, living in a nursing home, wanting to die. Everyone who has worked in a nursing home knows of such patients. Typically, doctors wait for pneumonia to strike. When it does, they do not use antibiotics, but instead 'allow nature to take its course'. Since pneumonia may take a long time to come, though, some of the more thoughtful health-care professionals regret that they do not have the courage to respond more actively to a persistent and well-founded request for aid in dying.[11] In the Netherlands in 1971 Dr Geertruida Postma did have the courage to act. Perhaps she had more courage than others because in this case the woman asking to die was her mother.

Dr Postma's mother had suffered a brain haemorrhage that left her partly paralysed, deaf, and able to speak only with difficulty. In the nursing home where she lived, she had to be tied into a chair to avoid falling. She repeatedly begged her daughter to end her life. Finally, Dr Postma said, 'When I watched my mother, a human wreck, hanging in that chair, I couldn't stand it anymore'. She gave her mother an injection of morphine that ended her life. She then told the director of the nursing home, who reported the death to the police.

Dr Postma was charged with mercy killing, which was (and remains) a statutory offence in the Netherlands. The prescribed penalty was twelve years in gaol. Dr Postma was found guilty, but was given only a one-week suspended sentence, and put on probation for a year. The outcome suggested some degree of acceptance for what she had done. This was reinforced when other doctors signed an open letter to the Netherlands minister of justice, saying that they had committed the same crime. A handful of people in Dr Postma's village decided to form a Society for Voluntary Euthanasia. Within a decade, it had grown to 25,000 members.[12]

After the Postma case, the Royal Dutch Medical Association reconsidered its attitude to voluntary euthanasia. In 1973, when every other medical association unequivocally supported the Hippocratic tradition that doctors must not assist their patients to die, the Royal Dutch Medical Association opened the door just a crack. Although the association said that voluntary euthanasia should remain illegal, it suggested that if a doctor, after considering all the aspects of a patient's circumstances, shortened the life of a patient who was incurably ill and in the process of dying, a court should decide whether there was a conflict of duties that could justify the doctor's action.

This 'conflict of duties' defence was used in a crucial case decided by the High Court of the Netherlands in 1984. Known as the Alkmaar case, from the district in which the initial trial took place, it dealt with the death of a patient referred to in the court records as Mrs B. She was ninety-five years old. On the weekend before her death she was unable to eat or drink, and lost consciousness. On regaining consciousness, she pleaded with her doctor several times to put an end to her suffering, and said she did not want to experience again anything like what she had been through. The doctor discussed the matter with his assistant physician. They agreed that there was no prospect of Mrs B recovering her health. The doctor also discussed Mrs B's request with her son. Both the assistant physician and the son supported Mrs B's request for euthanasia. The doctor, considering that Mrs B's suffering was unbearable, finally decided to end her life. He was charged with mercy killing.

In his defence, the doctor said that he had faced an emergency situation: the legal duty not to kill had been in conflict with his duty as a physician to relieve his patient's unbearable suffering. Both the lower court and the Court of Appeals rejected this argument. The doctor was convicted, although no punishment was imposed. The doctor appealed to the High Court, which held that the Court of Appeals should have investigated whether the emergency situation had existed as the doctor had claimed. The High Court suggested that this matter should be considered, taking into account 'responsible medical opinion measured by the prevailing standards of medical ethics'. This decision implied that where a patient was in an unbearable situation that would not improve, and the patient's suffering could not be relieved in any other way, a doctor who acted on the patient's explicit, persistent and well-informed request for euthanasia would not be guilty of an offence. The decision in the Alkmaar case was later confirmed in other cases.[13]

By the time the Alkmaar case was decided, the Royal Dutch Medical Association had taken a firmer stance in favour of voluntary euthanasia. It proposed that euthanasia should be permissible under the following conditions:

• Only a medical practitioner should carry out euthanasia.

• There should be an explicit request from the patient which leaves no room for doubt about the patient's desire to die.

• The patient's decision should be well-informed, free and persistent.

• The patient must be in a situation of unbearable pain and suffering without hope of improvement.

• There must be no other measures available to make the patient's suffering bearable.

• The doctor must be very careful in reaching the decision and should seek a second opinion from another independent doctor.[14]

Because a conflict of duties defence was available, the Dutch ministry of justice decided not to prosecute doctors for carrying out euthanasia or for assisting in suicide, if a set of conditions similar to those laid down by the Royal Dutch Medical Association was met. These conditions do not require that the patient should be in a terminal condition, but only that the situation must be unbearable, and without hope of improvement.

This situation was regularised by the Dutch parliament in 1993. Although the parliament did not repeal the law that makes mercy killing a criminal offence, it established in law a procedure for doctors to report medical decisions resulting in euthanasia to the public prosecutor. The public prosecutor was instructed to decide on a case-by-case basis whether prosecution should follow, on the principle that legal action should be initiated if it was not clear that the mercy killing was carried out at the express request of the patient. With the support of the Christian Democrats, who under the Roman Catholic prime minister, Ruud Lubbers, led the coalition government, this proposal passed the lower house of parliament by 91 votes to 45. It passed the upper house by a much narrower margin, but that was because of the opposition of small parties who regarded it as a 'spineless compromise' and urged full legalisation of voluntary euthanasia.[15]

THE COMING STRUGGLE FOR THE RIGHT TO DIE

We have seen how a number of people who were very ill managed to end their lives. The desire among the citizens of modern democracies for control over how they die is growing. The failure of attempts to ban Derek Humphry's book *Final Exit*—which describes ways of ending your life, including lists of lethal drugs and the quantities you will need—shows that the information people need to kill themselves painlessly can no longer be suppressed. The astonishing success of the book—it rose to No. 1 on the *New York Times* list of best-selling 'how-to and advice' books—indicates how many people want that information. No United States prosecutor attempted to stop the sale of the book. In Australia, it was for a time declared a prohibited import, but an Australian edition was then released, for sale only to those over eighteen years of age.[16]

The desire for control over how we die marks a sharp turning away from the sanctity of life ethic. It will not be satisfied by the concessions to patient autonomy within the framework of that ethic—a right to refuse 'extraordinary means' of medical treatment, or to employ drugs like morphine that are 'intended' to relieve pain, but have the 'unintended but foreseen side-effect' of shortening life. The right to refuse medical treatment can help only in the limited number of cases in which it leads to a swift and painless death. Most cancer patients, for instance, are not in this situation. They are more likely to be helped by liberal injections of morphine, but even that is not a solution for people like Janet Adkins or Lillian Boyes. In the case of Carla, too, though she had a continuous infusion of morphine, she did not want to die by a gradually increasing dose, which would most likely have put her into a state of drowsy confusion for some days before death came. She preferred to die at a time of her own choosing, with her family around her. For most people who are very ill, the desire for control over death is best satisfied with the assistance of a medical practitioner. That is why the traditional ethic will be unable to accommodate the present demand for control over how we die.

Nearly all of the deaths I have just described are particularly sad because they came to people still in middle age. Yet if we focus on how these people died, Carla's death seems clearly better than the others. She had the best possible medical attention, right up to the moment of death. Her family could be with her, and even her priest. Nothing had to be furtive. There was no need to fear failure. No-one had to lie awake afterwards wondering if the police would knock.

The issue that is about to be fought out in the courts of several countries is whether people should be allowed to choose to die in the way Carla died. Change may come if juries persist in refusing to convict, as the jury refused to convict Kevorkian of assisting Thomas Hyde to commit suicide. It may also come through legal argument. Sue Rodriguez's challenge to the Canadian prohibition of assisted suicide failed narrowly. Meanwhile, the day after Kevorkian's acquittal in the Hyde case, in Washington state, US District Judge Barbara Rothstein declared unconstitutional a state law preventing doctors from helping terminally ill patients to commit suicide. Like Judge Richard Kaufman in Michigan, Rothstein found that the law violated the liberty of terminally ill patients. She also found that to permit the refusal of life-support systems for terminally ill people, but not to allow a doctor to help a patient to commit suicide, is a violation of rights to equal protection granted by the Fourteenth Amendment. The decision is being appealed and the issue will probably be decided by the Supreme Court.[17]

It may seem strange that a judge can suddenly find a law that has existed for 140 years to be contrary to a constitution that was written over two hundred years ago; but the United States constitution is a living tradition of legal interpretation, not a static document. In terms of this tradition, for the Supreme Court to find that there is a constitutional right to suicide would be no more startling than its finding, two decades ago, that there was a constitutional right to abortion. Moreover, since the Supreme Court's abortion decision in *Roe v. Wade* is now itself a precedent, the present argument for a constitutional right to suicide arguably has a stronger legal basis than the argument for a right to abortion had when the court accepted it.

The right to assistance in dying may come through referenda, rather than through the courts or legislatures. In a historic referendum in November 1994, Oregon became the first state to vote in favour of allowing doctors to do what Dr Timothy Quill did: to prescribe, for incurably ill patients who have requested assistance in dying, drugs that will, if the patient takes them, bring about a peaceful death. Previously, in 1991 and 1992, more far-reaching initiatives in the states of Washington and California had fallen short of a majority, gaining 46 per cent of the votes in each case. The Oregon decision has shown that citizens are prepared to support carefully-drafted reform laws that give individuals the right to medical assistance in dying.

When patients' rights to determine how they die are recognised in other countries as they are now recognised in the Netherlands and in Oregon, the Hippocratic tradition will undergo a further modification, as it did in the case of abortion. Good medical practice in the case of a terminally or incurably ill patient will come to be seen as including the provision of euthanasia, if the patient makes a free and well-informed request for it. But is that all that will change?

The most powerful objection to the legalisation of either voluntary euthanasia or physician-assisted suicide is that, once we begin to allow some people to kill others, we will find ourselves sliding down a slope that leads to killings of a kind that no-one wants. We may begin with strict controls designed to ensure that euthanasia is only carried out after a patient in an unbearable condition has repeatedly requested it but, so the argument runs, we shall gradually slide to euthanasia for people who are not capable of requesting it, or for people who are not suffering unbearably, but whose continued life puts a burden on their families. Then, perhaps, we shall move to euthanasia for those who have not asked for it, but whose treatment consumes scarce health-care resources that could be more effectively used elsewhere. In the end, say some opponents of legalisation, we will end up with a state that, like Nazi Germany, kills all those whom it considers to be unworthy of life.

The slippery slope argument helped to persuade the Supreme Court of Canada to decide against Sue Rodriguez. Justice Sopinka, who delivered the majority verdict, noted that in the Netherlands the assistance Sue Rodriguez was requesting would not be subject to prosecution. He then added:

> Critics of the Dutch approach point to evidence suggesting that involuntary active euthanasia (which is not permitted by the guidelines) is being practised to an increasing degree. This worrisome trend supports the view that a relaxation of the absolute prohibition takes us down 'the slippery slope'.[19]

Is the Netherlands a social laboratory that allows us to see how legalising voluntary euthanasia will lead us down the slippery slope? Justice Sopinka and a majority of the Supreme Court of Canada appear to think so. But is this right? What is the evidence that 'involuntary active euthanasia' is being practised 'to an increasing degree' in the Netherlands? Does the first decade of experience with open voluntary euthanasia in a modern nation provide any evidence by which we can gauge the validity of the slippery-slope argument?

To answer this question in a way that avoids muddle, we need to begin by being very specific about the terms we use. First, what did Justice Sopinka mean by 'involuntary active euthanasia'? Among bioethicists, this expression is rarely used, because to say that something is involuntary suggests that it is contrary to the will of the person affected, whereas to say that it is euthanasia suggests that it is a good death for that person. It is hard to see how killing a person who wants to go on living can be a good death. Bioethicists usually refer to euthanasia as either voluntary or non-voluntary, using the latter expression to refer to cases in which the patient is unable to express a desire about continued life—perhaps because he or she is an infant, or someone with advanced Alzheimer's disease who did not express any prior wishes about euthanasia before ceasing to be competent. It may be that Justice Sopinka meant 'non-voluntary active euthanasia' rather than 'involuntary active euthanasia'. But that would also be 'not permitted by the guidelines'. In any case, let us see what evidence there is of an increasing amount of either non-voluntary or involuntary euthanasia in the Netherlands.

Both those who believe that the Netherlands experience supports the slippery-slope argument, and those who oppose this view, draw their evidence from the study carried out in 1990 for the government-appointed committee of inquiry. To assess the issue properly, we need to look in a little more detail at what the study did and did not find.[20]

The first important point to note is that the study was not concerned only with voluntary euthanasia and assisted suicide. The investigators wanted to put voluntary active euthanasia into the context of all medical decisions which the doctor knows may hasten the death of the patient. These include non-treatment decisions (to withdraw or withhold treatment or, for example, not to resuscitate a patient whose heart has stopped) and decisions to alleviate pain and symptoms by giving drugs that the doctor knows may cause the patient to die more rapidly. In no country except the Netherlands have these medical decisions been investigated with a comparable breadth or rigour.

The study showed that active euthanasia and assisted suicide are far less common than other medical decisions that were known to shorten life or to carry the risk of shortening it. A total of 48,700 deaths were associated with these 'end of life' medical decisions: 22,500 were associated with decisions to withdraw or withhold treatment, and another 22,500 with decisions to alleviate pain and symptoms by giving drugs that the doctor knew may cause the patient to die more rapidly. Of the remainder, as we have already seen, 2300 deaths were the result of active voluntary euthanasia, and 400 were medically assisted suicides. In almost all of these 2700 deaths the patient was terminally ill, usually with some form of cancer, and in three-quarters of them it was estimated that the provision of euthanasia or assistance in suicide shortened life by less than four weeks. There were about three times as many requests for euthanasia or assistance in suicide as there were deaths from these causes, which suggests that doctors were not eager to act on these requests, and often found other ways of providing an acceptable level of comfort.

The remaining 1000 deaths have caused the most concern. They were cases in which a doctor supplied, prescribed or administered a drug with the explicit purpose of hastening the end of life, but without an explicit request from the patient. Although these 1000 cases were only a small fraction—barely 2 per cent—of all the deaths related to medical decision-making, critics of the Dutch situation have pounced on them. Here, they say, is all the evidence we need: 1000 people a year are being put to death without their consent. Isn't this definitely a 'worrisome trend' as Mr Justice Sopinka put it?

Before we reach this conclusion, however, there are some additional points to be considered. The authors of the study describe these 1000 cases as 'patients who were near death and clearly suffering grievously'. The drug most often used was morphine, either alone or in combination with a sedative. In 600 of the cases there had been some patient involvement in a discussion about ending life, although it had not yet reached the stage of an explicit request. In almost all the cases where there had been no discussion, this was because the patient was not capable of discussing it, usually being either permanently unconscious or in a state of 'reduced consciousness'. The exceptions were two cases dating back to the early 1980s, when doctors had not felt comfortable discussing these matters openly.

Thus while there appears to be a limited amount of non-voluntary euthanasia being practised in the Netherlands in extreme circumstances, no cases of 'involuntary euthanasia' came to light during the period of study. No-one was put to death against her or his will. In 71 per cent of cases, the medical decision had shortened life by less than a week, and by more than six months in only one of ninety-seven cases discussed in interviews with doctors.[21]

These facts may soften our attitude to the fact that there were 1000 cases in which doctors actively ended the patient's life without the patient's explicit consent. But even if, in every case in which a doctor ended a patient's life without consent, we could accept that the doctor was justified, would it not still be true that this violated the guidelines accepted by the courts? Does this not vindicate the slippery-slope argument by showing that non-voluntary active euthanasia is being practised to an increasing degree?

Here the answer is very clear: the Dutch figures cannot possibly show an 'increasing practice' of anything, because to show that we would need figures from two or more different years, preferably separated by a substantial gap. No such figures exist. The authors of the Dutch study are therefore surely right when they say, after discussing attempts to use their study as a basis for a slippery-slope argument, 'We conclude that no empirical data can be marshalled to support the slippery slope argument against the Dutch'.[22]

If there are no figures comparing the practice of euthanasia in the Netherlands at earlier and later times, we may still want to know whether Dutch doctors end the lives of their patients without an explicit request more often than doctors in other countries. Again, however, there is simply no basis for giving a definite answer to this question. Remember that the 1000 deaths that critics focus on are cases of patients dying in conditions of considerable suffering. The Dutch study found a much larger number of cases, perhaps as many as 8000, in which doctors gave drugs more to relieve pain or symptoms than explicitly to end life, but hastening death was nevertheless part of the purpose of giving the drugs. To say what is one's primary or secondary purpose is obviously not going to be easy in these situations. (As Kevorkian proved, when he persuaded the jury—or did he?—that he had supplied Thomas Hyde with carbon monoxide, tubing and a mask in order to relieve suffering rather than to cause death.) Doctors everywhere give patients who are dying from painful illnesses large doses of morphine or sedatives that may shorten their lives. They do this knowing that, if the drug does shorten the patient's life, it will be better for the patient than continued suffering. Had Dr Nigel Cox not been honest enough to record the potassium chloride he gave Lillian Boyes in the notes, he would never have been reported to the police. When he was convicted, Ann Bastow, a nurse, wrote to the *Times*:

> Every experienced hospital nurse will, I am sure, have assisted a doctor to end the life of a terminally ill patient, although some may be unwilling to admit it. Dr Cox has been made a scapegoat for people like myself. The shame of it all is that he has had to stand trial alone, representing thousands of caring doctors and nurses who have committed exactly the same crime.[23]

Three Australian studies have shown that active voluntary euthanasia is relatively common in that country, even though the law regards it as murder. In a study of doctors in Victoria, almost half who had treated incurably ill adult patients said that they had been asked by a patient to hasten death, and 29 per cent of these doctors said that they had taken active steps to bring about the death of a patient who had requested this. Of those who had done this, 80 per cent had done it more than once. A separate study of doctors in New South Wales gave virtually identical results. A survey of Australian nurses showed that 23 per cent had been asked by a doctor to engage in an action that would directly and actively end a patient's life, and 85 per cent of those asked had done so. More than 80 per cent had done so more than once. In addition, a small number of nurses—5 per cent—had complied with a patient's request to directly end his or her life, without having been asked by a doctor to do so.[24] A Californian survey of medical practitioners showed a broadly similar picture, with 23 per cent of doctors who had been asked by a patient to hasten death having done so.[25] Given these results, we can only guess at how common active non-voluntary euthanasia is in Australia, the USA, or in any other country other than the Netherlands. Is it more common in the Netherlands than elsewhere? There is no reason to believe that it is, but no-one really knows.

There is one more point that needs to be made before we leave the Dutch situation and its critics. The critics invariably focus on the 1000 cases in which doctors gave drugs with the intention of ending life without the patient's explicit consent. They do not mention the much larger number of cases in which doctors withdrew or withheld treatment that could have prolonged life, again without the patient's explicit consent. This happened in 70 per cent of the instances of withdrawal or withholding of medical treatment, a total of 15,750 deaths. In 88 per cent of these cases, the patient was not able to be consulted, leaving 12 per cent, or 1890, in which the patient was capable of being consulted, but was not. The Dutch study also tells us that in almost half of the total number of cases of withdrawal or withholding of medical treatment, this was done with the explicit purpose of hastening death. (In the remainder, the doctor 'took into account the probability that the end of life would be hastened'.)

Such cases of withdrawing treatment are also a normal part of medical practice in other countries. They are often instances of intentionally shortening life, and they can end life just as surely as giving potassium chloride. (When Tony Bland's feeding tube was withdrawn, his death was just as certain as, and no less intentional than, any death that takes place as a result of medical decision-making in the Netherlands.) There is some evidence suggesting that death after the withdrawal of treatment is a common occurrence. We have already seen this in the case of severely disabled newborn infants. It is probably more common still in elderly people. One American study of deaths in a nursing home found that 190 patients developed fever, but eighty-one of these received no specific treatment for it. Forty-eight of these patients from whom treatment was withheld died.[26]

If we don't want doctors to hasten the deaths of their patients without an explicit request, why are we not as concerned about this when it happens as a result of withdrawing treatment as when it results from an injection? Quite possibly, permitting active voluntary euthanasia actually reduces the number of patients whom doctors allow to die by withdrawing treatment without their explicit request. Removing the legal prohibition and the social taboo on active voluntary euthanasia has contributed to a much more open atmosphere about these questions. Hence it seems plausible that in the Netherlands there are *fewer* life-shortening decisions taken by doctors without the consent of their patients than elsewhere.[27] We don't know if this is the case: all we can say with confidence is that there is no evidence to the contrary.

'Thou shalt not kill' is the best known of the ten commandments. When doctors intentionally and actively kill their patients, no matter how close to death the patient is, or how much the patient has pleaded for death, the doctor is breaking the strongest moral rule that we have been taught. Yet what was once unthinkable for the medical profession is now happening. Voluntary euthanasia is firmly established in the Netherlands. It has the steady support of approximately 80 per cent of the Dutch population.[28] Apparently they do not see any 'worrisome trend'. Both Protestant and Roman Catholic hospital chaplains approve of it and are regularly involved in giving support to patients who choose euthanasia. More than half the doctors interviewed for the Dutch study had performed euthanasia or assisted with suicide at some time. A further 34 per cent considered it conceivable that they would do so, in certain circumstances. Only 12 per cent said that they would never perform euthanasia or assist with suicide, and of these, two-thirds would refer a patient who wanted euthanasia to a colleague who might be willing to do it. This left just 4 per cent of Dutch medical practitioners who refuse to have anything to do with requests for euthanasia.[29] This is an astonishingly small figure, considering that as recently as 1987 the World Medical Association reaffirmed its view that euthanasia, defined as 'the act of deliberately ending the life of a patient, even at the patient's own request' is unethical.[30]

What has happened in the Netherlands will have an effect on the practice of medicine everywhere, and on our ideas about the sanctity of human life. When Dutch doctors can directly, intentionally and openly kill their patients—and the heavens have not fallen—drawing subtle distinctions between acts and omissions begins to seem like splitting hairs. The Dutch experience makes us look at the important questions: was there a medical decision affecting the end of the patient's life? If so, was the patient consulted, and was the decision in accordance with the patient's wish? If not, why not?

The Dutch experience with euthanasia may not be easily replicable in other countries. Americans, in particular, would do well to remember that the Netherlands is a welfare state that provides a high standard of health care and social security to all its citizens. No patients need to ask for euthanasia because they are unable to afford good health care. In addition, everyone in the Netherlands has his or her own family doctor, and usually stays with that doctor for many years. Thus doctors and patients get to know each other well over a long relationship—a very different situation from modern medical practice in some other countries. So the Dutch system will not be a suitable model for all countries to follow. In the United States, where there is a greater emphasis on individual rights, and religious fundamentalists have more political clout, change seems more likely to come as it did in Oregon, by way of a right to physician-assisted suicide than by the legal acceptance of active voluntary euthanasia. But nothing seems more certain than that, in the next decade—and possibly much sooner—the citizens of several other countries will join the Dutch in finding a way to gain control of how they die.

BEYOND THE
DISCONTINUOUS MIND

'Human', to the discontinuous mind, is an absolute concept.
There can be no half measures. And from this flows much evil.

RICHARD DAWKINS, 1993

AN UNUSUAL INSTITUTION

In the Netherlands, a few years ago, an observer reported on the lives of some people confined in a new kind of institution. These people had a special condition that did not handicap them at all physically, but intellectually they were well below the normal human level; they could not speak, although they made noises and gestures. In the institutions in which such people were usually kept, they tended to spend much of their time making repetitive movements, and rocking their bodies to and fro. This institution was an unusual one, in that its policy was to allow the inmates the maximum possible freedom to live their own lives and form their own community. This freedom extended even to sexual relationships, which led to pregnancy, birth and child-rearing. The observer was interested in finding out how people without language would behave under these conditions.

The behaviour of the inmates was far more varied than in the more conventional institutional settings. They rarely spent time alone, and they appeared to have no difficulty in understanding each other's gestures and vocalisations. They were physically active, spending a lot of time outside, where they had access to about two acres of relatively natural forest, surrounded by a wall.

They co-operated in many activities, including on one occasion—to the consternation of the supervisors—an attempt to escape that involved carrying a large fallen branch to the wall, and propping it up as a kind of ladder that made it possible to climb to the other side.

The observer was particularly impressed by what he called the 'politics' of the community. A defined leader soon emerged. His leadership—and it was always a 'he'—depended, however, on the support of other members of the group. The leader had privileges, but also, it seemed, obligations. He had to cultivate the favour of others by sharing food and other treats. Fights would develop from time to time, but they would usually be followed by some conciliatory gestures, so that the loser could be readmitted into the society of the leader. If the leader became isolated, and allowed the others to form a coalition against him, his days at the top were numbered.

A simple ethical code could also be detected within the community. Its two basic rules, the observer commented, could be summed up as 'one good turn deserves another', and 'an eye for an eye and a tooth for a tooth'. The breach of the first of these rules apparently led to a sense of being wronged. On one occasion Henk was fighting with Jan, and Gert came to Jan's assistance. Later, Henk attacked Gert, who gestured to Jan for help, but Jan did nothing. After the fight between Gert and Henk was over, Gert furiously attacked Jan.

The mothers were with one exception competent at nursing and rearing their children. The mother-child relationships were close, and lasted many years. The death of a baby led to prolonged grieving. Because sexual relationships were not monogamous, it was not always possible to tell who the father of the child was, and fathers did not play a significant role in the rearing of the children.

In view of the very limited mental capacities that these inmates had been credited with, the observer was impressed by instances of behaviour that clearly showed intelligent planning. In one example, two young mothers were having difficulty stopping their small children from fighting. An older mother, a considerable authority figure in the community, was dozing nearby. One of the younger mothers woke her, and pointed to the squabbling children. The older mother made the appropriate noises and gestures, and the children, suitably intimidated, stopped fighting. The older mother then went back to her nap.

In order to see just how far ahead these people could think, the observer devised an ingenious test of problem-solving ability. One inmate was presented with two series of five locked boxes made of clear plastic, each of which opened with a different, but readily identifiable, key. The keys were visible in the boxes. One series of five boxes led to a food treat, whereas the other series led to an empty box. The key to the first box in each series lay beside it. It was necessary to begin by choosing one of these two initial boxes; and to end up with the treat, one had mentally to work through the five boxes to see which choice would lead to the box with the treat. The inmate was able to succeed in this complex task.

The inmates' own awareness of what they were doing was well shown by their extensive practice of deceit. On one occasion, after a fight, it was noticeable that the loser limped badly when in the presence of the victor, but not when alone. Presumably, by pretending to be more seriously hurt than he really was, he hoped for some kind of sympathy, or at least mercy, from his conqueror. But the most elaborate forms of deceit were concerned with—no surprise here for any observer of human behaviour—sexual relationships. Although monogamy was not practised, the leader tried to prevent others having sex with his favourites. To get around this, flirtations leading up to sexual intercourse were conducted with a good deal of discretion, so as not to attract the leader's attention.

I have described this community in some detail because I want to raise an ethical question about the way in which people with this condition were regarded by those who looked after them. In the eyes of their supervisors the inmates did not have the same kind of right to life as normal human beings. Though treated with care and consideration for their welfare, they were seen as clearly inferior, and their lives were accorded much less value than the lives of normal human beings. When one of them was killed, in the course of a dispute over who should be leader, the killing was not considered equivalent to the killing of a normal human being. Nor were they eligible for the same kind of medical attention that, throughout the Netherlands, was available for normal human beings. Moreover in other institutions—not the one I have just described—people with this condition are deliberately infected with diseases such as hepatitis, in order to test the efficacy of experimental drugs or vaccines. In some cases they die as a result of the experiment.

How should we regard this situation? Is it a moral outrage? Or is it ethically defensible, given the more limited intellectual capacities of these people?

Your answer to this question may vary according to the mental image you formed of the inmates of the community I have described. I referred to them as 'people'. In doing so I was using 'people' as the colloquial plural of 'person' and for that term I had in mind the definition offered by the seventeenth-century English philosopher John Locke: 'A thinking intelligent being that has reason and reflection and can consider itself as itself, the same thinking thing, in different times and places'.[1] But because the term 'person', like 'people', is commonly used only of members of the species *Homo sapiens,* my use of the term may have led you to think that the community I was describing was made up of intellectually disabled human beings. My use of Dutch names probably reinforced that assumption. In that case, you probably also thought it very wrong that the lives of these people were accorded less value than those of normal human beings; and the mention of their use as experimental subjects very likely caused shock and a sense of outrage.

Perhaps some readers, however, were able to guess that I was not describing human beings at all. The 'special condition' that these people have is their membership of the species *Pan troglodytes*. They are a community of chimpanzees, living in Arnhem Zoo, not far from Amsterdam.[2] If you guessed this, you may not have been so shocked that the supervisors thought the value of the lives of the inmates was markedly less than that of normal humans; perhaps you were not even disturbed by the use of the inmates in lethal experiments.

In all the cases I have discussed so far, the human nature of the life in question has set the whole framework of the ethical discussion. I began this chapter with a subterfuge to make each reader aware of the extent to which his or her attitudes vary according to whether it is a human or nonhuman being who is killed—even when the actual capacities of the being are known, though its species is not. Becoming aware of this is a first step towards a critical examination of another part of the foundations of our ethical attitudes to life and death. I have already noted the curious fact that the term 'pro-life' is used to describe people who oppose killing human fetuses but are quite happy to support the killing of calves, pigs and chickens. This is in itself powerful testimony to the extent to which the killing of any human beings, even fetal human beings, seems to us an overwhelmingly more important issue than the killing of nonhuman animals. But here, too, we shall find that the traditional ethic now looks decidedly shaky.

WHOSE ORGANS MAY WE TAKE?

The reader will recall Baby Theresa and Baby Valentina, anencephalic infants whose parents' wishes for them to become organ donors were frustrated by court rulings that organs could not be removed before death. In 1992, shortly after these two babies died, Dr Thomas Starzl, a Pittsburgh transplant surgeon, removed the liver from a healthy baboon and transplanted it into the body of a man who was dying from a liver disease. The baboon, a healthy, sentient, intelligent, responsive animal, was killed immediately after the liver was taken; the patient died about two months later.[3] No court stepped in to prevent the use of the baboon's liver. Although some animal rights groups protested, most of the discussion at the time brushed over the fact that the transplant had involved the death of a baboon, and focused instead on whether this procedure could offer new hope for a large number of people needing organ transplants.

Attempts to transplant organs from animals into human beings go back a long way. The first to try may have been Dr James Hardy, of the University of Mississippi Medical Center, who in 1964 grafted the heart of a chimpanzee into a sixty-four-year-old man. The heart beat for ninety minutes before the patient died.[4] Twenty years later Dr Leonard Bailey of Loma Linda University Medical Center in California transplanted the heart of a baboon into a baby, known as Baby Fae, who had a lethal heart defect. She died three weeks after surgery. The operation met with an almost universal chorus of disapproval, from the general public, from news commentators, and from bioethicists alike. Many thought that it was wrong because it amounted to human experimentation: Dr Bailey had very little ground for believing that a cross-species transplant, or 'xenotransplant' as it is now commonly called, would succeed. Some commentators suggested that Dr Bailey should have done experiments on transplanting organs between different species of nonhuman animals first, and should have moved to xenotransplantation with humans only when he had a good record of success from animal experimentation. Others believed that Dr Bailey had performed such a bizarre operation only in order to score a world 'first', and to gain publicity for himself and his transplant team. What was missing from this chorus of disapproval was any general concern for the baboon whose heart had been removed. With the exception of a small number of animal rights advocates, the fact that a healthy baboon had been killed in order to provide a heart for Baby Fae aroused no object-ion.[5] As a result research into this field continued. In 1987 the American National Institutes of Health agreed to give $3.36 million to the Columbia Presbyterian Medical Center in New York for research on implanting chimpanzee hearts in human bodies.[6]

The traditional sanctity of life ethic forbids us to kill and take the organs of a human being who is not, and never can be, even minimally conscious; and it maintains this refusal even when the parents of the infant favour the donation of the organs. At the same time, this ethic accepts without question that we may rear baboons and chimpanzees in order to kill them and use their organs. Why does our ethic draw so sharp a distinction between human beings and all other animals? Why does species membership make such a difference to the ethics of how we may treat a being?

IN GOD'S IMAGE AND AT THE CENTRE OF THE UNIVERSE

There have been cultures, especially in the east, that have held that all life is sacred, including the lives of nonhuman animals. There have been other cultures that have had a much more restricted view of the sanctity of life, punishing only the unprovoked killing of a member of the tribe or national group, and accepting as ethically unproblematic the killing of outsiders, or of unwanted newborn infants. The western tradition is unusual in its emphasis on the sanctity of every human life, but only of human life.

The origins of this distinctive western view are not difficult to trace. The starting point is the Hebrew view of creation, as put forward in Genesis:

> And God said, Let us make man in our image, after our likeness: and let them have dominion over the fish of the sea, and over the fowl of the air, and over the earth, and over every creeping thing that creepeth upon the earth.

So God created man in his own image, in the image of God created he him; male and female created he them.

And God blessed them, and God said unto them, be fruitful and multiply, and replenish the earth, and subdue it; and have dominion over the fish of the sea, and over the fowl of the air, and over every living thing that moveth upon the earth.[7]

Human beings are here seen as special because they alone of all living things were made in the image of God. In addition, God gave them power over all the other living things. To these two critical marks of distinction between human beings and non-human animals, a third came to be added, first in later Jewish writings, and then with much more emphasis under Christianity: the belief that humans, alone of all living things, have immortal souls, and so will survive death.

Jesus appears never to have directly addressed the question of our relations with nonhuman animals. This absence of comment—in marked contrast to, for example, the teachings of Buddha—conveys a clear impression that only humans really count. Jesus's own behaviour also provides two examples of indifference to nonhuman life. In a fit of anger at finding no figs on a fig tree, he curses the tree, which withers and dies. (The tree had no figs because it was not the season for figs.) On another occasion, Jesus casts out devils and makes them go into a herd of pigs, who then hurl themselves into the sea and drown. Augustine, the most influential of the early church fathers, did not doubt that these actions were deliberate, and intended to teach us something about the value of nonhuman life:

Christ himself shows that to refrain from the killing of animals and the destroying of plants is the height of superstition, for judging that there are no common rights between us and the beasts and trees, he sent the devils into a herd of swine and with a curse withered the tree on which he had found no fruit...Surely the swine had not sinned, nor had the tree.[8]

In the middle ages, Thomas Aquinas incorporated the philosophy of Aristotle into Christian thinking. So much was Aquinas indebted to Aristotle that he refers to him simply as 'the Philosopher', as if there were no others. Aristotle's ideas fitted well into the Christian view of the special status of human beings, because Aristotle thought that everything in nature exists for a purpose, and the ultimate purpose of the less rational is to serve the needs of the more rational. Thus plants exist to serve animals for food, and the nonhuman animals exist in order to provide food and clothing for human beings.[9] This position is not representative of Greek thought as a whole. Pythagoras, for example, had a much more egalitarian view of our place amongst other animals—but that view has had no real influence on Christian thinking. On the other hand, the views of Aquinas became the semi-official philosophy of the Roman Catholic Church. So lasting was this influence that in the middle of the nineteenth century Pope Pius IX refused to allow a Society for the Prevention of Cruelty to Animals to be established in Rome, on the grounds that to do so would imply that human beings have duties toward animals.[10]

During and after the Renaissance, philosophers challenged some aspects of the scholastic philosophy of Aquinas and other medieval thinkers, but not the special place given to human beings. Human beings were unique because, although part of the physical world of animals, they had immortal souls and so were linked to the angels and to God. Marsilio Ficino, one of the most influential of the Italian philosophers of the Renaissance, described humans as 'the centre of nature, the middle of the universe, the chain of the world'.[11]

In the seventeeth century the French philosopher René Descartes, often regarded as the founder of modern philosophy, took this view one step further, digging the gulf between humans and animals still deeper. Influenced by the new and highly successful science of mechanics, he held that all material things, including animals, are governed by mechanistic principles like those that govern the movements of a clock. Consciousness, on the other hand, is something quite separate from matter. Human beings belong, as the Renaissance philosophers had said, to both the material world and the world of immortal souls. It is our possession of an immortal soul that makes it possible for us to be conscious, and to have thoughts. Animals, on the other hand, do not have immortal souls, and so cannot be conscious. They are machines. Although they may squeal when wounded, this does not mean that they feel pain. A clock can also make noises. If the actions of animals are more complex than those of a clock, that is because they are more complex machines, as we would expect of machines made by God rather than by human beings.[12]

More than a century later, in the philosophy of Immanuel Kant, the human-centred view of ethics reached its most sophisticated development. Kant's view is still recognisably part of the tradition that goes back on the one hand to Aristotle, and on the other to the consistent Christian doctrine that human beings partake of both the material world and the spiritual world. From Aristotle, Kant takes the view that animals 'are there merely as a means to an end. That end is man.' From the Christian doctrine, Kant retained the picture of human beings as split between two worlds. One was, as always, the material world, governed by physical laws. The other, however, Kant presented in a characteristic Enlightenment form, as the world of reason. It was because animals could not reason, and 'are not self-conscious' that they exist 'merely as a means to an end'. Humans, on the other hand, as reasoning, self-conscious and autonomous beings, must be respected as ends in themselves.[13]

With this kind of religious and philosophical background, it is no wonder that western ethical thinking singled out *human* life as sacrosanct, and paid little attention to the taking of the lives of nonhuman animals. To end a human life is to end the life of a being made in the image of God. It is also to consign a being to his or her immortal destiny—that is, to heaven or hell for all eternity. Who could tell how that fate might have differed if life had continued a little longer? In the end our reckoning is to God. In more philosophical terms, to kill a human being is to kill a self-conscious, autonomous being, who is to be respected as an end in his or her self.

In contrast to all this, to kill a nonhuman animal is to kill a being over whom God has already given us dominion. He will not call us to account for the death, as he would for the death of a human being. To kill a nonhuman animal is to kill a merely material thing, a being that is not even conscious, or at least not self-conscious, and whose role in life is to serve as a means to our ends, including our needs for food and clothing—not, in other words, anything to worry about.

THE WESTERN TRADITION UNDER ATTACK

For thousands of years, the human-centred western tradition ruled without serious opposition. It first encountered difficulties when the Copernican system of astronomy replaced the older Greek model. No longer could one believe that the earth was the literal centre of the universe, around which everything else revolved. This led the Italian humanist Giordano Bruno to assert that 'man is no more than an ant in the presence of the infinite'. When he refused to recant this and other heresies, he was burned at the stake. Galileo, forewarned by this example, was more prudent. Later, when the church could no longer suppress the Copernican idea, it managed instead to absorb it. Humans were not at the centre of the universe any more, but they were still made in the image of God. There were also less overtly religious reasons— those of Descartes or Kant—for maintaining the special sanctity of human life when compared with all other creatures.

In the nineteenth century a more formidable threat to the western tradition emerged. It was neatly summed up in an entry that Charles Darwin wrote in his notebook in 1838: 'Man in his arrogance thinks himself a great work, worthy of the interposition of a deity. More humble and, I believe, true to consider him created from animals.'[14]

This thought did not arise out of nowhere. Already, in the eighteenth century, a fascination had developed with the great apes, and some scientists had had heretical thoughts about our relationship with them. When the Swedish biologist Carl Linnaeus devised our modern system of classifying plants and animals into species, genus, family, order, phylum and kingdom, he found that he had developed a set of criteria that put human beings and chimpanzees into the same genus. This caused him great concern, because it went against the idea of human beings as a separate creation, an idea staunchly upheld by the Swedish Lutheran Church and all other Christian churches at the time. So Linnaeus fudged the application of his own criteria, and left humans alone in the genus *Homo*, and even in our own special family, Hominidae. But he was not proud of what he had done. In 1788 he wrote to a friend:

> I demand of you, and of the whole world, that you show me a generic character...by which to distinguish between Man and Ape. I myself most assuredly know of none. I wish somebody would indicate one to me. But, if I had called man an ape, or vice versa, I would have fallen under the ban of all the ecclesiastics. It may be that as a naturalist I ought to have done so.[15]

Lord Monboddo, a Scottish pioneer of anthropology, went further. In his major work, *On the Origin and Progress of Language*, Monboddo described the similarities between ourselves and the 'Ouran Outang' (a term he probably used to cover both orangutans and chimpanzees) and concluded that 'it appears certain that they are of our species'.[16]

Linnaeus had been afraid to follow his best scientific instincts. Monboddo was bolder, but lacked scientific stature, and few took his subversive ideas seriously. Half a century later Darwin combined courage with true scientific greatness. At first, though, he proceeded with caution. It took another twenty-one years from the date of his notebook entry before he considered himself ready to publish, in *The Origin of Species*, the theory that the different species of plants and animals have evolved by the natural selection of random mutations. Even then Darwin did not dare to state explicitly that human beings have also evolved in this manner. He gave just the barest hint of it, saying that his work would illuminate 'the origin of man and his history'. To publish more about our own species would, he thought, 'only add to the prejudices against my views'.[17] Darwin therefore waited another dozen years, until his theory of evolution had achieved a fair degree of acceptance within the scientific world, before he released *The Descent of Man*, in 1871.

Darwin's theory, embodied in these two great works, undermined the foundations of the entire western way of thinking on the place of our species in the universe. He taught us that we too were animals, and had a natural origin as the other animals did. As Darwin emphasised in *The Descent of Man*, the differences between us and the nonhuman animals are differences of degree, not of kind. Nor did he rest his case on physical similarities alone. The third and fourth chapters of *The Descent of Man* show that we can find the roots of our own capacities to love and to reason, and even of our moral sense, in the nonhuman animals.

No intelligent and unbiased student of the evidence could any longer believe in the literal truth of Genesis. With the disproof of the Hebrew myth of creation, the belief that human beings were specially created by God, in his own image, was also undermined. So too was the story of God's grant of dominion over the other animals. No wonder that Darwin's theory was greeted with a storm of resistance, especially from conservative Christians. Nor is it surprising that in these circles opposition to Darwin's theory continues to smoulder.

The difference Darwin makes is more momentous than many

people appreciate. Even Thomas Huxley, Darwin's courageous defender, tried to play it down. In a lecture he gave in 1860, he insisted that 'no one is more strongly convinced than I am of the gulf between civilized man and the brutes...Our reverence for the nobility of mankind will not be lessened by the knowledge that man is, in substance and in structure, one with the brutes.'[18] But if our substance and our structure is the same as that of the other animals—if we *are* an animal, rather than a specially created being made in the image of God—how can this not reduce the gulf between us and them? Huxley's statement is a transparent attempt to reduce opposition to the acceptance of Darwin's theory. This tactic was successful, at least in the short term. The theory of evolution was accepted by all serious biological scientists. In the longer term, however, the use of this tactic meant that for a century after the publication of *The Descent of Man*, the gulf between humans and nonhuman animals in terms of ethical status remained unbridged. Was Darwin's devastating blow to the western view of human beings going to be absorbed, as the Copernican revolution had been absorbed previously?

WHO IS *HOMO*?

For a full century, the western view of the special status of humans did the intellectual equivalent of defying gravity; its foundations had been knocked out from under it, and yet it remained upright. Then a series of further shocks rocked it, bringing the task that Darwin began much nearer to completion. This series of shocks came from several directions in quick succession.

One shock came out of the new concern with the damage we are doing to the ecosystems of our planet, to other species of animals, and to our own air and water. This gave rise to a reassessment of our attitude to the natural world. In 1967, when the ecological movement was just beginning, it received an important intellectual boost from an article called 'The Historical

Roots of Our Ecological Crisis'. The author was Lynn White, Jr, Professor of History at the University of California, Los Angeles. White argued that the ecological crisis could be traced back to the nature of the western tradition, out of which modern technology and science had developed. Behind this tradition lay the victory of Christianity over paganism, a victory that brought with it the idea that the proper human attitude to nature is one of domination and mastery. Though himself a Christian, White called Christianity 'the most anthropocentric religion the world has seen' and called for a new kind of Christianity that would 'depose man from his monarchy over creation and set up a democracy of all God's creatures'.[19] Other ecological thinkers rejected Christianity altogether. They explored eastern and especially Buddhist traditions which began from a more harmonious view of nature and the place of humans within it. Whatever the source, there was a clear trend in favour of seeing ourselves as part of nature rather than masters over it.

A second shock came in the 1970s, with the emergence of the animal liberation or animal rights movement, which demanded an end to 'speciesism'. That term, coined by the Oxford psychologist Richard Ryder in 1970, has now entered the *Oxford English Dictionary*, where it is defined as 'discrimination against or exploitation of certain animal species by human beings, based on an assumption of mankind's superiority'. As the term suggests, there is a parallel between our attitudes to nonhuman animals, and the attitudes of racists to those they regard as belonging to an inferior race.[20] In both cases there is an inner group that justifies its exploitation of an outer group by reference to a distinction that lacks real moral significance. While acknowledging the acceptance of a basic principle of equality among all human beings as a progressive step, animal liberationists pointed out that the idea of human equality still left most sentient creatures outside the charmed circle. If we are now able to see that the fact that a human being belongs to a different *race* is not a good reason for giving less consideration to the interests of that being, then why, animal liberationists asked, should the fact that a being belongs to a different *species* be a good reason for doing so? The animal liberation movement demanded that we go beyond a speciesist morality, and give equal consideration to the interests of all beings who can feel pleasure or pain, irrespective of species.

Within a decade of its founding, the animal liberation movement had grown remarkably, influencing public debate in every area of the treatment of animals, from product testing on animals to factory farming, from the use of animals for fur and in circuses to the whaling industry. Part of the strength of the movement was its solid philosophical base. The animal liberation movement is unique among recent political movements in the extent to which its ideas and support have come from academic philosophers. This has meant that the case against speciesism has been put more rigorously than might otherwise have been the case. Many philosophers now accept that a difference of species alone cannot provide an ethically defensible basis for giving the interests of one being more consideration than another. Colin McGinn, distinguished professor of philosophy at Rutgers University, New Jersey, has described this as 'a won argument'.[21] There are, no doubt, still philosophers who would disagree with that statement; and, in the community as a whole, animal liberationists remain a small minority. Their challenge to our automatic assumption of species superiority has nevertheless had an enormous impact on both our thought and our practice.

A third shock came from our growing knowledge of nonhuman animals, and especially of the great apes. Jane Goodall was the first human being to be so well accepted by a group of free-living chimpanzees that she could spend hundreds of hours observing them at close range in their natural habitat. Dian Fossey carried out similar studies of gorillas in Rwanda. The work of these two women led to books read by millions, and started a public fascination with our nearest relatives that has continued through films and television programs. Their observations have repeatedly broken down the barriers which we have erected between ourselves and other animals. People used to say that one distinguishing mark of our species was that only humans use tools. Then Goodall saw chimpanzees use sticks in order to fish for termites inside a termite nest. Other scientists reported that some seals will use rocks in order to break open shellfish, and various birds use thorns or small sticks to probe insects out of bark. So we retreated a little, and said that only humans make tools. This point of demarcation collapsed when Goodall reported that chimpanzees shape their sticks by stripping off leaves and small branches until they get the right kind of implement for the task. Since then chimpanzees have been seen to make and use a variety of other tools. One has even used a stone to turn another stone into a sharp-edged cutting tool. Nor are they the only animal to make tools. Capuchin monkeys, for instance, can shape bone fragments with a stone before using them as probes or cutting tools.[22]

A different kind of study helped to break down another barrier: the belief that human uniqueness lies in our capacity for language. Early attempts to teach chimpanzees to speak failed, because they simply do not have the vocal chords needed to produce words. When two American scientists brought an infant chimpanzee called Washoe into their home and raised her exactly as if she were a deaf human child, using American Sign Language to communicate with her and with each other in her presence, they found that she learned to understand and use a large number of signs. When she matured and had an adoptive son, she taught him signs, which he then used to communicate with other chimpanzees as well as with humans. Washoe has also been filmed signing to herself when no-one else is around. Gorillas and orang-utans have learned American Sign Language too. Koko, a gorilla, has a vocabulary of over 1000 words, and can understand a much larger number of words in spoken English as well. Chantek, an orang-utan, has used signs to tell lies. For example, he stole a pencil eraser, put it in his mouth, and signed 'food eat', as if to say that he had swallowed it. He had really kept the eraser in his cheek, and later it was found in his bedroom in a place where he commonly hid things. Although there have been attempts to suggest that what the apes are doing is not 'really' language but just a response to cues provided by human beings, the immense amount of data now accumulated, including the data on apes signing to each other or to themselves, now makes this explanation untenable.[23]

These studies show that our nearest relatives are more like us than we supposed. The gulf between us has also been narrowed from the opposite direction. Starting in the 1960s with some highly speculative popular books like Robert Ardrey's *African Genesis* and *The Territorial Imperative*, Desmond Morris's *The Naked Ape* and Lionel Tiger and Robin Fox's *The Imperial Animal*, we have begun to take more seriously the essential Darwinian insight that we are animals too. Though there is much in the earlier books that cannot be accepted, a more careful and solidly based field of scientific study has applied evolutionary theory to the behaviour of social mammals with illuminating results. Since we too are social mammals, this work helps to explain human behaviour, and to show it to be more biologically constrained and less distinct from that of other social mammals than we had thought. It remains true that we reason better than the other social mammals, but the objectives to which we apply our reason are generally ones we share with them: to obtain food, to gain sexual partners, to rise in social status, to protect our family, and to defend our territory. Even the most basic moral principles by which we constrain our behaviour, like the rule of reciprocity, and the obligations we have to our kin, as well as constraints on our sexual behaviour, are things we share with other animals.[24] All of this has helped to make us see that we are animals, and not as different from other animals as we had thought.

What may prove the final blow to the traditional western view of the distinctness of human beings is now coming from new knowledge in genetics, and its implications for the way scientists classify humans and our nearest ancestors. For many years, most biologists assumed that humans evolved as a separate branch from the other great apes, including the chimpanzees and gorillas. This was a natural enough assumption, given the strength of our belief in how special we are. More recent techniques in molecular biology have enabled us to measure quite precisely the degree of genetic difference between different animals. We now know that we share 98.4 per cent of our DNA with chimpanzees. This is a very slight genetic difference. It is, for example, less than that between two different species of gibbon, which are separated by 2.2 per cent; or between the red-eyed and white-eyed vireos, two closely related North American bird species, the genes of which differ by 2.9 per cent. More significant still is the fact that the difference between us and chimpanzees is less than the 2.3 per cent that separates the DNA of chimpanzees from that of gorillas. In other words, we—not the gorillas—are the chimpanzees' nearest relatives. And all of the African apes—chimpanzees, gorillas and humans—are more closely related to each other than any of them are to orang-utans.

On the basis of this discovery, some leading scientists, among them Richard Dawkins, lecturer in zoology at the University of Oxford, and Jared Diamond, professor of physiology at the University of California, Los Angeles, have suggested that it is time to do what Linnaeus lacked the courage to do: change the way in which we classify ourselves and the other African apes. As we saw, Linnaeus classified humans not only as a separate species, *Homo sapiens*, but also as a separate genus, *Homo*, and even a separate family, Hominidae. That is how things have remained since the eighteenth century. Our nearest relative, the chimpanzee, is not *Homo* but *Pan* (there are two species, *Pan troglodytes* and *Pan paniscus*) while the gorilla is a separate genus, *Gorilla gorilla*, and the apes as a whole belong to the family Pongidae. We now have decisive evidence that this two hundred-year-old categorisation has no basis other than the desire to separate us from other animals. All taxonomists agree that the two species of gibbon belong in the same genus, and the same is true of the red-eyed and white-eyed vireos. We are closer to the chimpanzees than the different species of gibbons, or the different species of vireos, are to each other. We are also approximately as close to the gorillas as these different species are to each other. There is only one proper conclusion to draw. Since the rules of naming in zoology give priority to the name that was first proposed, this means that the two species of chimpanzee should be renamed *Homo troglodytes* and *Homo paniscus*, and the gorilla, *Homo gorilla*. Or to follow Jared Diamond's more colourful way of putting it, we are 'the third chimpanzee'.[25]

So we belong to the same family and the same genus as chimpanzees and gorillas. Still, it may be said, we remain a distinct species, and that is enough to allow us to draw a clear line between human beings and all other animals. It is true that we remain a distinct species, but how clear is the line that this enables us to draw? Stephen Clark, professor of philosophy at Liverpool University, and R. I. M. Dunbar, professor of biological anthropology at University College, London, have both argued recently that the way in which we divide beings into species does not reflect a natural order of things, or a reality out there in the world, but rather the subjective judgments of those doing the classifying. The boundaries between species are not laid down by nature; they reflect our ways of classifying living things. We often group together in the same species beings that look very different—the pekinese and the wolfhound, for example—while separating beings that look very alike, as many different species of birds do. As Dunbar puts it:

> The biological reality is that the great apes are just populations of animals that differ only slightly more in their degree of genetic relatedness to you and me than do other populations of humans

living elsewhere in the world. They just look a bit different to those other populations that we commonly call 'human', but not all that different, and by no means as different as, say, spiders do.[26]

What then of the definition of a species as a group that can interbreed? Apart from the practical problems that the pekinese and wolfhound might have, one reason why this idea is no longer a standard definition of species is the phenomenon of the so-called 'ring species'. Here is Richard Dawkins' example of a ring-species:

> The best-known case is herring gull versus lesser black-backed gull. In Britain these are clearly distinct species, quite different in colour. Anybody can tell them apart. But if you follow the population of herring gulls westward around the North Pole to North America, then via Alaska across Siberia and back to Europe again, you will notice a curious fact. The 'herring gulls' gradually become less and less like herring gulls and more and more like lesser black-backed gulls until it turns out that our European lesser black-backed gulls actually are the other end of a ring that started out as herring gulls. At every stage around the ring, the birds are sufficiently similar to their neighbours to interbreed with them. Until, that is, the ends of the continuum are reached, in Europe. At this point the herring gull and the lesser black-backed gull never interbreed, although they are linked by a continuous series of interbreeding colleagues all the way around the world.

Dawkins then draws a pointed conclusion:

> The only thing that is special about ring species like these gulls is that the intermediates are still alive. *All* pairs of related species are potentially ring species. The intermediates must have lived once. It is just that in most cases they are now dead.[27]

So if we cannot interbreed with chimpanzees, or with half-human, half-chimpanzee beings who can interbreed with chimpanzees, this is merely due to the deaths of the intermediate types. In any case, why do we assume that a human being and a chimpanzee could not produce a child? It is true that there is a difference in the number of chromosomes, chimpanzees having 48 and humans 46. But siamangs and lar gibbons—two distinct species of ape living in Malaysia and Indonesia—have interbred, despite the fact that they have different numbers of chromosomes (50 and 44 respectively).[28] So the possibility of human and chimpanzee interbreeding cannot be ruled out.

WHO IS A PERSON?

This chapter began with a description of the life of a community, the nonhuman nature of which was concealed by my use of the term 'person'. We often use 'person' as if it meant the same as 'human being'. In recent discussions in bioethics, however, 'person' is now often used to mean a being with certain characteristics such as rationality and self-awareness. There is a solid historical basis for this use. It is, as we saw, consistent with the definition given by John Locke in the seventeenth century. 'Person' comes from the Latin 'persona', which initially meant a mask worn by an actor in a play, and later came to refer to the character the actor played. The word was introduced into philosophical discourse by the Stoic philosopher Epictetus, who used it to mean the role one is called to play in life. It was then taken up by early Christian thinkers grappling with the problem of understanding the doctrine of the trinity—what was the relationship between God the Father, God the Son, and the the Holy Ghost? In 325 the Council of Nicea settled the issue by saying that the trinity is one substance and three persons. But what was a person? Since neither God the Father nor the Holy Ghost were human beings, it was evident that a person did not have to be a human being. In the sixth century the philosopher Boethius confirmed this by defining 'person' as 'an individual substance of rational nature', a definition subsequently used by Aquinas and other writers and supplemented by Locke with the element of awareness of one's own existence at different times and places.[29]

So a person is not *by definition* a human being. But the only nonhuman persons Boethius and Aquinas contemplated were spiritual beings like God and the Holy Ghost. Are there other, more tangible persons who are not human? Is the following a description of a person?

> She communicates in sign language, using a vocabulary of over 1000 words. She also understands spoken English, and often carries on 'bilingual' conversations, responding in sign to questions asked in English. She is learning the letters of the alphabet, and can read some printed words, including her own name. She has achieved scores between 85 and 95 on the Stanford–Binet Intelligence Test.
>
> She demonstrates a clear self-awareness by engaging in self-directed behaviours in front of a mirror, such as making faces or examining her teeth, and by her appropriate use of self-descriptive language. She lies to avoid the consequences of her own misbehaviour, and anticipates others' responses to her actions. She engages in imaginary play, both alone and with others. She has produced paintings and drawings which are representational. She remembers and can talk about past events in her life. She understands and has used appropriately time-related words like 'before', 'after', 'later', and 'yesterday'.
>
> She laughs at her own jokes and those of others. She cries when hurt or left alone, screams when frightened or angered. She talks about her feelings, using words like 'happy', 'sad', 'afraid', 'enjoy', 'eager', 'frustrate', 'made' and, quite frequently, 'love'. She grieves for those she has lost—a favourite cat who has died, a friend who has gone away. She can talk about what happens when one dies, but she becomes fidgety and uncomfortable when asked to discuss her own death or the death of her companions. She displays a wonderful gentleness with kittens and other small animals. She has even expressed empathy for others seen only in pictures.[30]

Many people react with scepticism to such descriptions of a nonhuman animal, but the abilities of the gorilla Koko described here are broadly similar to those reported quite independently by observers of other great apes, including chimpanzees and orang-utans. On the evidence presented, there seems little doubt that Koko is 'a thinking intelligent being that has reason and reflection and can consider itself as itself, the same thinking thing, in different times and places'. So, it would seem, are many other great apes, and not only those who have learnt a human language. After spending most of her life observing free-living chimpanzees in the Gombe region of Tanzania, Jane Goodall wrote:

> Certainly all of us who have worked closely with chimpanzees over extended periods of time have no hesitation in asserting that chimpanzees, like humans, show emotions similar to—sometimes probably identical to—those which we label joy, sadness, fear, despair and so on...They can plan for the immediate future...And they clearly have some kind of self-concept.[31]

There are other persons on this planet. The evidence for personhood is at present most conclusive for the great apes, but whales, dolphins, elephants, monkeys, dogs, pigs and other animals may eventually also be shown to be aware of their own existence over time and capable of reasoning. Then they too will have to be considered as persons. But what difference does it make, whether a nonhuman animal is a person or not? In one respect, it makes little difference. Whether or not dogs and pigs are persons, they can certainly feel pain and suffer in a variety of ways, and our concern for their suffering should not depend on how rational and self-aware they might be. All the same, the term 'person' is no mere descriptive label. It carries with it a certain moral standing. Just as, in law, the fact that a corporation can be a person means that a corporation can sue and be sued, so too, once we recognise a nonhuman animal as a person, we will soon begin to attribute basic rights to that animal.

Our isolation is over. Science has helped us to understand our evolutionary history, as well as our own nature and the nature of other animals. Freed from the constraints of religious conformity, we now have a new vision of who we are, to whom we are related, the limited nature of the differences between us and other species, and the more or less accidental manner in which the boundary between 'us' and 'them' has been formed. Adopting this new vision will change forever the way in which we make ethical decisions about beings who are alive and belong to our species, but lack the capacities that some members of other species possess. Why should we treat the life of an anencephalic human child as sacrosanct, and feel free to kill healthy baboons in order to take their organs? Why should we lock chimpanzees in laboratory cages and infect them with fatal human diseases, if we abhor the idea of experiments conducted with intellectually disabled human beings whose mental level is similar to that of the chimpanzees?

The new vision leaves no room for the traditional answer to these questions, that we human beings are a special creation, infinitely more precious, in virtue of our humanity alone, than all other living things. In the light of our new understanding of our place in the universe, we shall have to abandon that traditional answer, and revise the boundaries of our ethics. One casualty of that revision will be any ethic based on the idea that what really matters about beings is whether they are human. This will have dramatic effects, not only on our relations with nonhuman animals, but on the entire traditional sanctity of life ethic. For once we remove the assumption that an animal must be human in order to have some kind of right to life, then we will have to start looking at the characteristics and capacities that an animal must possess in order to have that right. When we do that, however, we will not be able to avoid noticing that, if we set the standard anywhere above the bare possession of life itself, some human beings will fail to meet it. Then it will become very difficult to continue to maintain that these humans have a right to life, while simultaneously denying the same right to animals with equal or superior characteristics and capacities.

PART III

Towards a Coherent Approach

IN PLACE OF THE
OLD ETHIC

THE STRUCTURE OF ETHICAL REVOLUTIONS

Four hundred years ago our views about our place in the universe underwent a crisis. The ancients used a model of the solar system devised by Ptolemy, according to which the earth was the centre of the universe and all the heavenly bodies revolved around it. Even the ancients knew, however, that this model did not work very well. It did not predict the positions of the planets with sufficient accuracy. So it was assumed that, as the planets moved in great circles around the earth, they also moved in smaller circles around their own orbits. This helped to patch up the model, but it didn't fix all the problems, and further adjustments were required. These adjustments were again an improvement, but still did not quite get it right. It would have been possible to add yet another modification to the basic geocentric model—but then Copernicus proposed a radically new approach. He suggested that the planets, including the earth, revolve around the sun. This remarkable new view met stiff resistance, because it required us to give up our cherished idea that we are the centre of the universe. It also clashed with the Judeo-Christian view of human beings as the pinnacle of creation. If we are the reason why everything else was made, why do we have such an undistinguished address?

The resistance to the Copernican theory was not, however, simply due to human pride, hidebound conservatism, or religious prejudice. The truth is that, in predicting the movements of the planets, Copernicus was not really any more accurate than the latest patched-up version of Ptolemy's old system. For Copernicus too had made a mistake. He clung to the idea that the heavenly bodies move in perfect circles, when really, as Kepler was later to show, the orbits of the planets are slightly elliptical. So there were some who continued to believe in the ancient model of the universe, and looked for better ways of making it fit the facts. The Copernican theory nevertheless triumphed, not because it was more accurate than the old one, but because it was a fresh approach, full of promise.[1]

Like cosmology before Copernicus, the traditional doctrine of the sanctity of human life is today in deep trouble. Its defenders have responded, naturally enough, by trying to patch up the holes that keep appearing in it. They have redefined death so that they can remove beating hearts from warm, breathing bodies, and give them to others with better prospects, while telling themselves that they are only taking organs from a corpse. They have drawn a distinction between 'ordinary' and 'extraordinary' means of treatment, which allows them to persuade themselves that their decision to withdraw a respirator from a person in an irreversible coma has nothing to do with the patient's poor quality of life. They give terminally ill patients huge doses of morphine that they know will shorten their lives, but say that this is not euthanasia, because their declared intention is to relieve pain. They select severely disabled infants for 'non-treatment' and make sure that they die, without thinking of themselves as killing them. By denying that an individual human being comes into existence before birth, the more flexible adherents of the sanctity of life doctrine are able to put the life, health, and well-being of a woman ahead of that of a fetus. Finally, by putting a taboo on comparisons between intellectually disabled human beings and nonhuman animals, they have preserved the species boundary as the boundary of the sanctity of life ethic, despite overwhelming evidence that the differences between us and other species are differences of degree rather than of kind.

The patching could go on, but it is hard to see a long and beneficial future for an ethic as paradoxical, incoherent and dependent on pretence as our conventional ethic of life and death has become. New medical techniques, decisions in landmark legal cases and shifts of public opinion are constantly threatening to bring the whole edifice crashing down. All I have done is to draw together and put on display the fatal weaknesses that have become apparent over the last two or three decades. For anyone who thinks clearly about the whole range of questions I have raised, modern medical practice has become incompatible with belief in the equal value of all human life.

It is time for another Copernican revolution. It will be, once again, a revolution against a set of ideas we have inherited from the period in which the intellectual world was dominated by a religious outlook. Because it will change our tendency to see human beings as the centre of the *ethical* universe, it will meet with fierce resistance from those who do not want to accept such a blow to our human pride. At first, it will have its own problems, and will need to tread carefully over new ground. For many the ideas will be too shocking to take seriously. Yet eventually the change will come. The traditional view that all human life is sacrosanct is simply not able to cope with the array of issues that we face. The new view will offer a fresh and more promising approach.

REWRITING THE COMMANDMENTS

What will the new ethical outlook be like? I shall take five commandments of the old ethic that we have seen to be false, and show how they need to be rewritten for a new ethical approach to life and death. But I do not want the five new commandments to be taken as something carved in stone. I do not really approve of ethics carved in stone anyway. There may be better ways of remedying the weaknesses of the traditional ethic. The title of this book suggests an ongoing activity: we can rethink something more than once. The point is to start, and to do so with a clear understanding of how fundamental our rethinking must be.

First Old Commandment:
Treat all human life as of equal worth

Hardly anyone really believes that all human life is of equal worth. The rhetoric that flows so easily from the pens and mouths of popes, theologians, ethicists and some doctors is belied every time these same people accept that we need not go all out to save a severely malformed baby; that we may allow an elderly man with advanced Alzheimer's disease to die from pneumonia, untreated by antibiotics; or that we can withdraw food and water from a patient in a persistent vegetative state. When the law sticks to the letter of this commandment, it leads to what everyone agrees now is an absurdity, like Joey Fiori's survival for almost two decades in a persistent vegetative state, or the continuation of respirator support for the anencephalic Baby K. The new approach is able to deal with these situations in the obvious way, without struggling to reconcile them with any lofty claims that all human life is of equal worth, irrespective of its potential for gaining or regaining consciousness.

First New Commandment:
Recognise that the worth of human life varies

This new commandment allows us frankly to acknowledge—as the British judges did when presented with the facts about Tony Bland's existence—that life without consciousness is of no worth at all. We can reach the same view—again, as British judges did in considering the condition of Baby C—about a life that has no possibility of mental, social or physical interaction with other human beings. Where life is not one of total or near total deprivation, the new ethic will judge the worth of continued life by the kind of balancing exercise recommended by Lord Justice Donaldson in the case of Baby J, taking into account both predictable suffering, and possible compensations.

Consistent with the first new commandment, we should treat human beings in accordance with their ethically relevant characteristics. Some of these are inherent in the nature of the being. They include consciousness, the capacity for physical, social and mental interaction with other beings, having conscious preferences for continued life, and having enjoyable experiences. Other relevant aspects depend on the relationship of the being to others, having relatives for example who will grieve over your death, or being so situated in a group that if you are killed, others will fear for their own lives. All of these things make a difference to the regard and respect we should have for a being.

The best argument for the new commandment is the sheer absurdity of the old one. If we were to take seriously the idea that all human life, irrespective of its capacity for consciousness, is equally worthy of our care and support, we would have to root out of medicine not only open quality of life judgments, but also the disguised ones. We would then be left trying to do our best to prolong indefinitely the lives of anencephalics, cortically dead infants, and patients in a persistent vegetative state. Ultimately, if we were really honest with ourselves, we would have to try to prolong the lives of those we now classify as dead because their brains have entirely ceased to function. For if human life is of equal worth, whether it has the capacity for consciousness or not, why focus on the death of the brain, rather than on the death of the body as a whole?

On the other hand, if we do accept the first new commandment, we overcome the problems that arise for a sanctity of life ethic in making decisions about anencephalics, cortically dead infants, patients in a persistent vegetative state, and those who are declared to be brain dead by current medical criteria. In none of these cases is the really important issue one of how we define death. That question has had so much attention only because we are still trying to live with an ethical and legal framework formed by the old commandment. When we reject that commandment, we will instead focus on ethically relevant characteristics like the capacity for enjoyable experiences, for interacting with others, or for having preferences about continued life. Without consciousness, none of these are possible; therefore, once we are certain that consciousness has been irrevocably lost, it is not ethically relevant that there is still some hormonal brain function, for hormonal brain function without consciousness cannot benefit the patient. Nor can brain-stem function alone benefit a patient, in the absence of a cortex. So our decisions about how to treat such patients should not depend on lofty rhetoric about the equal worth of all human life, but on the views of families and partners, who deserve consideration at a time of tragic loss. If a patient in a persistent vegetative state has previously expressed wishes about what should happen to her or him in such circumstances, they should also be taken into account. (We may do this purely out of respect for the wishes of the dead, or we may do it in order to reassure others, still alive, that their wishes will not be ignored.) At the same time, in a public health-care system, we cannot ignore the limits set by the finite nature of our medical resources, nor the needs of others whose lives may be saved by an organ transplant.

Second Old Commandment:
Never intentionally take innocent human life

The second commandment should be rejected because it is too absolutist to deal with all the circumstances that can arise. We have already seen how far this can be taken, in the Roman Catholic Church's teaching that it is wrong to kill a fetus, *even if that would be the only way to prevent both the pregnant woman and the fetus dying.*

For those who take responsibility for the consequences of their decisions, this doctrine is absurd. It is horrifying to think that in the nineteenth and early twentieth century it was probably responsible for the preventable and agonising deaths of an unknown number of women in Roman Catholic hospitals or at the hands of devout Roman Catholic doctors and midwives. This could occur if, for example, the head of the fetus became stuck during labour, and could not be dislodged. Then the only way of saving the woman was to perform an operation known as a craniotomy, which involves inserting a surgical implement through the vagina and crushing the cranium, or skull, of the fetus. If this was not done, the woman and fetus would die in childbirth. Such an operation is obviously a last resort. Nevertheless, in those difficult circumstances, it seems appalling that any well-intentioned health-care professional could stand by while both woman and fetus die. For an ethic that combines an exceptionless prohibition on taking innocent human life with the doctrine that the fetus is an innocent human being, however, there could be no other course of action. If the Roman Catholic Church had said that performing a craniotomy is permissible, it would have had to give up either the absolute nature of its prohibition on taking innocent human life, or its view that the fetus is an innocent human being. Obviously, it was—and remains—willing to do neither. The teaching still stands. It is only because the development of obstetric techniques now allows the fetus to be dislodged and removed alive that the doctrine is no longer causing women to die pointlessly.

Another circumstance in which the second old commandment needs to be abandoned is—as the British law lords pointed out in deciding the Bland case—when life is of no benefit to the person living it. But the only modification to the absolute prohibition on taking human life that their lordships felt able to justify in that case—to allow a life to be taken intentionally by withholding or omitting treatment—still leaves the problem of cases in which it is better to use active means to take innocent human life. The law found Dr Nigel Cox guilty of the attempted murder of Mrs Lillian Boyes, despite the fact that she begged for death, and knew that she had nothing ahead of her but a few more hours of agony. Needless to say, no law, no court, and no code of medical ethics, would have required Dr Cox to do everything in his power to prolong Mrs Boyes' life. Had she suddenly become unable to breathe on her own, for instance, it would have been quite in accordance with the law and the traditional ethical view not to put her on a respirator—or if she was already on one, to take it away. The very thought of drawing out the kind of suffering that Mrs Boyes had to endure is repugnant, and would have been regarded as wrong under the traditional ethic as well as the new one. But this only shows how much weight the traditional ethic places on the fine line between ending life by withdrawing treatment, and ending it by a lethal injection. The attitude of the traditional ethic is summed up in the famous couplet:

> Thou shalt not kill; but need'st not strive
> Officiously to keep alive.

These lines are sometimes uttered in revered tones, as if they were the wisdom of some ancient sage. One doctor, writing in the *Lancet* to defend the non-treatment of infants with spina bifida, referred to the lines as 'The old dictum we were taught as medical students'.[2] This is ironic, for a glance at the poem from which the couplet comes—Arthur Hugh Clough's 'The Latest Decalogue'—leaves no doubt that the intention of this verse, as of each couplet in the poem, is to point out how we have failed to heed the spirit of the original ten commandments. In some of the other couplets, this is unmistakeable. For example:

> No graven images may be
> Worshipped, except the currency.

Clough would therefore have supported an extended view of responsibility. Not killing is not enough. We are also responsible for the consequences of our decision not to strive to keep alive.[3]

Second New Commandment:
Take responsibility for the consequences of your decisions

Instead of focusing on whether doctors do or do not intend to end their patients' lives, or on whether they end their patients' lives by withdrawing feeding tubes rather than giving lethal injections, the new commandment insists that doctors must ask whether a decision that they foresee will end a patient's life is the right one, all things considered.

By insisting that we are responsible for our omissions as well as for our acts—for what we deliberately don't do, as well as for what we do—we can neatly explain why the doctors were wrong to follow the Roman Catholic teaching when a craniotomy was the only way to prevent the deaths of both mother and fetus. But there is a price to pay for this solution to the dilemma too: unless our responsibility is limited in some way, the new ethical approach could be extremely demanding. In a world with modern means of communication and transport, in which some people live on the edge of starvation while others enjoy great affluence, there is always something that we could do, somewhere, to keep another sick or malnourished person alive. That all of us living in affluent nations, with disposable incomes far in excess of what is required to meet our needs, should be doing much more to help those in poorer countries achieve a standard of living that can meet their basic needs is a point on which most thoughtful people will agree; but the worrying aspect of this view of responsibility is that there seems to be no limit on how much we must do. If we are as responsible for what we fail to do as we are for what we do, is it wrong to buy fashionable clothes, or to dine at expensive restaurants, when the money could have saved the life of a stranger dying for want of enough to eat? Is failing to give to aid organisations really a form of killing, or as bad as killing?

The new approach need not regard failing to save as equivalent to killing. Without some form of prohibition on killing people, society itself could not survive. Society can survive if people do not save others in need—though it will be a colder, less cohesive society. Normally there is more to fear from people who would kill you than there is from people who would allow you to die. So in everyday life there are good grounds for having a stricter prohibition on killing than on allowing to die. In addition, while we can demand of everyone that he or she refrain from killing people who want to go on living, to demand too much in the way of self-sacrifice in order to provide assistance to strangers is to confront head-on some powerful and near-universal aspects of human nature. Perhaps a viable ethic must allow us to show a moderate degree of partiality for ourselves, our family and our friends. These are the grains of truth within the misleading view that we are responsible only for what we do, and not for what we fail to do.

To pursue these questions about our responsibility to come to the aid of strangers would take us beyond the scope of this book—but two conclusions are already apparent. First, the distinction between killing and allowing to die is less clear-cut than we commonly think. Rethinking our ethic of life and death may lead us to take more seriously our failure to do enough for those whose lives we could save at no great sacrifice to our own. Second, whatever reasons there may be for preserving at least a part of the traditional distinction between killing and allowing to die— for example, maintaining that it is worse to kill strangers than to fail to give them the food they need to survive—these reasons do not apply when, like Lillian Boyes, a person wants to die, and death would come more swiftly and with less suffering if brought about by an act (for example, giving a lethal injection) than by an omission (for example, waiting until the patient develops an infection, and then not giving antibiotics).

Third Old Commandment:
Never take your own life, and always try to prevent others taking theirs

For nearly two thousand years, Christian writers have condemned suicide as a sin. When we should die, said Thomas Aquinas, is

God's decision, not ours.[4] That view became so deeply embedded in Christian nations that to attempt suicide was a crime, in some cases punished—ideologues lack a sense of irony—by death. The prohibition on suicide was one element of a general view that the state should enforce morality and act paternalistically towards its citizens.

This view of the proper role of the state was first powerfully challenged by the nineteenth-century British philosopher John Stuart Mill, who wrote in his classic *On Liberty*: 'The only purpose for which power can be rightfully exercised over any member of a civilised community, against his will, is to prevent harm to others. His own good, either physical or moral, is not a sufficient warrant.'[5]

Incurably ill people who ask their doctors to help them die at a time of their own choosing are not harming others. (There could be rare exceptions, for example if they have young children who need them; but people who are so ill as to want to die are generally in no position to care adequately for their children.) The state has no grounds for interfering, once it is satisfied that others are not harmed, and the decision is an enduring one that has been freely made, on the basis of relevant information, by a competent adult person. Hence the new version of the third commandment is the direct opposite of the original version.

Third New Commandment:
Respect a person's desire to live or die

John Locke, as we saw, defined a 'person' as a being with reason and reflection that can 'consider itself as itself, the same thinking thing, in different times and places'. This concept of a person is at the centre of the third new commandment. Only a person can *want* to go on living, or have plans for the future, because only a person can even understand the possibility of a future existence for herself or himself. This means that to end the lives of people, against their will, is different from ending the lives of beings who are not people. Indeed, strictly speaking, in the case of those who are not people, we cannot talk of ending their lives against or in accordance with their will, because they are not capable of having a will on such a matter. To have a sense of self, and of one's continued existence over time, makes possible an entirely different kind of life. For a person, who can see her life as a whole, the end of life takes on an entirely different significance. Think about how much of what we do is oriented towards the future—our education, our developing personal relationships, our family life, our career paths, our savings, our holiday plans. Because of this, to end a person's life prematurely may render fruitless much of her past striving.

For all these reasons, killing a person against her or his will is a much more serious wrong than killing a being that is not a person. If we want to put this in the language of rights, then it is reasonable to say that only a person has a right to life.[6]

Fourth Old Commandment:
Be fruitful and multiply

This biblical injunction has been a central feature of Judeo-Christian ethics for thousands of years. The Jewish outlook regarded large families as a blessing. Augustine said that sexual intercourse without procreative intent is a sin, and to try actively to prevent procreation 'turns the bridal chamber into a brothel'. Luther and Calvin were equally forceful in their encouragement of procreation, with Calvin even referring to Onan's act of 'spilling his seed on the ground' as 'to kill before he is born the son who was hoped for'. As late as 1877, the British government prosecuted Annie Besant and Charles Bradlagh for distributing a book on contraception, and around the same time in America the Comstock law prohibited the mailing or importation of contraceptives. In the twentieth century, until World War II, several European powers, among them France and Germany, continued to have national policies of increasing population in order to be able to support large armies. In some American states, old laws against the use of contraceptives survived until 1965, when the Supreme Court struck them down on the grounds that they were an invasion of privacy.[7]

Restrictions on abortion should be seen against this background view that more people are a good thing. The biblical injunction may have been apt for its time, but with world population having risen from two billion in 1930 to over five billion today, and projected to go to eleven billion by the middle of the next century, it is unethical to encourage more births. It may seem that in developed countries with low population densities, like Australia, Canada or the United States, there is ample room for a much larger population; but all nations put their wastes down the same atmospheric and oceanic sinks, and the average Australian or North American uses several times his or her share of these sinks. If this situation continues, it will either mean that people in developing countries cannot achieve a lifestyle like ours, with similar outputs of carbon dioxide and other wastes; or, if they do, then each of us will share responsibility for global warming that will speed up the melting of the polar icecaps, and so lead to a rise in sea levels. This will cause devastating floods in low-lying coastal areas, including the delta areas of Bangladesh and Egypt where forty-six million people live. Entire island nations like Tuvalu, the Marshall Islands, and the Maldives could disappear beneath the waves.[8] Global warming may also mean devastating droughts in areas that now feed millions. Irrespective of how few people there may be per square kilometre, additional people living in developed countries add to the strain we are placing on the ecosystems of our planet.

The new version of the fourth commandment therefore takes a different perspective.

Fourth New Commandment:
Bring children into the world only if they are wanted

What do the original and new versions of the fourth command-ment have to do with the questions discussed in this book? The two versions underpin very different views of how we should treat human life before a person comes into existence.

Consider, for example, an embryo in a laboratory. The crucial characteristic that makes it wrong to kill such an embryo, some would say, is that it has the potential to become a person, with all the characteristics that mature humans usually possess, including a degree of rationality and self-awareness that will far surpass that of a rat or a fish. But the fact that the embryo could become a person does not mean that the embryo is now capable of being harmed. The embryo does not have, and never has had, any wants or desires, so we cannot harm it by doing something contrary to its desires. Nor can we cause it to suffer. In other words the embryo is not, now, the kind of being that can be harmed, any more than the egg is before fertilisation. In the absence of any meaningful sense in which the embryo can be harmed, the argument from potential seems to presuppose that it is good to promote the existence of new human beings. Otherwise, why would the fact that the embryo has a certain potential require us to realise that potential?

There are (or soon will be) as many people on this planet as it can reasonably be expected to support. If it is not wrong to kill an embryo because of the wrong it does to an existing being, then the fact that killing it will mean that one fewer person comes into existence does not make it wrong either. Those who use the potential of the embryo as an argument against abortion are rather like Calvin who, as we saw, objected to Onan's practice of spilling his seed on the ground, because this killed 'the son who was hoped for'. Suppose that we really were hoping for a son. Sup-pose, too, that if we did not conceive a son now, then it would become impossible for us to conceive one at all. Then Calvin's objection would be sound. But if we are not hoping for another son, then the argument will pass us by.

Fifth Old Commandment:
Treat all human life as always more precious than any nonhuman life
The fifth and last of the traditional commandments that make up the sanctity of life ethic is so deeply embedded in the western mind that even to compare human and nonhuman animals is to risk causing offence. At the time of the controversy over the Reagan administration's 'Baby Doe' rules, I wrote a commentary on the issue for *Pediatrics*, the journal of the American Academy of Pediatrics. My commentary contained this sentence:

> If we compare a severely defective human infant with a nonhuman animal, a dog or a pig, for example, we will often find the non human to have superior capacities, both actual and potential, for rationality, self-consciousness, communication, and anything else that can plausibly be considered morally significant.

The editor received more than fifty letters protesting against my views in this commentary, several condemning the editor for allowing it to be published. Many of the correspondents protested particularly against the comparison of the intellectual abilities of a human being and a dog or a pig. Yet the sentence that so disturbed them is not only true, but *obviously* true.[9]

Opposition to comparisons between humans and animals has been even stronger in Germany. In 1989 an organisation called 'Lebenshilfe' invited me to speak at a European symposium on 'Bioengineering, Ethics and Disability'. Lebenshilfe is the major German organisation for parents of intellectually disabled infants. When my invitation became more widely known, a number of groups began to campaign against my participation, citing passages from my book *Practical Ethics* (which had been translated into German) as evidence for the fact that I held views so shocking that they ought not even to be discussed. Among the passages often cited during this campaign was one similar to the sentence just quoted from my *Pediatrics* article. Astonishingly, the campaign succeeded: Lebenshilfe withdrew its invitation to me, only a few days before the symposium was due to open. Then, when that was not enough to appease the protesters, Lebenshilfe cancelled the entire symposium. Evidently shaken by these events, the following year Lebenshilfe adopted a set of 'Ethical Foundational Statements', which included the following: 'The uniqueness of human life forbids any comparison—or, more specifically, equation—of human existence with other living beings, with their forms of life or interests'.[10]

This prohibition is simply a last-ditch defence of the human-centred view of the universe that, as we saw, was severely battered by Copernicus and Galileo, and to which Darwin gave what ought to have been its final blow. We like to think of ourselves as the darlings of the universe. We do not like to think of ourselves as a species of animal. But the truth is that there is no unbridgeable gulf between us. Instead there is an overlap. The more intellectually sophisticated nonhuman animals have a mental and emotional life that in every significant respect equals or surpasses that of some of the most profoundly intellectually disabled human beings. This is not my subjective value-judgment. It is a statement of fact that can be tested and verified over and over again. Only human arrogance can prevent us seeing it.

Fifth New Commandment:
Do not discriminate on the basis of species

Some people will be happy to accept the previous four new commandments, but will have doubts about this one, because they associate the rejection of a bias in favour of our own species with an extreme form of species-egalitarianism that treats every living thing as of equal worth.[11] Obviously, since the new ethical outlook I have been defending rejects even the view that all *human* lives are of equal worth, I am not going to hold that *all* life is of equal worth, irrespective of its quality or characteristics. These two claims—the rejection of speciesism, and the rejection of *any* difference in the value of different living things—are quite distinct. Belief in the equal value of all life suggests that it is as wrong to uproot a cabbage as it would be to shoot dead the next person who rings your doorbell. We can reject speciesism, however, and still find many good reasons for holding that there is nothing wrong with pulling up a cabbage, while shooting the next person to ring your doorbell is utterly dreadful. For example, we can point out that cabbages lack the kind of nervous system and brain associated with consciousness, and so are not capable of experiencing anything. To uproot the cabbage therefore does not frustrate its conscious preferences for continuing to live, deprive it of enjoyable experiences, bring grief to its relatives, nor cause alarm to others who fear that they too may be uprooted. To shoot the next person to ring your doorbell is likely to do all of these things.

In listing the possible reasons why it is wrong to shoot the next person to ring your doorbell, I never mentioned species. Perhaps a flying saucer has just landed in your front garden, and a friendly alien has rung the bell. If the alien is capable of having conscious preferences for continuing to live, that is a reason for not killing it. The same applies if the living alien will have enjoyable experiences, or if the alien has relatives who will grieve for its death, or other companions who will fear that they too may now be shot. So the four possible reasons I mentioned for regarding it as wrong to kill the person ringing your doorbell will apply to the alien just as they would apply to the girl from next door who wants to retrieve her ball. The rejection of speciesism implies only that the *species* of the doorbell ringer is irrelevant.

Why isn't species a legitimate reason? For essentially the same reason as we now exclude race or sex. The racist, sexist and speciesist are all saying: the boundary of my group also marks a difference of value. If you are a member of my group, you are more valuable than if you are not—no matter what other characteristics you may lack. Each of these positions is a form of group protectiveness, or group selfishness. Throughout human history, we have broadened the circle of those whose interests we take into account, from the tribe to the nation, from the nation to the race, and from the race to the species. We now take for granted the inadequacy of having made the circle narrower than our entire species; but we do not notice that the circle remains an arbitrarily exclusionary one. It still leaves beings outside who are very like us in morally important respects. For instance, in the very respects that British judges have recently said are relevant to deciding whether there is a duty to preserve life, some nonhuman animals are more like normal humans than are some seriously damaged members of our own species. Dogs are conscious beings. They can feel pain, and they evidently enjoy many aspects of their lives. In that respect they are like you and me, and unlike Tony Bland after the tragedy at the Hillsborough Stadium. Or to take another example: if the ability to interact with others is an essential part of what it is to be *us*, then a normal chimpanzee is more like us than was Baby C, who was described by the Court of Appeal as 'permanently unable to interact mentally, socially and physically'.

Many people will want to cling to the superior status of the *human* being. We are so used to talk of *human* rights, *human* dignity, and the infinite value of *human* life, that we will not easily abandon the idea that to be *human* is in itself to be very special. In part, the problem is that the very word 'human' is not a purely descriptive term. It can mean simply a member of the species *Homo sapiens*, but it can also have built into it the very qualities that we think make human beings special. This is the sense listed by the *Oxford English Dictionary* as 'Having or showing the qualities or attributes proper to or distinctive of man'. As an illustration of this usage, the dictionary offers the following quotation from Harriet Martineau's *Society in America*, published in 1837: 'Every prison visitor has been conscious, on first conversing privately with a criminal, of a feeling of surprise at finding him so human.'

Clearly there would be no surprise at finding the prisoner to be a member of the species *Homo sapiens*! Martineau meant, and her readers will immediately have understood, that she was referring to the discovery that criminals have wants, feelings, desires, and other characteristics very like our own. Henry Longfellow put the two senses of the word together in one line from his popular poem 'The Song of Hiawatha': 'Every human heart is human'.[12]

Pedantic as it may be to correct a poetic utterance, the ethical significance of distinguishing between the two senses could be put by saying that *not* every human heart is human, whereas some nonhuman hearts *are* human. The heart of the anencephalic Baby Valentina was the heart of a member of the species *Homo sapiens* but, no matter how long Valentina had lived, her heart would never have beaten faster when her mother came into the room, because Valentina could never feel emotions of love or concern for anyone. The heart of the gorilla Koko, on the other hand, is not the heart of a member of the species *Homo sapiens*, but it is a heart capable of relating to others, and of showing love and concern for them. In the second sense of the term 'human', Koko's heart is more human than Valentina's.

If, as I hope, this lengthy discussion has put to rest possible doubts about the new fifth commandment, it remains only to say what its implications are for the issues discussed in this book. Because membership of the species *Homo sapiens* is not ethically relevant, any characteristic or combination of characteristics that we regard as giving human beings a right to life, or as making it generally wrong to end a human life, may be possessed by some nonhuman animals. If they are, then we must grant those nonhuman animals the same right to life as we grant to human beings, or consider it as seriously wrong to end the lives of those nonhuman animals as we consider it to end the life of a human being with the same characteristic or combination of characteristics. Likewise, we cannot justifiably give more protection to the life of a human being than we give to a nonhuman animal, if the human being clearly ranks lower on any possible scale of relevant characteristics than the animal. Baby Valentina clearly ranks lower on any possible scale of relevant characteristics than Koko. Yet as the law now stands, a surgeon could kill Koko in order to take her heart and transplant it into a human being, while to take Valentina's heart would have been murder. In terms of the revised ethical outlook, that is wrong. The right to life is not a right of members of the species *Homo sapiens*; it is—as we saw in discussing the third new commandment—a right that properly belongs to persons. Not all members of the species *Homo sapiens* are persons, and not all persons are members of the species *Homo sapiens*.

SOME ANSWERS

All we have so far is a rough sketch of how the five crumbling pillars of the old ethic might be replaced with solid new material, better able to support a structure that will guide our decisions about live and death into the next century. More thought and discussion are needed to develop these broad proposals into a working ethic. But we have to keep living in the house we are rebuilding. We cannot move out during the renovations, because decisions about life and death need to be made all the time. We cannot live without an ethic, and we cannot buy a new one ready-made. So despite the preliminary nature of our sketch of the new ethic, it is not premature to see what answers it gives to some of the issues I have discussed.

Brain death, anencephaly, cortical death and the persistent vegetative state

Our examination of the sanctity of life ethic began with brain death. We saw then that the decision to regard people as dead whose brains have irreversibly ceased to function is an ethical judgment. To cease to support the bodily functions of such people is normally a justifiable ethical decision, in accordance with the first and fifth new commandments, for the most significant ethically relevant characteristic of human beings whose brains have irreversibly ceased to function is not that they are members of our species, but that they have no prospect of regaining consciousness. Without consciousness, continued life cannot benefit them. There may, of course, be other issues: the need for the family to have time to adjust to a tragic loss, the preservation of organs that could save the lives of others, and occasionally, as with Trisha Marshall and Marion Ploch, a pregnancy. Exactly the same holds for patients in a persistent vegetative state, once we can be certain that there is no possibility of restoring consciousness. It holds, too—apart from the impossibility of pregnancy—for anencephalics and cortically dead infants.

This does not mean that the decision to end the life of an irreversibly unconscious patient is simple or automatic. The considerations of family feelings are both subtle and important, particularly if the patient is an infant or young person, and the loss of consciousness was unexpected. But the new approach does make the decision more manageable. There are some situations in which all the considerations point in the same direction. The cases of Baby Theresa and Baby Valentina were exactly such situations. When the parents of an anencephalic baby would like their child to be used as a source of organs to save the life of another infant, the fact that the anencephalic baby is alive should not stop us from doing the obvious thing: taking the heart from the baby who cannot benefit from continued life, and giving it to the one who can. Similarly, the new commandments would have solved the dilemma posed by Dr Frank Shann at the Royal Children's Hospital conference on the status of anencephalic and cortically dead infants: provided that the parents of the cortically dead baby were willing to give their consent to the donation of his heart, the baby with the heart defect could have been saved.

Abortion and the brain-dead pregnant woman

The first, fourth and fifth new commandments have implications for the abortion controversy. What ethically relevant characteristics does the fetus have? The fact that it is a member of the species *Homo sapiens* does not answer this question. The argument from the potential of the embryo has already been examined and found wanting. In terms of the actual capacities of the fetus, there is little to suggest that it would be wrong to end its life. Probably at some point in its development in the womb the fetus does become conscious. This may happen around the tenth week of gestation when brain activity can first be detected. Even then, brain-wave activity measurable by an EEG does not become continuous until the thirty-second week, so it may be that the fetus is only intermittently conscious until that stage, which is well past the date when it becomes viable.[13] Suppose, though, that the fetus is capable of feeling pain at the earliest possible date, ten weeks. Is the capacity to feel pain a sufficient reason to grant a being a right to life? If we think that it is, we will have to grant the same right to (at least) every normal vertebrate animal, since there is more evidence for brain activity and a capacity to feel pain even in vertebrates with relatively small brains, like frogs and fish, than there is in the fetus at ten weeks of gestation. If we baulk at so radical a change in our attitudes to nonhuman animals, we shall have to hold that the fetus may be killed for relatively trivial reasons, like those that we now consider justify us in killing rats (say, to test new food colourings) or fish (because some people prefer tuna to tofu).

An intermediate position would be that we may kill both fetuses and nonhuman animals at a similar level of awareness, if we can do so in a way that does not cause pain or distress, or if, despite the fact that some pain or distress is caused, the need to kill the fetus or nonhuman animal is sufficiently serious to outweigh the pain or distress caused. This would mean that we would have to stop the routine product safety-tests now carried out on rats and other animals, because these cause the animals to become ill, and often to die in considerable distress, and the products generally do not serve any need that could not be served by an existing product. (It may not be a popular comparison to make, but rats are indisputably more aware of their surroundings, and more able to respond in purposeful and complex ways to things they like or dislike, than a fetus at ten, or even at thirty-two weeks' gestation.) Fishing, too, would have to stop, except when practised by those who have no other way of getting enough to eat. Most commercially caught fish die slowly of suffocation, as they lie gasping in the air. Recreational anglers inflict pain and distress by inducing fish to bite on a barbed metal hook. In the case of abortion, whether pain and distress is caused to the fetus would depend not only on how developed the fetus is, but also on the method used. This intermediate position would allow unrestricted early abortions, and would not entirely exclude late abortions, if a method of abortion that killed the fetus painlessly were used, or if the reason for the abortion were sufficiently serious to outweigh the pain that might be caused.

It follows that there are no grounds for opposing abortion before the fetus is conscious, and only very tenuous grounds for opposing it at any stage of pregnancy. In fact, since a woman's reasons for having an abortion are invariably far more serious than the reasons most people in developed countries have for eating fish rather than tofu, and there is no reason to think that a fish suffers less when dying in a net than a fetus suffers during an abortion, the argument for not eating fish is much stronger than the argument against abortion that can be derived from the possible consciousness of the fetus after ten weeks. What has been said here of fish would also be true, in different ways, of the commercially reared and killed animals we commonly eat—quite apart from any ethically relevant characteristics that animals like cows and pigs may have in addition to their capacity to suffer. So while one may consistently be an ethical vegetarian and still accept even late abortions, those who oppose late abortions on the grounds of fetal distress will need to be ethical vegetarians if their position is to be consistent and non-speciesist.

Resolving the issue of abortion in this way has direct implications for the dilemma with which this book began: the brain-dead woman who is pregnant. Since neither the actual characteristics of the fetus, nor its potential, are a reason for keeping it alive, such women can normally be allowed to become dead in every sense. The only ground for not doing so would be the strong desire of the father of the child, or of other close relatives of the pregnant woman, that the child should live. The issue then ceases to be one of a life or death decision for the fetus, and becomes a question of whether the medical resources required should be used to satisfy this desire rather than others.

Infants

In the modern era of liberal abortion laws, most of those not opposed to abortion have drawn a sharp line at birth. If, as I have argued, that line does not mark a sudden change in the status of the fetus, then there appear to be only two possibilities: oppose abortion, or allow infanticide. I have already given reasons why the fetus is not the kind of being whose life must be protected in the way that the life of a person should be. Although the fetus may, after a certain point, be capable of feeling pain, there is no basis for thinking it rational or self-aware, let alone capable of seeing itself as existing in different times and places. But the same can be said of the newborn infant. Human babies are not born self-aware, or capable of grasping that they exist over time. They are not persons. Hence their lives would seem to be no more worthy of protection than the life of a fetus.

Must we accept this shocking conclusion? Or does birth somehow make a difference, in some way that has so far been overlooked? Perhaps our focus on the status of the fetus and the infant has led us to neglect other aspects of the situation. Here are two ways in which birth may make a difference, not so much to the fetus/infant and its claim to life, but to others who are affected by it.

First, after birth the pregnant woman is no longer pregnant. The baby is outside her body. Thus her claim to control her own body and her own reproductive system is no longer enough to determine the life or death of the newborn baby. As I argued, this right in itself was never enough to resolve the abortion issue. Still, that does not mean that it was without any weight at all, and so the fact that at birth it no longer applies will make some difference to how we think of the newborn infant.

The second difference birth makes is that if the baby's mother does not want to keep her child, it can be cared for by someone else who does. This reason for preserving infant life is strong in a society in which there are more couples wanting to adopt a baby than there are babies needing adoption. It is no reason at all for preserving infant life if there are babies in need of adoption, and no-one willing to adopt them. The coming of effective contraception and safe legal abortion have moved most developed nations sharply into the former status (though not, unfortunately, if we focus on babies with major disabilities, whom very few couples are willing to adopt). In these societies there is an important reason to protect the lives of babies, even those unwanted by their parents. In other societies that have difficulty coping with unwanted children and so have traditionally accepted infanticide, this is not a reason for preserving infant life.

So birth does make a difference to the status of the infant. But the difference is one of degree, and it remains true that the new approach, drawing on the third new commandment and the idea of a person on which that commandment is based, will not consider the newborn infant entitled to the same degree of protection as a person. There are other issues at stake as well. First, as we saw in the British Court of Appeal decisions in the cases of Baby C and Baby J, the future prospects of life may be so bleak that it is kinder to the baby, both now and in the future, to 'treat it to die'. That decision must depend crucially on the wishes of the parents. Their desire to keep and cherish the child can make an enormous difference to its prospects; conversely, the quality of life of a child abandoned to an institution, without loving parents, can be much less acceptable. The views of the parents, as the people most closely concerned with the infant, should also be given great weight simply because of the effects, both good and bad, that the continued life of their child will have on them and any other children they may have. In general, therefore, decisions about the future of severely disabled newborn infants should be made, not by judges who will have nothing to do with the child after their judgment is delivered, but by the parents, in consultation with their doctor.[14]

What of Baby Doe, or of John Pearson, the baby that Dr Leonard Arthur was charged with murdering? These were both Down syndrome babies, rejected by their parents. People with Down syndrome have a distinctive appearance, are poorly co-ordinated, and are intellectually disabled to varying degrees; but they are not in pain, or in need of frequent operations. Many people with Down syndrome have a cheerful temperament, and can be warm and loving. In contrast to Baby C and Baby J, their lives could not be described as full of suffering, without compensating positive elements. Why then did so eminent a doctor as Sir Douglas Black feel able to say, at Arthur's trial, that 'it is ethical that a child suffering from Down syndrome...should not survive'? Why did half of a sample of American general paediatricians say that they would not oppose a parental refusal of surgery for a Down syndrome infant with blockage of the digestive system? Why did the Supreme Court of Indiana refuse to order that Baby Doe should be given the operation that would have saved his life?

Here is one answer to these questions. Shakespeare once described life as an uncertain voyage. As parents, or intending parents, we want our children to set out on that voyage as well equipped as possible for whatever it may bring. The expression 'our children' need not refer to particular, already existing children. If we have no children, but are planning to have some, we may well want to provide the children we hope to have with a good start on life's uncertain voyage. That will be better for our children—in the generic sense. But it is not *only* because we believe it will be better for our children that we may choose not to bring up a child with Down syndrome. Having children is a central part of *our* uncertain voyage as well. We will look after them and guide their lives until they are in their teens; after they become independent of us, we will still love them and share their joys and sorrows.

To have a child with Down syndrome is to have a very different experience from having a normal child. It can still be a warm and loving experience, but we must have lowered expectations of our child's abilities. We cannot expect a child with Down syndrome to play the guitar, to develop an appreciation of science fiction, to learn a foreign language, to chat with us about the latest Woody Allen movie, or to be a respectable athlete, basketballer or tennis player. Even when an adult, a person with Down syndrome may not be able to live independently; and for someone with Down syndrome to have children of their own is unusual and can give rise to problems. For some parents, none of this matters. They find bringing up a child with Down syndrome a rewarding experience in a thousand different ways. But for other parents, it is devastating.

Both for the sake of 'our children', then, and for our own sake, we may not want a child to start on life's uncertain voyage if the prospects are clouded. When this can be known at a very early stage of the voyage we may still have a chance to make a fresh start. This means detaching ourselves from the infant who has been born, cutting ourselves free before the ties that have already begun to bind us to our child have become irresistible. Instead of going forward and putting all our efforts into making the best of the situation, we can still say no, and start again from the beginning. That is what Molly Pearson was doing when, told that she had given birth to a Down syndrome baby, she said to her husband, 'I don't want it, Duck'.

It must be extraordinarily difficult to cut oneself off from one's own child, and prefer it to die, so that another child with better prospects can be born. Yet many women think like this when they discover that they are pregnant with an abnormal child. We saw that there was broad public support for Sherri Finkbane's efforts to abort a fetus after she had taken thalidomide during pregnancy. Today, prenatal diagnosis is routine for older women, who are more at risk of having a baby with Down syndrome. It is premised on the assumption that if the test shows a fetus with Down syndrome or other abnormalities, an abortion will follow. When the pregnancy was a wanted one, the couple will usually then try to conceive another child.

In our culture, it is only before the baby is born that we openly accept this idea of saying no to a new life that does not have good prospects. But we saw earlier that many other cultures say no shortly after birth as well. Kung women who give birth when they still have a child too young to walk probably do not find it easy to go to the bushes and smother the newborn infant, but doing this does not prevent them being loving mothers to the children that they do choose to bring up. Japanese mothers are renowned for their devotion to their children and this, as we have seen, was compatible with the tradition of 'mabiki', or 'thinning' of infants. Japanese midwives who attended births did not assume that the baby was to live; instead they always asked if the baby was 'to be left' or 'to be returned' to wherever it was thought to have come from. Needless to say, in Japan as in all these cultures, a baby born with an obvious disability would almost always be 'returned'.[15]

The official western reaction to these practices is that they are shocking examples of the barbaric standards of non-Christian morality. I do not share this view. My dissent has nothing to do with cultural relativism. Some non-western practices—for example, female circumcision—are wrong and should, if possible, be stopped. But, in the case of infanticide, it is our culture that has something to learn from others, especially now that we, like them, are in a situation where we must limit family size. I do not mean, of course, that infanticide should become a means of limiting family size. Contraception is obviously the best way to do this, since there is no point in going through an unwanted pregnancy and birth; and, for the same reason, abortion is much better than infanticide. But, for reasons we have already discussed, in regarding a newborn infant as not having the same right to life as a person, the cultures that practised infanticide were on solid ground.

Despite the dominance of the traditional western ethic, some parents do think of their infants as replaceable. Here is a journal entry written by Peggy Stinson when Andrew, her extremely premature and seriously brain-damaged son had been in intensive care for two months:

> I keep thinking about the other baby—the one that won't be born. The IICU [Infant Intensive Care Unit] is choosing between lives. It may already be too late for the next baby. If Andrew's life is strung out much longer, will we have the money, the emotional resources, the nerve to try again?

Another two months went by before Peggy returned to this topic in her journal. Andrew's condition had not changed.

> Thirty-fifth birthday coming up next week; haven't got forever to try for another child...At this rate we'll have neither Andrew nor the next child, who because of Andrew's extended course, will have lost the chance to exist at all.
>
> Jeff [a doctor at the hospital] once said that our 'next child' was theoretical, abstract—its interests couldn't be considered. Strictly speaking that may be so, but that next baby seems real enough to me. To Bob too. Decision this week to change that abstraction into a real person before it's too late.[16]

It is rare to find a couple reflecting openly on the choice between an existing baby and the 'next child' who they will conceive and raise only if the existing one dies. But there are many couples who realise that to give enough love and care to a severely disabled child would make it very difficult to bring up another child. A couple considering whether to terminate a pregnancy when the fetus has been diagnosed as having Down syndrome is in a similar situation to the Stinsons. The couple could, of course, continue the pregnancy, bring up the child with Down syndrome, and then have another child. But most couples have a sense of how many children they plan to have, and so to allow one pregnancy to lead to a child effectively precludes the existence of another child. It is implausible that the choice between one life or another does not enter the minds of many parents with disabled newborn infants. It is not Peggy Stinson's thoughts that are so unusual, but her willingness to write them down and publish them. We know that once our children's lives are properly underway, we will become committed to them; for that very reason, many couples do not want to bring up a child if they fear that both the child's life and their own experience of child-rearing will be clouded by a major disability.

Shakespeare's image of life as a voyage is consistent with the idea that the seriousness of taking life increases gradually, parallel with the gradual development of the child's capacities that culminate in its life as a full person. On this view birth marks the beginning of the next stage of development, but important changes continue to happen in the weeks and months after birth as well. These changes are not only in the capacities of the baby, but also in the attachment of the parents and the acceptance of the infant into the family and the wider moral community. Many cultures have a ceremony to mark this acceptance. In ancient Greece, the infant could only be exposed on the mountainside before it had been named. (Christening may be a relic of such ceremonies.)

All of this may help to show that the ethical approach towards newborn infants proposed here is consonant with some strands of our thought about the wrongness of killing, although certainly not with all of them. Neither the first nor the second new commandment condemns Molly Pearson and her husband, or the parents of Baby Doe, for wanting their newborn Down-syndrome infants to die. There is no sharp ethical distinction between what they did, and what most pregnant women do when they are offered an abortion because the fetus they are carrying has Down syndrome. In both cases, the decision is not primarily the concern of the state, nor of the doctors—it chiefly concerns the family into whom the baby is born.

There remains, however, the problem of the lack of any clear boundary between the newborn infant, who is clearly not a person in the ethically relevant sense, and the young child, who is. In our book, *Should the Baby Live?*, my colleague Helga Kuhse and I suggested that a period of twenty-eight days after birth might be allowed before an infant is accepted as having the same right to life as others. This is clearly well before the infant could have a sense of its own existence over time, and would allow a couple to decide that it is better not to continue with a life that has begun very badly. The boundary is, admittedly, an arbitrary one, and this makes it problematic. We accept other arbitrary boundaries based on age, like eligibility for voting or for holding a driving licence—but a right to life is a more serious matter. Could we return to a view of infants more like that of ancient Greece, in which a public ceremony a short time after birth marked not only the parents' decision to accept the child but also society's conferral on it of the status of a person? The strongest argument for treating infants as having a right to life from the moment of birth is simply that no other line has the visibility and self-evidence required to mark the beginning of a socially recognised right to life. This is a powerful consideration; maybe in the end it is even enough to tilt the balance against a change in the law in this area. On that I remain unsure.[17]

People

The third new commandment recognises that every person has a right to life. We have seen that the basic reason for taking this view derives from what it is to be a person, a being with awareness of her or his own existence over time, and the capacity to have wants and plans for the future. There is also a powerful social and political reason for protecting the lives of those who are capable of fearing their own death. Universal acceptance and secure protection of the right to life of every person is the most important good that a society can bestow upon its members. Without it there is, as the seventeenth-century English philosopher Thomas Hobbes said, 'continual fear and danger of violent death. And the life of man solitary, poor, nasty, brutish and short.'[18] Only a being able to see herself as existing over time can fear death and can know that, if people may be killed with impunity, her own life could be in jeopardy. Neither infants nor those nonhuman animals incapable of seeing themselves as existing over time can fear their own deaths (although they may be frightened by threatening or unfamiliar circumstances, as a fish in a net may be frightened). It is reasonable to regard more seriously crimes that cause fear in others, and threaten the peaceful coexistence on which society depends. This provides another reason for recognising that every person has a right to life, or in other words that it is a greater wrong to take the life of a person than to take the life of any other being.

A right is something one can choose to exercise or not to exercise. I have a right to a percentage of the money my publisher earns by selling this book, because I wrote it and then made an agreement with my publisher for it to be published on this basis. But I can waive this right, if I wish to do so. I could pass the royalties on to an overseas aid organisation, or to the next homeless person I meet, or even tell my publisher to keep them. Similarly, the most important aspect of having a right to life is that one can choose whether or not to invoke it. We value the protection given

by a right to life only when we want to go on living. N(
fear being killed at his or her own persistent, infoi
autonomous request. On the contrary, the evidence s
many people approaching the end of their lives fear suffering
much more than death. Hence the very argument that so powerfully supports recognition and protection of every person's right to
life also supports the right to medical assistance in dying when this
is in accordance with a person's persistent, informed and
autonomous request.

As we saw, the right to medical assistance in dying has been
accepted as legitimate in the Netherlands, and those who want to
exercise it in other countries are increasingly finding ways around
existing laws. But respect for a person's right to live or die
also suggests that, where a person is capable of expressing a view
about continuing to live, life-sustaining treatment should not
be withdrawn without the patient's consent. The second new
commandment indicates that doctors cannot take refuge in the
idea that in withdrawing treatment, they are only 'letting nature
take its course'. On the contrary, they are responsible for the
decision taken, which was to let the patient die rather than to
postpone death.

THE BASIS OF THE NEW APPROACH
TO LIFE AND DEATH

The new approach to life and death decisions is very different
from the old one. But it is important to realise that the ethics of
decision-making about life and death are only one part of ethics,
important as they are. In particular, before leaving the sketch of
the new ethic I have drawn, I want to emphasise that to deny that
a being has a right to life is not to put it altogether outside the
sphere of moral concern. A being that is not a person does not
have the same interest in continuing to live into the future that a
person usually has, but it will still have interests in not suffering,

and in experiencing pleasure from the satisfaction of its wants. Since neither a newborn human infant nor a fish is a person, the wrongness of killing such beings is not as great as the wrongness of killing a person. But this does not mean that we should disregard the needs of an infant to be fed, and kept warm and comfortable and free of pain, for as long as it lives. Except where life is at stake, these needs should be given the weight they would be given if they were the needs of an older person. The same is true, with the necessary changes for its different needs, of the fish. Fish can surely feel pain. Their pain matters just as much, in so far as rough comparisons can be made, as similar pains experienced by a person. We do both infants and fish wrong if we cause them pain or allow them to suffer, unless to do so is the only way of preventing greater suffering.

Even when these limits to the scope of the changes I propose are understood, many will be sceptical about the need for so great a change in our ethics. There is a common view that reason and argument play no role in ethics, and therefore we have no need to defend our ethical views when they are challenged. Some people are more ready to reason about the merits of football players or chocolate cake recipes than they are about their belief in the sanctity of human life. This is a force for conservatism in ethics. It allows people to listen to a criticism of their own views, and then say: 'Oh yes, well that is your opinion, but I think differently'—as if that is the end of the discussion. I hope I have shown that it is not so easy to ignore the fact that our standard view of the ethics of life and death is incoherent.

As we have just seen, the differences between the old and the new approach arise from just five key ethical commandments. In fact, the case for a drastic change to the old ethic is even simpler and more rationally compelling than that. Just as changing one or two lines of a complex computer program can completely alter the image that appears on your screen, so changing two central assumptions is enough to bring about a complete transformation of the old ethic. The first of these assumptions is that we are responsible for what we intentionally do in a way that we are not responsible for what we deliberately fail to prevent. The second is that the lives of all and only members of our species are more worthy of protection than the lives of any other being. These are the assumptions behind the second and fifth of the commandments that we discussed earlier.

Each of these assumptions has a religious origin. The roots of the first lie in the Judeo-Christian idea of the moral law as set down in simple rules that allow for no exceptions, and the second springs from the same tradition's idea that God created man in his own image, granted him dominion over the other animals, and bestowed an immortal soul on human beings alone of all creatures. Taken independently of their religious origins, both of the crucial assumptions are on very weak ground. Can doctors who remove the feeding tubes from patients in a persistent vegetative state really believe that there is a huge gulf between this, and giving the same patients an injection that will stop their hearts beating? Doctors may be trained in such a way that it is psychologically easier for them to do the one and not the other, but both are equally certain ways of bringing about the death of the patient. As for the second assumption, what I have already said should be sufficient to show that it is not rationally defensible.

If we did nothing to the old ethic apart from abandoning these two assumptions, we would still have to construct an entirely new ethic. We could construct it differently from the ethic I have sketched out. We could, for instance, insist that, just as it is always wrong intentionally to take human life, so it is always wrong deliberately to refrain from saving human life. This would be a consistent position, but not an attractive one. It would force us to do whatever we could to keep people alive, whether they wanted to be kept alive or not, and irrespective of whether they could ever recover consciousness. That would surely be a pointless and often cruel exercise of our medical powers. There would be other, even more far-reaching but on the whole much more desirable consequences for our responsibilities towards those in other countries who need food and other forms of aid that we can spare. In a similar manner, having abandoned the distinction between humans and nonhuman animals, we could refuse to adopt a distinction between persons and those who are not persons, and instead insist that every living thing or, perhaps more plausibly, every being capable of experiencing pleasure or pain, has an equal right to life. So a new ethical approach can take many different forms. But without its two crucial but shaky assumptions, the old ethic cannot survive. The question is not whether it will be replaced, but what the shape of its successor will be.

21 *San Francisco Chronicle*, 4 August 1993; *Miami Herald*, 24 April 1993; *Toronto Star*, 22 June 1993.

22 See, for example, the United States Uniform Determination of Death Act. Note that the Harvard committee had referred to the absence of central nervous system 'activity' rather than function. The use of the term 'function' rather than 'activity' makes the definition of brain death more permissive, because, as the United States President's Commission recognised (*Defining Death*, p. 74), electrical and metabolic activity may continue in cells or groups of cells after the organ has ceased to function. The commission did not think that the continuation of this activity should prevent a declaration of death.

23 'Rethinking brain death', pp. 62–74; Amir Halevy and Baruch Brody, 'Brain Death: Reconciling Definitions, Criteria and Tests', *Annals of Internal Medicine*, vol. 119, 1993, pp. 519–25; Robert Veatch, 'The Impending Collapse of the Whole-Brain Definition of Death', *Hastings Center Report*, vol. 23, no. 4, 1993, pp. 18–24.

3. Dr Shann's Dilemma

1 D. Shewmon, 'Anencephaly: Selected Medical Aspects', *Hastings Center Report*, vol. 18, no. 5, 1988, pp. 11–19.

2 Neil Campbell, 'Some Anatomy and Physiology', in K. Sanders and B. Moore (eds), *Anencephalics, Infants and Brain Death Treatment Options and the Issue of Organ Donation*, Law Reform Commission of Victoria, Melbourne, 1991, p. 13.

3 'Anencephaly: Selected Medical Aspects', p. 11–19.

4 Diane Gianelli, 'Doctors Argue Futility of Treating Anencephalic Baby', *American Medical News*, vol. 37, no. 11, 21 March 1994, p. 5; Linda Greenhouse, 'Court Order to Treat Baby With Partial Brain Prompts Debate on Costs and Ethics', New York Times, 20 February 1994.

5 Frank Shann, 'The cortically dead infant who breathes', in *Anencephalics, Infants and Brain Death Treatment Options*, p. 28.

6 Neil Campbell, 'The Arguments For', in *Anencephalics, Infants and Brain Death Treatment Options*, p. 109.

7 Steve Keeley, 'The Arguments Against', in *Anencephalics, Infants and Brain Death Treatment Options*, p. 114.

8 Henry Beecher, 'The New Definition of Death, Some Opposing Views', unpublished paper presented at the meeting of the American Association for the Advancement of Science, December 1970, p. 4, quoted from Robert Veatch, *Death, Dying and the Biological Revolution*, Yale University Press, New Haven, 1976, p. 39.

9 *Defining Death*, p. 83.

10 *Defining Death*, p. 40.

11 *Cruzan v. Director, Missouri Department of Health* (1990) 110 S. Ct., pp. 2886–7. For a philosophical defence of a similar view, see Jeff

McMahon, *Killing at the Margins of Life*, Oxford University Press, New York, forthcoming, 1995.

12 *Birmingham News*, 31 March 1992 and *USA Today*, 30 March 1992, quoted in Gregory Pence, *Classic Cases in Medical Ethics*, 2nd ed., McGraw–Hill, forthcoming 1995.

13 *La Stampa*, 16 April 1992; *La Repubblica*, 17 April 1992.

14 Danish Council of Ethics, *Death Criteria: A Report*, Danish Council of Ethics, Copenhagen, 1989, cited by Reid Cushman and Soren Holm, 'Death, Democracy, and Public Ethical Choice', *Bioethics*, vol. 4, 1990, p. 246.

4. Tony Bland and the Sanctity of Human Life

1 *Airedale N.H.S. Trust v. Bland (C.A)*, 19 February 1993, 2 Weekly Law Reports, p. 350. Page numbers given without further identifying details in subsequent footnotes to this chapter are to this report of the case.

2 The Multi-Society Task Force on PVS, 'Medical aspects of the persistent vegetative state', *New England Journal of Medicine*, vol. 330, 1994, pp. 1499–1508.

3 *Cruzan v. Director, Missouri Department of Health* (1990) 110 S. Ct., p. 2841. The passage from the judgement of Sandra Day O'Connor is quoted from the *New York Times*, 27 June 1990; for further details, see George Annas, 'Nancy Cruzan and the Right to Die', *New England Journal of Medicine*, vol. 323, 1990, p. 670; and Marcia Angell, 'Prisoners of Technology: the case of Nancy Cruzan', *New England Journal of Medicine*, vol. 322, 1990, pp. 1226–8.

4 Michael de Courcy Hinds, 'Uncharted Law for a Man Between Life and Death', *New York Times*, 6 June 1994.

5 p. 333; the passage was quoted again by Lord Goff of Chieveley in his judgment in the House of Lords, p. 364.

6 pp. 374, 385.

7 p. 331.

8 p. 387.

9 Sanford H. Kadish, 'Respect for Life and Regard for Rights in the Criminal Law', in Stephen F. Barker (ed.), *Respect for Life in Medicine, Philosophy, and the Law*, Johns Hopkins University Press, Baltimore, 1977, p. 72.

10 *Age*, 3 July 1986; cited in Helga Kuhse, *The Sanctity of Life Doctrine in Medicine: A Critique*, Oxford University Press, Oxford, 1987, p. 10.

11 pp. 330–1.

12 p. 339.

13 p. 348.

14 p. 355.

15 For the distinction between biological and biographical life, see James Rachels, *The End of Life*, Oxford University Press, Oxford, 1986.

16 p. 361.
17 p. 372.
18 p. 379.
19 p. 386.
20 p. 400.
21 p. 383.
22 p. 388.
23 p. 379.
24 R. v. Adams, 1959, quoted by Derek Morgan, 'Letting babies die legally', *Institute of Medical Ethics Bulletin*, May 1989, p. 13. See also Patrick Devlin, *Easing the Passing: The Trial of Dr John Bodkin Adams*, Faber & Faber, London, 1986, pp. 171, 209.
25 *Crimes Act* 1900 (New South Wales), s. 18 (1)(a).
26 Ralph Porzio, in *In the Matter of Karen Quinlan: The Complete Legal Briefs, Court Proceedings, and Decisions in the Superior Court of New Jersey*, University Publications of America, Frederick, Maryland, 1982, vol. 1, pp. 202–6; quoted by Gregory Pence, *Classic Cases in Medical Ethics*, 2nd ed., McGraw-Hill, New York, forthcoming 1995.
27 See 'In the Matter of Karen Quinlan, an Alleged Incompetent', in B. Steinbock (ed.), *Killing and Letting Die*, Prentice-Hall, Englewood Cliffs, New Jersey, 1980, p. 31.
28 *The Sanctity of Life Doctrine in Medicine: A Critique*, ch. 4.
29 In re Quinlan, 70 N.J. 10 355 A.2d (1976); see pp. 647, 665, 670.
30 p. 400.
31 pp. 346, 348.
32 p. 362.
33 *The Sanctity of Life Doctrine in Medicine: A Critique*, p. 11.
34 John Keown, 'Courting Euthanasia? Tony Bland and the Law Lords', *Ethics & Medicine*, vol. 9, no. 3, 1993, p. 37.
35 Luke Gormally, 'Definitions of Personhood: Implications for the Care of PVS Patients', *Ethics & Medicine*, vol. 9, no. 3, 1993, p. 48.
36 p. 368.
37 p. 384.
38 p. 369.
39 p. 399.
40 p. 387.
41 pp. 388–9.
42 pp. 379–80.

5. Uncertain Beginnings

1 Robert and Peggy Stinson, *The Long Dying of Baby Andrew*, Little, Brown, Boston, 1983, p. 46.
2 The issue was explicitly addressed in the Holy Office Decree *De craniotomia et abortu*, issued in 1889 (*Acta Sanctae Sedis*, 22–748), and was

frequently reiterated; see also the 1930 encyclical of Pius XI, *Casti Connubii*, and the account in John Connery, 'Abortion: Roman Catholic Perspectives' in Warren T. Reich (ed.), *Encyclopedia of Bioethics*, The Free Press, New York, 1978, vol. 1., pp. 12–13.

3   The first passage quoted is from Matilda Gage, in *Revolution,* vol. 1, no. 14, 9 April 1868, pp. 215–6; the second is from an article signed 'E.V.B.' in *Woman's Advocate* (Dayton, Ohio), vol. 1, no. 20, 8 April 1869, p. 16. I owe both references to James Mohr, *Abortion in America: The Origins and Evolution of National Policy, 1800–1900*, Oxford University Press, New York, 1978, p. 112. Other points in this and the preceding and following paragraphs are also drawn from Mohr's book.

4   *Abortion in America*, pp. 262–3.

5   World Medical Association, *Hippocratic Oath*, Geneva, 1948; reprinted in S. Gorovitz et al. (eds), *Moral Problems in Medicine*, Prentice-Hall, Englewood Cliffs, NJ, 1976, Appendix B.

6   H.L.A. Hart, 'Abortion Law Reform: The English Experience' in Robert L. Perkins (ed.), *Abortion: Pro and Con*, Schenkman, Cambridge, Mass., 1974, p. 190.

7   *Abortion in America*, p. 253. For details of the Finkbane Case see Gregory Pence, *Classic Cases in Medical Ethics*, 2nd ed., McGraw-Hill, New York, forthcoming 1995, ch. 6; and *New York Times*, 25 July, 2–7 August, 19–20 August, 1962.

8   *Classic Cases in Medical Ethics* 2nd ed., ch. 6, drawing on Michael Barone (ed.), *The Almanac of American Politics*, rev. ed., Macmillan, New York, 1990.

9   *Classic Cases in Medical Ethics*, 2nd ed., ch. 6, based on *Abortion and Women's Health*, The Alan Guttmacher Institute, New York, 1990, pp. 19–27.

10 *General Social Surveys, 1972–1987, Cumulative Codebook*, National Opinion Research Center, University of Chicago, Chicago, 1987; cited by D. C. Wertz and J. C. Fletcher (eds), *Ethics and Human Genetics: A Cross-Cultural Perspective*, Springer-Verlag, Berlin and New York, 1989, p. 446.

11 Norman Ford, *When Did I Begin?*, Cambridge University Press, Cambridge, 1988. See also P. Singer, H. Kuhse et al. (eds), *Embryo Experimentation*, Cambridge University Press, Cambridge, 1990, especially the essay by H. Kuhse and P. Singer, 'Individuals, Humans and Persons: the Question of Moral Status'.

12 See Helga Kuhse, 'A Report from Australia: When a Human Life has Not Yet Begun—According to the Law', *Bioethics*, vol. 2, 1988, pp. 334–42; Stephen Buckle, Karen Dawson and Peter Singer, 'The syngamy debate: when *precisely* does a human life begin?' in *Embryo Experimentation*, pp. 213–25.

13 For details of the case of the orphaned frozen embryos, see Peter Singer and Deane Wells, *Making Babies: The New Science and Ethics of Conception*, Charles Scribner's Sons, New York, 1985, pp. 86–7; the embryos were subsequently found not to be viable.

14 'World unites to fight soaring population', *New Scientist*, 23 April 1994, p. 5.

15 John T. Noonan, 'An Almost Absolute Value in History' in John T. Noonan (ed.), *The Morality of Abortion*, Cambridge, Mass., 1970, pp.56–7.

16 J. Grudzinskas and A. Nysenbaum, 'Failure of human pregnancy after implantation', *Annals of the New York Academy of Sciences*, vol. 442, 1985, pp. 39–44; C. Roberts and C. Lowe, 'Where have all the conceptions gone?', *Lancet*, 1975, vol. 1, pp. 498–9, J. Muller et al., 'Fetal loss after implantation', *Lancet*, 1980, vol. 2, pp. 554–6. For further discussion see Peter Singer and Karen Dawson, 'IVF Technology and the Argument from Potential', *Philosophy and Public Affairs*, 1988, vol. 17, pp. 87–104.

17 Marilee C. Allen, et al., 'The Limit of Viability—Neonatal Outcome of Infants Born at 22 to 25 weeks' Gestation', *New England Journal of Medicine*, vol. 329, 1993, pp. 1597–1601.

18 *Akron v. Akron Center for Reproductive Health, Inc.*, 1983, 103 Supreme Court 2481.

19 My previous discussion is in Peter Singer and Deane Wells, *The Reproduction Revolution*, Oxford University Press, Oxford, 1984, pp. 134–6; see also Leslie Cannold, 'Women's Response to Ectogenesis and the Relevance of Severance Abortion Theory', a thesis for the degree of Master of Bioethics at the Centre for Human Bioethics, Monash University.

20 Hans-Martin Sass, 'The Moral Significance of Brain-Life Criteria', in F. K. Beller and R. F. Weir (eds), *The Beginning of Human Life*, Kluwer Academic Publishers, Dordrecht, 1994, pp. 57–70. The idea behind Sass's 'brain life' proposal has been around for a long time: see, for example, Bernard Häring, *Medical Ethics*, Fides, Notre Dame, Ind., 1973, pp. 81–5, and the other references that Sass gives on pp. 61 and 63.

21 *The Beginning of Human Life*, p. 62; but J. C. Larroche has reported neuronal activity even earlier, at forty-nine days: 'The marginal layer in the neocortex of a 7-week-old human embryo', *Anatomical Embryology*, vol. 162, 1981, pp. 301–12, cited by Rodrigo Kuljis, 'Development of the Human Brain: The Emergence of the Neural Substrate for Pain Perception and Conscious Experience', in *The Beginning of Human Life*, p. 54.

22 See D. G. Jones, 'Brain birth and personal identity', *Journal of Medical Ethics*, vol. 15, 1989, pp. 173–8, 185; cited by Sass in *The Beginning of Human Life*, p. 63.

6. Making Quality of Life Judgments

1 Mark Selikowitz, *Down Syndrome: The Facts*, Oxford University Press, Oxford, 1990, p. 123.

2 The information in this paragraph about Vanderbilt University Hospital and the New Mexico paediatrician comes from the American Academy of Pediatrics' submission to the court hearing mentioned in the next paragraph; the remaining details are from *Newsday* (Long Island, NY), 13 November 1983; quoted by Gregory Pence, *Classic Cases in Medical Ethics*, 2nd ed., McGraw-Hill, New York, forthcoming 1995.

3 Ronald Reagan, 'Abortion and the Conscience of the Nation', *Human Life Review*, vol. 9, no. 2, Spring 1983, pp. 13–14.

4 *Otis Bowen v. American Hospital Association et al.*, US Supreme Court. 106 S. Ct. 2101. No. 84-15-9, 9 June 1986.

5 Loretta M. Kopelman, Thomas G. Irons and Arthur E. Kopelman, 'Neonatologists Judge the "Baby Doe" Regulations', *New England Journal of Medicine*, vol. 318, no. 11, 17 March 1988, pp. 677–83.

6 Eric Harrison and Tracy Shryer, 'Weeping Father Pulls Gun, Stops Infant's Life Support', *Los Angeles Times*, 27 April 1989; Matt O'Connor and Shawn Pogatchnik; 'Jury won't indict dad in boy's death', *Chicago Tribune,* 19 May 1989; Anon, 'Man who let son die is cleared by coroner', *New York Times*, 22 May 1989.

7 For the surveys of paediatricians, see A. Shaw et al., 'Ethical Issues in Pediatric Surgery: A National Survey of Pediatricians and Pediatric Surgeons', *Pediatrics*, vol. 60, 1977, pp. 588–99; 'Treating the Defective Newborn', *Hastings Center Report*, vol. 6, no. 2, April 1976; and David Todres et al., 'Pediatricians' Attitudes Affecting Decision-Making in Defective Newborns', *Pediatrics*, vol. 60, 1977, pp. 197–201. The Gallup poll was reported in the *Chicago Sun-Times*, 2 June 1983, and is quoted from Jeff Lyon, *Playing God in the Nursery*, Norton, New York, 1985, p. 78.

8 Helga Kuhse, Peter Singer and Cora Singer, 'The Treatment of Newborn Infants with Major Handicaps: A Survey of Obstetricians and Paediatricians in Victoria', *Medical Journal of Australia*, vol. 2, 17 September 1983, pp. 274–8.

9 See Z. Szawarski and A. Tulczynski, 'The treatment of defective newborns—a survey of paediatricians in Warsaw', *Journal of Medical Ethics*, vol. 14, 1988, pp. 11–17 and Z. Szawarski, 'A Report from Poland: Treatment and Non-Treatment of Defective Newborns', *Bioethics*, vol. 4, 1990, pp. 143–53; Barbara Bay and Michael Burgess, 'A survey of Calgary paediatricians attitudes regarding the treatment of defective newborns', *Bioethics,* vol. 5, 1991, pp. 139–49; Carole Outterson, 'Newborn Infants with Severe Defects: A Survey of Paediatric Attitudes and Practices in the UK', *Bioethics* , vol. 7, 1993, pp. 420–35.

10 For details of the trial, see the unpublished transcript of the official court reporters, Marten, Meredith & Co. Ltd, 36/8 Whitefriars St., London. Arthur's acquittal was reported in the *Times*, 6 November 1981; the opinion poll results were published in the same paper on 10 November. For a fuller discussion see Helga Kuhse, 'A Modern Myth. That Letting Die is not the Intentional Causation of Death: Some Reflections on the Trial and Acquittal of Dr Leonard Arthur', *Journal of Applied Philosophy*, vol. 1, 1984, pp. 21–38.

11 *In Re B* (1981) 1 Weekly Law Reports, p. 1245; quoted by Derek Morgan, 'Letting babies die legally', *Institute of Medical Ethics Bulletin*, May 1989, p. 15.

12 Derek Morgan, *Institute of Medical Ethics Bulletin*, pp. 14–15.

13 *Times*, 20 October 1990; *Lancet*, vol. 336, 1990, p. 1121; *Re J (a minor)*, 1990, 3 *All England Rights*, 1990, 930.

14 *Record of Investigation into Death*, Case No 3149/89, 21 October 1991, state coroner's office, South Melbourne; quoted from Helga Kuhse, 'Quality of Life and the Death of "Baby M"', *Bioethics*, vol. 6, 1992, p. 235.

15 'Quality of Life and the Death of "Baby M"', p. 236.

16 R.B. Zachary, 'Life with Spina Bifida', *British Medical Journal*, 3 December 1977, p. 1461.

17 These examples are drawn from Helga Kuhse and Peter Singer, *Should the Baby Live?*, Oxford University Press, Oxford, 1985, ch. 5, where more detailed references can be found.

7. Asking for Death

1 'Dr Kevorkian's Legal Victory', editorial, *New York Times*, 16 December 1993.

2 *Age*, Melbourne, 4 May 1994; *New York Times*, 3 May 1994. For earlier accounts, see *New York Times*, 22 February 1993; 5 August 1993; 18 August 1993; 23 October 1993; 29 October 1993; 11 November 1993; 14, 15, 16 December 1993; Associated Press reports 23 April 1994, 2 May 1994; and see also Gregory Pence, *Classic Cases in Medical Ethics*, 2nd ed., McGraw-Hill, New York, forthcoming 1995, to which I owe several of these references.

3 'Death and Dignity: A Case of Individualized Decision Making', *New England Journal of Medicine*, vol. 324, 1991, pp. 691–4.

4 Timothy Quill, 'Death and Dignity: A Case of Individualized Decision Making'; *New York Times*, 22 July 1991.

5 *Age*, 14 September 1993; for a fuller account see Helga Kuhse (ed.), *Willing to Listen, Wanting to Die*, Penguin, Ringwood, 1994.

6 *Sue Rodriguez v. The Attorney General of Canada and the Attorney General of British Columbia, Canada Supreme Court Reports*, Part 4, 1993, vol. 3, pp. 519–632.

7 *Age*, 16 February 1994; *Times-Colonist* (British Columbia), 18 February 1994.

8   *Sunday Times*, 20 September 1992, p. 26; *British Medical Journal*, vol.
    305, 26 September 1992, p. 731; *Lancet*, vol. 340, 26 September 1992,
    pp. 757–8, 782–3; *Bulletin of Medical Ethics*, September 1992, pp. 3–4;
    Guardian Weekly, 29 November 1992, p. 25.
9   This account summarises that given by Pieter Admiraal, 'Listening and
    Helping to Die: The Dutch Way', in *Willing to Listen, Wanting to Die.*
10 P. J. van der Maas, J. J. M. van Delden, L. Pijnenborg, *Euthanasia and
    other Medical Decisions Concerning the End of Life*, Health Policy
    Monographs, vol. 2, Elsevier, Amsterdam, 1992.
11 See, for example, Sue Harper, 'Terminal Care in Nursing Homes', in
    Willing to Listen, Wanting to Die.
12 Derek Humphry and Ann Wickett, *The Right to Die: Understanding
    Euthanasia*, Harper & Row, New York, 1988, pp. 180–82.
13 See J.K.M. Gevers, 'Legal Developments Concerning Active Euthanasia
    on Request in The Netherlands', *Bioethics* , vol. 1, 1987, pp. 156–62.
14 'Legal Developments Concerning Active Euthanasia on Request in
    The Netherlands', p. 158.
15 Ministry of Justice, The Hague, *News Release*, November 1993; *Facts on
    File World News Digest*, 25 February 1993; *Press Association Newsfile*,
    30 November 1993.
16 Derek Humphry, *Final Exit*, Hemlock Society, Oregon, 1991; Penguin,
    Ringwood, 1991. See *Time*, 19 August 1991, p. 55, for a discussion of
    the book's success and the absence of attempts to suppress it.
17 'Judge rules against assisted-suicide law', *Oregonian*, 4 May 1994.
18 Derek Humphry, *Lawful Exit: The Limits of Freedom for Help in Dying*,
    The Norris Lane Press, Junction City, Oregon, 1993, pp. 98, 103.
19 *Sue Rodriguez v. The Attorney General of Canada and the Attorney General
    of British Columbia*, Canada Supreme Court Reports, Part 4, 1993, vol. 3,
    p. 603.
20 In addition to the government-instigated study carried out by P.J. van
    der Maas and colleagues, I shall also draw for additional information on
    a study by G. van der Wal, 'Euthanasie en hulp bij zelfodling door
    huisartsen' [Euthanasia and assisted suicide performed by general
    practitioner], Rotterdam 1992; of which some findings are given in
    English in *Euthanasia in the Netherlands: The State of the Debate*, Royal
    Dutch Medical Association, Utrecht, February 1993. In what follows
    I have been much assisted by Helga Kuhse, 'Voluntary Euthanasia and
    Public Policy: Some Important Distinctions and What We Can Learn
    From the Netherlands Experience', a paper presented at a conference
    organised by the Centre for Human Bioethics, Monash University,
    15 November 1993. See also Margaret Battin, 'Voluntary Euthanasia
    and the Risks of Abuse: Can We Learn Anything from the
    Netherlands?', *Law, Medicine and Health Care*, vol. 20, nos 1 and 2,
    Spring–Summer 1992, pp. 133–43.

21 On this topic, in addition to *Euthanasia and Other Medical Decisions Concerning the End of Life*, pp. 66–7, 181–2, see J. J .M van Delden, Loes Pijnenborg and Paul J. van der Maas, 'The Remmelink Study: Two Years Later', *Hastings Center Report*, vol. 23, no. 6, November–December 1993, p. 24. See also Loes Pijnenborg et al., 'Life-Terminating Acts without Explicit Request of the Patient', *Lancet*, vol. 341, 1993, pp. 1196–9.

22 'The Remmelink Study: Two Years Later', p. 26.

23 *Times*, 23 September 1992.

24 The studies are, in the order cited: Helga Kuhse and Peter Singer, 'Doctors' practices and attitudes regarding voluntary euthanasia', *Medical Journal of Australia*, vol. 148, 1988, pp. 623–7; Peter Baume and Emma O'Malley, 'Euthanasia: attitudes and practices of medical practitioners', *Medical Journal of Australia*, vol. 161, 18 July 1994, pp. 137–64; Helga Kuhse and Peter Singer, 'Voluntary euthanasia and the nurse: an Australian survey', *International Journal of Nursing Studies*, vol. 30, no. 4, 1993, pp. 311–22.

25 *Survey of California Physicians Regarding Voluntary Euthanasia for the Terminally Ill*, National Hemlock Society, Los Angeles, 1988.

26 N. K. Brown and D. J. Thompson, 'Nontreatment of fever in extended-care facilities', *New England Journal of Medicine*, vol. 300, 1979, pp. 1246–50; cited in *Euthanasia and Other Medical Decisions Concerning the End of Life*, p. 184.

27 'The Remmelink Study: Two Years Later', p. 27.

28 Margaret Pabst Battin, *The Least Worst Death*, Oxford University Press, New York, 1994, p. 136, based on information provided by Dr Else Boorst-Eilers.

29 'The Remmelink Study: Two Years Later', p. 24.

30 *Declaration on Euthanasia*, World Medical Association, 1987; see *Los Angeles Times*, 12 October 1987.

8. Beyond the Discontinuous Mind

1 John Locke's definition of a person is to be found in his *Essay on Human Understanding*, first published 1690, various editions, bk. II, ch. 9, par. 29.

2 The description comes from Frans de Waal's fascinating book, *Chimpanzee Politics*, Jonathan Cape, London, 1982. I made only two changes: I gave human names to the chimpanzees involved in the fight, and I added an account of the experiment involving the two series of boxes, which was actually carried out quite separately by J. Döhl and B. Rensch, and is described in greater detail by Jane Goodall in *The Chimpanzees of Gombe*, Harvard University Press/Belknap Press, Cambridge, Mass., 1986, p. 31.

3 *New York Times*, 30 June 1992 and 6 September 1992.

4 Kathy Eyre, 'Animal-Human Transplants', Associated Press, 5 September 1988, cited in Dale Peterson and Jane Goodall, *Visions of Caliban*, Houghton Mifflin, Boston, 1993, p. 227.

5 For discussion of the Baby Fae case, see the six commentaries collected under the heading 'The Subject is Baby Fae', *Hastings Center Report*, vol. 15, no. 1, February 1985, pp. 8–13.

6 Nick Taylor, 'Heart to heart: Can a chimp transplant save a human life?' *New York Magazine*, 13 July 1987, pp. 44–8; cited in Dale Peterson and Jane Goodall, *Visions of Caliban*, Houghton Mifflin, Boston, 1993, p. 228.

7 Genesis 1: 24–28, Authorised Version.

8 Augustine, *The Catholic and the Manichaean Ways of Life*, tr. D.A. Gallagher and I.J. Gallagher, The Catholic University Press, Boston, 1966, p. 102. For the incident of the pigs, see Mark, 5:1–13, and for that of the fig tree, Mark, 11:12–21.

9 Aristotle, tr. John Warrington, *Politics*, J.M. Dent & Sons, London, 1959, p. 6.

10 E.S. Turner, *All Heaven in a Rage*, Michael Joseph, London, 1964, p. 163.

11 Marsilio Ficino, *Theologica Platonica*, first published 1474, various editions, III, 2 and XVI, 3.

12 René Descartes, *Discourse on Method*, first published 1637, various editions, vol. 5; see also his letter to Henry More, 5 February 1649.

13 The quotations come from Immanuel Kant, *Lectures on Ethics*, tr. L. Infield, Harper Torchbooks, New York, 1963, pp. 239–40. On the basis for respect for human beings as ends in themselves, see Kant's *The Foundations of the Metaphysics of Morals*, first published 1785, various editions, in *The Philosophy of Immanuel Kant*, vol. 4, trans. L. W. Beck, University of Chicago Press, Chicago, 1949, p. 87.

14 Charles Darwin, *Notebooks, 1836–1844*, ed. Paul H. Barrett et al., Cornell University Press, Ithaca, 1987, p. 300. James Rachels takes this passage as the theme of his *Created from Animals: The Moral Implications of Darwinism*, Oxford University Press, Oxford, 1990, which is an illuminating exploration of the topic dealt with in the following paragraphs.

15 Letter from Linnaeus to J. G. Gmelin, 1788, cited by George Seldes, *The Great Thoughts*, Ballantine, New York, 1985; quoted from Carl Sagan and Ann Druyan, *Shadows of Forgotten Ancestors*, Random House, New York, 1992, p. 274.

16 Lord J. B. Monboddo, *Of the Origin and Progress of Language*, Kincaid & Creech, Edinburgh, 1773–92. I owe the reference to Stephen Clark, 'Apes and the Idea of Kindred', in Paola Cavalieri and Peter Singer (eds), *The Great Ape Project: Equality Beyond Humanity*, Fourth Estate,

London, 1993, pp. 113–4.

17 Charles Darwin, *The Descent of Man*, John Murray, London, 1871, p. 1.

18 T. H. Huxley, *Man's Place in Nature*, first published 1863, University of Michigan Press, Ann Arbor, 1959, pp. 129–30, 132.

19 First published in *Science*, vol. 155, 1967, pp. 1203–7, and often reprinted, for example in Garrett de Bell (ed.), *The Environmental Handbook*, Ballantine/Friends of the Earth, New York, 1970, pp. 12–26. The passages quoted are from pp. 20 and 24 of this reprinting.

20 See Richard Ryder, *Animal Revolution: Changing Attitudes Towards Speciesism*, Blackwell, Oxford, 1989.

21 Colin McGinn, 'Eating Animals is Wrong', *London Review of Books*, 24 January 1991, p. 14.

22 See W. C. McGrew, *Chimpanzee Material Culture*, Cambridge University Press, Cambridge, 1992; Yukimaru Sugiyama, 'Tool use by wild chimpanzees', *Nature,* vol. 367, 27 January 1994, p. 327; *New Scientist*, 5 March 1994.

23 See Roger Fouts and Deborah Fouts, 'Chimpanzees' Use of Sign Language'; H. Lyn White Miles, 'Language and the Orang-utan: The Old "Person" of the Forest'; and Francine Patterson and Wendy Gordon, 'The Case for the Personhood of Gorillas', all in *The Great Ape Project*.

24 See the selection of readings in Peter Singer (ed.), *Ethics*, Oxford University Press, Oxford, 1994, Part IB.

25 Jared Diamond, *The Rise and Fall of the Third Chimpanzee*, Harper-Collins, New York, 1991; the relevant passage is reprinted in *The Great Ape Project*, pp. 88–101. The preceding paragraph draws on Diamond's account.

26 R.I.M. Dunbar, 'What's in a Classification?' in *The Great Ape Project*, pp. 111–12; see also Stephen Clark, 'Apes and the Idea of Kindred', in the same volume, pp. 113–25.

27 Richard Dawkins, 'Gaps in the Mind', in *The Great Ape Project*, p. 82.

28 Richard H. Tuttle, 'A Trans-Specific Agenda', *Science*, vol. 264, 22 April 1994, pp. 602–3.

29 A. Trendelenburg, 'A Contribution to the History of the Word Person', *Monist*, vol. 20, 1910, pp. 336–63. I owe this reference to Paola Cavalieri.

30 Francine Patterson and Wendy Gordon, 'The Case for the Personhood of Gorillas', in *The Great Ape Project*, pp. 58–9.

31 Jane Goodall, 'Chimpanzees—Bridging the Gap' in *The Great Ape Project*, pp. 13–4.

9. In Place of the Old Ethic

1 The classic account of the shift from the Ptolemaic to Copernican models is Thomas Kuhn, *The Structure of Scientific Revolutions*, University

of Chicago Press, Chicago, 1972.

2 Dr. L. Haas, from a letter in the *Lancet*, 2 November 1968; quoted from S. Gorovitz (ed.), *Moral Problems in Medicine*, Prentice-Hall, Englewood Cliffs, NJ, 1976, p. 351.

3 Clough's 'The Latest Decalogue' can be found in Helen Gardner (ed.), *The New Oxford Book of English Verse*, Oxford University Press, Oxford, 1978.

4 Thomas Aquinas, *Summa Theologica*, II, ii, Question 64, Article 5.

5 John Stuart Mill, *On Liberty*, J.M. Dent & Sons, London, 1960, pp. 72–3.

6 This position is associated with Michael Tooley's influential article, 'Abortion and Infanticide', *Philosophy and Public Affairs*, vol. 2, 1972, pp. 37–65; for a slightly different argument to the same conclusion, see also Michael Tooley, *Abortion and Infanticide*, Oxford University Press, Oxford, 1983. Similar views have been defended by several philosophers and bioethicists, among them H. Tristram Engelhardt, Jr, *The Foundations of Bioethics*, Oxford University Press, New York, 1986; R. G. Frey, *Rights, Killing and Suffering*, Blackwell, Oxford, 1983; Jonathan Glover, *Causing Death and Saving Lives*, Penguin, Harmondsworth, 1977; John Harris, *The Value of Life*, Routledge and Kegan Paul, London, 1985; Helga Kuhse, *The Sanctity of Life Doctrine in Medicine: A Critique*, Oxford University Press, Oxford, 1987; James Rachels, *The End of Life*, Oxford University Press, Oxford, 1986 and *Created from Animals*, Oxford University Press, Oxford, 1991. See also my own *Practical Ethics*, Cambridge University Press, Cambridge, 1979, 2nd ed., 1993.

7 For Augustine, see *Against Faustus*, bk 15. ch. 7; for Luther, 'Der Grosse Catechismus, 1529, 'On the Sixth Commandment' and for Calvin, *Commentaries on the First Book of Moses Called Genesis*, vol. 2, ch. 38, v. 8. I owe these references and other information in this paragraph to John T. Noonan, 'Contraception', in Warren T. Reich (ed.), *Encyclopedia of Bioethics*, The Free Press, New York, 1978, vol. I, pp. 204–16. The Supreme Court case referred to is *Griswold v. Connecticut*, 1965.

8 Jodi L. Jacobson, 'Holding Back the Sea' in Lester Brown et al., *State of the World, 1990: The Worldwatch Institute Report on Progress Towards a Sustainable Economy*, Worldwatch Institute, Washington, DC, 1990.

9 Peter Singer, 'Sanctity of Life or Quality of Life', *Pediatrics*, vol. 72, July 1983, pp.128–9; three protest letters were published with my reply in vol. 73, February 1984, pp. 259–63, but the remainder of the letters are unpublished.

10 Vorstand der Bundesvereinigung Lebenshilfe für geistig Behinderte, *Ethische Grundaussagen*, Marburg, 1990 (my trans.). For an account of

the events in Germany and their sequel up to 1991, see Peter Singer, 'On being silenced in Germany', *New York Review of Books*, 15 August 1991, reprinted in Peter Singer, *Practical Ethics*, pp. 337–59.

11 Albert Schweitzer's ethic of reverence for life *may* be making this wider claim; the contemporary American philosopher Paul Taylor certainly does make it. I discuss and reject these views in my *Practical Ethics*, pp. 276–84.

12 Henry Longfellow, *The Song of Hiawatha*, Introduction, 91; quoted from *The Oxford English Dictionary*, 2nd ed., Clarendon Press, Oxford, 1989, vol. VII, p. 474.

13 For an argument that it could be as late as 32 weeks, see Susan Taiwa, 'When is the capacity for sentience acquired during human fetal development?', *Journal of Maternal-Fetal Medicine*, vol. 1, 1992, pp. 153–65.

14 For a full defence of this position, see Helga Kuhse and Peter Singer, *Should the Baby Live?*, Oxford University Press, Oxford, 1985.

15 For sources and further details, see *Should the Baby Live?*, ch. 5.

16 Robert and Peggy Stinson, *The Long Dying of Baby Andrew*, Little, Brown, Boston, 1983, pp. 153, 266–7.

17 Here I have been influenced by Norbert Hoerster, 'Kindestötung und das Lebensrecht von Personen', *Analyse & Kritik,* vol. 12, 1990, pp. 226–44.

18 Thomas Hobbes, *Leviathan*, ch. 13.

SELECT BIBLIOGRAPHY

BOOKS

Aristotle, *Politics*, J.M. Dent & Sons, London, 1959.

Augustine, *The Catholic and the Manichaean Ways of Life*, tr. D. A. Gallagher and I. J. Gallagher, The Catholic University Press, Boston, 1966.

Margaret Pabst Battin, *The Least Worst Death*, Oxford University Press, New York, 1994.

F. K. Beller and R. F. Weir (eds), *The Beginning of Human Life*, Kluwer Academic Publishers, Dordrecht, 1994.

Paola Cavalieri and Peter Singer (eds), *The Great Ape Project: Equality Beyond Humanity*, Fourth Estate, London, and St Martin's Press, New York, 1993.

Charles Darwin, *The Descent of Man*, London, 1871.

Charles Darwin, *Notebooks, 1836–1844*, ed. Paul H. Barrett et al., Cornell University Press, Ithaca, 1987.

Patrick Devlin, *Easing the Passing: The Trial of Dr John Bodkin Adams*, Faber & Faber, London, 1986.

Frans de Waal, *Chimpanzee Politics*, Jonathan Cape, London, 1982.

Jared Diamond, *The Rise and Fall of the Third Chimpanzee*, HarperCollins, New York, 1991.

H. Tristram Engelhardt, Jr, *The Foundations of Bioethics*, New York, Oxford University Press, 1986.

Norman Ford, *When Did I Begin?*, Cambridge University Press, Cambridge, 1988.

R. G. Frey, *Rights, Killing and Suffering*, Blackwell, Oxford, 1983.

Jonathan Glover, *Causing Death and Saving Lives*, Penguin, Harmondsworth, 1977.

Jane Goodall, *The Chimpanzees of Gombe*, Harvard University Press/ Belknap Press, Cambridge, Mass., 1986.

Germain Grisez and Joseph Boyle, *Life and Death with Liberty and Justice: A Contribution to the Euthanasia Debate*, University of Notre Dame Press, Notre Dame, Indiana, 1979.

John Harris, *The Value of Life*, Routledge and Kegan Paul, London, 1985.

Derek Humphry, *Final Exit*, Hemlock Society, Oregon, 1991; Australian edition, Penguin, Ringwood, Victoria, 1991.

Derek Humphry, *Lawful Exit: The Limits of Freedom for Help in Dying*, The Norris Lane Press, Junction City, Oregon, 1993.

Derek Humphry and Ann Wickett, *The Right to Die: Understanding Euthanasia*, Harper & Row, New York, 1988.

Immanuel Kant, *The Foundations of the Metaphysics of Morals*, in *The Philosophy of Immanuel Kant*, vol. 4, trans. L. W. Beck, University of Chicago Press, Chicago, 1949.

Immanuel Kant, *Lectures on Ethics*, tr. L. Infield, Harper Torchbooks, New York, 1963.

Thomas Kuhn, *The Structure of Scientific Revolutions*, University of Chicago Press, Chicago, 1972.

Helga Kuhse, *The Sanctity of Life Doctrine in Medicine—A Critique*, Oxford University Press, Oxford, 1987.

Helga Kuhse (ed.), *Willing to Listen, Wanting to Die*, Penguin, Australia, 1994.

Helga Kuhse and Peter Singer, *Should the Baby Live?*, Oxford University Press, Oxford, 1985.

Jeff Lyon, *Playing God in the Nursery*, Norton, New York, 1985.

W.C. McGrew, *Chimpanzee Material Culture*, Cambridge University Press, Cambridge, 1992.

Jeff McMahan, *Killing at the Margins of Life*, Oxford University Press, New York, forthcoming 1995.

John Stuart Mill, *On Liberty*, J.M. Dent & Sons, London, 1960.

James Mohr, *Abortion in America: The Origins and Evolution of National Policy, 1800–1900*, Oxford University Press, New York, 1978.

Gregory Pence, *Classic Cases in Medical Ethics*, 2nd ed., McGraw-Hill, New York, forthcoming 1995.

Robert L. Perkins (ed.), Abortion: *Pro and Con*, Schenkmar, Cambridge, Mass., 1974.

Dale Peterson and Jane Goodall, *Visions of Caliban*, Houghton Mifflin, Boston, 1993.

President's Commission for the Study of Ethical Problems in Medicine, *Defining Death: A Report on the Medical, Legal and Ethical Issues in the Determination of Death*, US Government Printing Office, Washington, DC, 1981.

James Rachels, *Created from Animals: The Moral Implications of Darwinism*, Oxford University Press, Oxford, 1990.

James Rachels, *The End of Life*, Oxford University Press, Oxford, 1986.

Warren T. Reich (ed.), *Encyclopaedia of Bioethics*, The Free Press, New York, 1978.

David Rothman, *Strangers at the Bedside*, Basic Books, New York, 1991.

Richard Ryder, *Animal Revolution: Changing Attitudes Towards Speciesism*, Blackwell, Oxford, 1989.

Carl Sagan and Ann Druyan, *Shadows of Forgotten Ancestors*, Random House, New York, 1992.

Kathy Sanders and Bette Moore (eds), *Anencephalics, Infants and Brain Death Treatment Options and the Issue of Organ Donation*, Law Reform Commission of Victoria, Melbourne, 1991.

Mark Selikowitz, *Down Syndrome: The Facts*, Oxford University Press, Oxford, 1990.

Peter Singer (ed.), *Ethics*, Oxford University Press, Oxford, 1994.

Peter Singer, *Practical Ethics*, Cambridge University Press, Cambridge, 2nd ed., 1993.

Peter Singer, Helga Kuhse et al. (eds), *Embryo Experimentation*, Cambridge University Press, Cambridge, 1990.

Peter Singer and Deane Wells, *The Reproduction Revolution*, Oxford University Press, Oxford, 1984; American edition, *Making Babies*, Charles Scribner & Sons, New York, 1985.

Bonnie Steinbock (ed.), *Killing and Letting Die*, Prentice-Hall, Englewood Cliffs, New Jersey, 1980.

Robert and Peggy Stinson, *The Long Dying of Baby Andrew*, Little, Brown, Boston, 1983.

Michael Tooley, *Abortion and Infanticide,* Oxford University Press, Oxford, 1983.

E. S. Turner, *All Heaven in a Rage*, Michael Joseph, London, 1964.

P. J. van der Maas, J. J. M. van Delden, L. Pijnenborg, *Euthanasia and other Medical Decisions Concerning the End of Life*, Health Policy Monographs vol. 2, Elsevier, Amsterdam, 1992.

Robert Veatch, *Death, Dying and the Biological Revolution*, Yale University Press, New Haven, 1976.

D. C. Wertz and J. C. Fletcher (eds), *Ethics and Human Genetics: A Cross-Cultural Perspective*, Springer-Verlag, Berlin and New York, 1989.

ARTICLES

Pieter Admiraal, 'Listening and Helping to Die: The Dutch Way', in Helga Kuhse (ed.), *Willing to Listen, Wanting to Die*.

Marcia Angell, 'Prisoners of Technology: the case of Nancy Cruzan', *New England Journal of Medicine*, vol. 322, 1990, pp. 1226–8.

Anon, 'Crying Father Holds Doctors Off So Child in a Coma Can Die', *New York Times*, 27 April 1989.

George Annas, 'Nancy Cruzan and the Right to Die', *New England Journal of Medicine*, vol. 323, no. 10, 6 September 1990.

Christoph Anstötz, 'Should a Brain-Dead Pregnant Woman Carry Her Child to Full Term? The Case of the "Erlangen Baby"', *Bioethics*, vol. 7, 1993, pp. 340–50.

Margaret Battin, 'Voluntary Euthanasia and the Risks of Abuse: Can We Learn Anything from the Netherlands?', *Law, Medicine and Health Care*, vol. 20, nos 1–2, Spring–Summer 1992, pp. 133–43.

Barbara Bay and Michael Burgess, 'A survey of Calgary paediatricians attitudes regarding the treatment of defective newborns', *Bioethics*, vol. 5, 1991, pp. 139–49.

Henry Beecher, 'The New Definition of Death, Some Opposing Viewpoints', *International Journal of Clinical Pharmacology*, vol. 5, 1971, pp. 120–1.

J. L. Bernat, C. M. Culver, B. Gert, 'On the definition and criterion of death', *Annals of Internal Medicine*, vol. 94, 1981, pp. 389–94.

N. K. Brown and D. J. Thompson, 'Nontreatment of fever in extended-care facilities', *New England Journal of Medicine*, vol. 300, 1979, pp. 1246–50.

Stephen Buckle, Karen Dawson and Peter Singer, 'The syngamy debate: when *precisely* does a human life begin?' in Peter Singer, Helga Kuhse et al., *Embryo Experimentation*.

Neil Campbell, 'Some anatomy and physiology', in K. Sanders and B. Moore (eds), *Anencephalics, Infants and Brain Death Treatment Options and the Issue of Organ Donation*.

Stephen Clark, 'Apes and the Idea of Kindred', in Paola Cavalieri and Peter Singer, *The Great Ape Project: Equality Beyond Humanity*.

Don Colburn, 'AMA Ethics Panel Revises Rules on Withholding Food; In Irreversible Comas, Water and Nutrition May Be Stopped', *Washington Post*, 2 April 1986.

John Connery, 'Abortion: Roman Catholic Perspectives' in Warren T. Reich (ed.), *Encyclopedia of Bioethics*, The Free Press, New York, 1978, vol. 1, pp. 12–13.

Reid Cushman and Soren Holm, 'Death, Democracy, and Public Ethical Choice', *Bioethics*, vol. 4, 1990, pp. 237–252.

Richard Dawkins, 'Gaps in the Mind', in Paola Cavalieri and Peter Singer (eds), *The Great Ape Project: Equality Beyond Humanity*.

R.I.M. Dunbar, 'What's in a Classification?' in Paola Cavalieri and Peter Singer (eds), *The Great Ape Project: Equality Beyond Humanity*.

Roger Fouts and Deborah Fouts, 'Chimpanzees' Use of Sign Language' in Paola Cavalieri and Peter Singer (eds), *The Great Ape Project: Equality Beyond Humanity*.

Diane Gianelli, 'Doctors Argue Futility of Treating Anencephalic Baby', *American Medical News*, vol. 37, no. 11, 21 March 1994, p. 5.

J. K. M. Gevers, 'Legal Developments Concerning Active Euthanasia on Request in The Netherlands', *Bioethics*, vol. 1, 1987, pp. 156–62.

Jane Goodall, 'Chimpanzees—Bridging the Gap' in Paola Cavalieri and Peter Singer (eds), *The Great Ape Project: Equality Beyond Humanity*.

Luke Gormally, 'Definitions of Personhood: Implications for the Care of PVS Patients', *Ethics & Medicine*, vol. 9, no. 3, 1993.

Linda Greenhouse, 'Court Order to Treat Baby With Partial Brain Prompts Debate on Costs and Ethics', *New York Times*, 20 February 1994.

Amir Halevy and Baruch Brody, 'Brain Death: Reconciling Definitions, Criteria and Tests', *Annals of Internal Medicine*, vol. 119, no. 6, 1993, pp. 519–25.

Sue Harper, 'Terminal Care in Nursing Homes', in Helga Kuhse, *Willing to Listen, Wanting to Die*.

Eric Harrison and Tracy Shryer, 'Weeping Father Pulls Gun, Stops Infant's Life Support', *Los Angeles Times*, 27 April 1989.

H. L. A. Hart, 'Abortion Law Reform: The English Experience' in Robert L. Perkins (ed.), *Abortion: Pro and Con*, Schenkman, Cambridge, Mass., 1974.

Michael de Courcy Hinds, 'Uncharted Law for a Man Between Life and Death', *New York Times*, 6 June 1994.

Norbert Hoerster, 'Kindestötung und das Lebensrecht von Personen', *Analyse & Kritik*, vol. 12, 1990, pp. 226–44.

D. G. Jones, 'Brain birth and personal identity', *Journal of Medical Ethics*, vol. 15, 1989, pp. 173–8, 185.

Sanford H. Kadish, 'Respect for Life and Regard for Rights in the Criminal Law', in Stephen F. Barker (ed.), *Respect for Life in Medicine, Philosophy, and the Law*, Johns Hopkins University Press, Baltimore, 1977.

John Keown, 'Courting Euthanasia? Tony Bland and the Law Lords', *Ethics & Medicine*, vol. 9, no. 3, 1993.

Loretta M. Kopelman, Thomas G. Irons and Arthur E. Kopelman, 'Neonatologists Judge the "Baby Doe" Regulations', *New England Journal of Medicine*, vol. 318, no. 11, 17 March 1988, pp. 677–83.

Helga Kuhse, 'A Modern Myth. That Letting Die is not the Intentional Causation of Death: Some Reflections on the Trial and Acquittal of Dr Leonard Arthur', *Journal of Applied Philosophy*, vol. 1, 1984, pp. 21–38.

Helga Kuhse, 'Quality of Life and the death of "Baby M"', *Bioethics*, vol. 6, 1992, pp. 233–50.

Helga Kuhse, 'Voluntary Euthanasia and Public Policy: Some Important Distinctions and What We Can Learn From the Netherlands Experience', a paper presented at a conference organised by the Centre for Human Bioethics, Monash University, 15 November 1993.

Helga Kuhse, 'When a Human Life has Not Yet Begun—According to the Law', *Bioethics*, vol. 2, 1988, pp. 334–42.

Helga Kuhse and Peter Singer, 'Individuals, Humans and Persons: the Question of Moral Status' in Peter Singer, Helga Kuhse et al. (eds), *Embryo Experimentation*.

Helga Kuhse, Peter Singer and Cora Singer, 'The Treatment of Newborn Infants with Major Handicaps: A Survey of Obstetricians and Paediatricians in Victoria', *Medical Journal of Australia*, 17 September 1983, pp. 274–8.

Helga Kuhse and Peter Singer, 'Doctors' practices and attitudes regarding voluntary euthanasia', *Medical Journal of Australia*, vol. 148, 1988, pp. 623–7.

Helga Kuhse and Peter Singer, 'Voluntary euthanasia and the nurse: an Australian survey', *International Journal of Nursing Studies*, vol. 30, 1993, pp. 311–22.

Colin McGinn, 'Eating Animals is Wrong', *London Review of Books*, 24 January 1991.

H. Lyn White Miles, 'Language and the Orang-utan: The Old "Person" of the Forest' in Paola Cavalieri and Peter Singer (eds), *The Great Ape Project: Equality Beyond Humanity*.

Derek Morgan, 'Letting babies die legally', *Institute of Medical Ethics Bulletin*, May 1989, p. 13.

The Multi-Society Task Force on PVS, 'Medical aspects of the persistent vegetative state', *New England Journal of Medicine*, vol. 330, 1994, pp. 1499–508.

John T. Noonan, 'An Almost Absolute Value in History' in John T. Noonan (ed.), *The Morality of Abortion*, Cambridge, Mass., 1970.

John T. Noonan, 'Contraception', in Warren T. Reich (ed.), *Encyclopedia of Bioethics*, vol. I, pp. 204–16.

Carole Outterson, 'Newborn Infants with Severe Defects: A Survey of Paediatric Attitudes and Practices in the UK', *Bioethics*, vol. 7, 1993, pp. 420–35.

Francine Patterson and Wendy Gordon, 'The Case for the Personhood of Gorillas', in Paola Cavalieri and Peter Singer (eds), *The Great Ape Project: Equality Beyond Humanity*.

Loes Pijnenborg et al., 'Life-Terminating Acts without Explicit Request of the Patient', *Lancet*, vol. 341, 1993, pp. 1196–9.

Pope Pius XII, 'The Prolongation of Life: An Address of Pope Pius XII to an International Congress of Anesthesiologists', *The Pope Speaks*, vol. 4, 1957, p. 396.

Timothy Quill, 'Death and Dignity: A Case of Individualized Decision Making', *New England Journal of Medicine*, vol. 324, no. 10, 1991, pp. 691–4.

Ronald Reagan, 'Abortion and the Conscience of the Nation', *Human Life Review*, vol. IX, no. 2, Spring 1983.

Hans-Martin Sass, 'The Moral Significance of Brain-Life Criteria', in F. K. Beller and R. F. Weir (eds), *The Beginning of Human Life*.

Frank Shann, 'The Cortically Dead Infant Who Breathes' in K. Sanders and B. Moore (eds), *Anencephalics, Infants and Brain Death Treatment Options and the Issue of Organ Donation*.

A. Shaw et al., 'Ethical Issues in Pediatric Surgery: A National Survey of Pediatricians and Pediatric Surgeons', *Pediatrics*, vol. 60, 1977, pp. 588–99.

D. Shewmon, 'Anencephaly: Selected Medical Aspects', *Hastings Center Report*, vol. 18, no. 5, 1988, pp. 11–19.

Peter Singer, 'On being silenced in Germany', *New York Review of Books*, 15 August 1991; reprinted in Peter Singer, *Practical Ethics*, second edition.

Peter Singer, 'Sanctity of Life or Quality of Life', *Pediatrics*, vol. 72, July 1983, pp.128–9.

Peter Singer and Karen Dawson, 'IVF Technology and the Argument from Potential', *Philosophy and Public Affairs*, vol. 17, 1988, pp. 87–104.

Dashka Slater, 'Life after Death', *Express* (East Bay, California), 22 October 1993.

Z. Szawarski, 'A Report from Poland: Treatment and Non-Treatment of Defective Newborns', *Bioethics*, vol. 4, 1990, pp. 143–53.

Z. Szawarski and A. Tulczynski, 'The treatment of defective newborns—a survey of paediatricians in Warsaw', *Journal of Medical Ethics*, vol. 14, 1988, pp. 11–17.

Susan Taiwa, 'When is the capacity for sentience acquired during human fetal development?', *Journal of Maternal-Fetal Medicine*, vol. 1, 1992, pp. 153–65.

David Todres et al., 'Pediatricians' Attitudes Affecting Decision-Making in Defective Newborns', *Pediatrics*, vol. 60, 1977, pp. 197–201.

Tom Tomlinson, 'Misunderstanding Death on a Respirator', *Bioethics*, vol. 4, 1990, p. 253–64.

Michael Tooley, 'Abortion and Infanticide', *Philosophy and Public Affairs*, vol. 2, 1972, pp. 37–65.

A. Trendelenburg, 'A Contribution to the History of the Word Person', *Monist*, vol. 20, 1910, pp. 336–63.

Robert Truog, 'Rethinking brain death', in K. Sanders and B. Moore (eds), *Anencephalics, Infants and Brain Death Treatment Options and the Issue of Organ Donation*.

Richard H. Tuttle, 'A Trans-Specific Agenda', *Science*, vol. 264, 22 April 1994, pp. 602–3.

J. J. M. van Delden, Loes Pijnenborg and Paul J. van der Maas, 'The Remmelink Study: Two Years Later', *Hastings Center Report*, vol. 23, no. 6, November–December 1993.

Robert Veatch, 'The Impending Collapse of the Whole-Brain Definition of Death', *Hastings Center Report*, vol. 23, no. 4, 1993, p. 18–24.

Lidia Wasowicz, 'Tiny baby raises mighty ethical questions', *United Press International*, 10 August 1993.

Lynn White, Jr, 'The Historical Roots of Our Ecological Crisis', *Science*, vol. 155, 1967, pp. 1203–7.

Stuart Youngner et al., '"Brain Death" and Organ Retrieval: A Cross-sectional Survey of Knowledge and Concepts Among Health Professionals', *Journal of the American Medical Assocation*, vol. 261, 1989, p. 2209.

R.B. Zachary, 'Life with Spina Bifida', *British Medical Journal*, 3 December 1977.

MAJOR CASES CITED

Canada

Sue Rodriguez v. The Attorney General of Canada and the Attorney General of British Columbia, Canada Supreme Court Reports, part 4, vol. 3, pp. 519–632.

United Kingdom

Airedale N.H.S. Trust v. Bland, 19 February 1993, 2 Weekly Law Reports, pp. 316–400.

B (A Minor) (Wardship: Medical Treatment), In re, [1981] 1 Weekly Law Reports 1421 (C.A.).

C (A Minor) (Wardship: Medical Treatment), In re, [1989] 3 All England Reports 927 (C.A.).

J (A Minor) (Wardship: Medical Treatment), In re, 1990, 3 All England Reports, 930 (C.A.).

Reg. v. Cox, unreported, 18 September 1992, Ognall, J.

Reg. v. Adams, unreported, 8 April 1957, Devlin, J.

Reg. v. Arthur, unreported, 5 November 1981, Farquharson, J.

United States of America

Akron v. Akron Center for Reproductive Health, Inc, 103 Supreme Court 2481 (1983).

Otis Bowen v. American Hospital Association et al, U.S. Supreme Court. 106 Supreme Court 2101. No. 84-15-9, June 9, 1986.

Cruzan v. Director, Missouri Department of Health (1990) 110. Supreme Court, 2841.

Quinlan, In re, 70 New Jersey 10 355 A.2d (1976).

INDEX

153; active voluntary, Australian studies, 154-5; active v. passive, 75-80; brain-death legislation, 29-30; by team agreement (Netherlands), 141; of disabled newborns, 2; involuntary, no cases of, 153; non-voluntary, 75-80, 151; withdrawal of life-support, 58-80 *passim*; *see also* assisted suicide; voluntary euthanasia
evolution, theory of, 171-2, 176
experimentation on human embryo, 93-100 *passim*
'extraordinary' means of life-support, 70-3

Fae, Baby, 164
Falwell, Rev. Jerry, 106
family size, means of limiting, 215
Farquharson, Mr Justice, 122
fetus
    brain-wave activity, 208; consciousness, 208; denied status as 'human being', 188; efforts to save, 9-18; ethical difference in status after birth, 101, 210-11; ethically relevant characteristics, 208; parents reject abnormal, 214; quickening, 87; right to life, 85-6; viability, 101-2; *see also* embryo
Ficino, Marsilio, 167
Finkbane, Sherri, 91, 214
Fiori, Joey, 63
fishing, ethics of, 209
Ford, Father Norman, 94, 105

Galileo, 169
Gall, Dr Franz Paul, 14
Gellert, Annie, 44
Genesis, 165-6
genetics, close link between humans and apes, 177
Gesell, Judge Gerhard, 109-11
gibbon, 177, 178

global warming, 199
Goff of Chieveley, Lord, 67-8, 76-7
Goodall, Jane, 174, 182
gorillas, 177, 178
    personal characteristics, 181-2; renaming suggested, 178; studies of, 174; taught sign language, 175
Gormally, Luke, 75
Greece, ceremony presenting baby to public, 216, 217
Grisez, Germain, 30-1
Gründel, Johannes, 16
Guardianship Law (German), 15
gull, ring species phenomenon, 179

Hackethal, Julius, 13-15
Haid, Dr Bruno, 29
handicapped *see* disabled
Hardy, Dr James, 164
Harvard Brain Death Committee, 24-8, 33, 36, 47, 55; report: *Defining Death*, 28
Havard, Dr John, 123
hepatitis, 162
herring gull, 179
High Court (Britain), 124, 125
Highland General Hospital (US), 10
Hippocratic oath
    modernisation, 89; modified to accept euthanasia, 149; prohibits abortion, 88; prohibits killing patients, 132
Hobbes, Thomas, 218
Hoffmann, Lord Justice, 58, 66-7
Homo sapiens
    membership of species not ethically relevant, 204-6; not all 'persons', 202-6
hormones, brain regulates supply, 36
House of Lords (judicial), 60-80 *passim*
Howe, Dr J.G., 58-9
human behaviour, 176
human beings
    'centre of ethical universe'

concept challenged, 189; distinction abandoned between nonhuman animals, 222; distinction from apes subjective, 178-9; domination of animals challenged, 221-2; 'human' definition, 204-5; immortal souls, 166; made in God's image, 166; ring species interbreeding theory, 179-80; same genus as chimpanzees, 170; treatment according to ethically relevant characteristics, 191; 'unique' capacity for language, 175

human development, gradual nature, 130

human life
all of equal value, 65; 'all equally sacrosanct' rejected, 86; comparison with other beings, 202; difference of degree from nonhuman animals, 171; ethically relevant characteristics, 192; group protectivity, 204; human emotions define, 205; moment of beginning, 87-90, 94, 97, 101; 'moment' of conception, 94-5; moral status changes gradually, 130-1; more precious than nonhuman life, 201-2; of no benefit, 193; not to be taken intentionally, 192-4; quality, 65-8, 72; sanctity v. quality of life, 73-5, 131; significance of ending, 168-9; 'superior status', 204; traditional ethic, 4; value of 'intellectually handicapped' person, 162; worth of, 190

Humphry, Derek, *Final Exit*, 147

Huxley, Thomas, 172

Hyde, Thomas, 1, 134, 135, 148, 154

in vitro fertilisation, 93-100 *passim* micro-injection, 96, 99-100;

success rate, 97; *see also* infertility; medical technology

infanticide, 128-31, 214-15
acceptance by British public, 124, 125; medical, 115-31

infants *see* babies

infertility
techniques for overcoming, 95-7; *see also* in vitro fertilisation

intellectual abilities, human and nonhuman compared, 201

intention to end life, 68-73

irreversible coma, 26-7, 39 *see also* brain death

J., Baby, 191, 211-12

Jackson, Dr James, 11, 16-17

Japan
brain death definition, 33; brain death study, 31

Jesus, 166

John Paul II, Pope, 84-5

Judaism, attitude to abortion, 87

Judeo-Christian, view of human beings, 187

Kadish, Sanford, 65

Kant, Immanuel, 168

Kaufman, Judge Richard, 134, 148

Keeley, Dr Steve, 45

Keith of Kinkel, Lord, 67, 74

Kennan, Jim, 41

Keown, Dr John, 74-5

Kevorkian, Dr Jack, 1, 133-5, 136, 148, 154 *see also* suicide, machine

Koko (gorilla), 175, 181-2, 205, 206

Koop, Dr C. Everett, 109-12

Kuhse, Helga, 120

Kuhse, Helga (and Peter Singer), *Should the Baby Live?*, 217

Law Reform Commission of Victoria, 40-1

Lebenshilfe, 201-2
'Ethical Foundational Statements', 202

Absolute Value in History',
99-100
nurses, concept of death, 33-5
nursing home, patients die from
withheld treatment, 156

O'Connor, Justice Sandra Day, 102
oesophagus, not properly formed,
107
orang-utans, 170, 175-6, 177, 182
organ donors, 47, 54-5, 163-5
organ transplant, 33, 37, 188;
anencephalic babies as donors,
47; 'brain death' ethics, 2-3;
ethics of obtaining organs, 24-6;
experiments on nonhuman
animals, 164; heart, 22, 24, 44,
207; kidney, 23-4; nonhuman
animals' organs to humans,
163-5; research: chimpanzee
heart to human, 165
Owens, Dr Walter, 1, 107

pain, criterion for right to life, 208
Pan troglodytes (chimpanzee)
community, 159-63
parents, wishes about disabled baby,
212
patients
ask doctor to hasten death, 155;
benefit to, 64-8 *passim*; incapable
of discussing end of life, 153;
informed decision, 132;
terminally ill, 188; wishes to be
considered, 61-4, 192
Pearce, Margaret, 44
Pearson, John, 121-3, 128-9, 212
Pearson, Molly, 121, 214, 217
persistent vegetative state, 27, 39,
207 *see also* brain death
'person'
definition, 162, 180-3, 197, 218;
desire to continue life, 197-8;
moral standing, 182; not all *Homo
sapiens*, 202-6; right to life, 218;
see also Pan troglodytes

(chimpanzee) community
personal security vital, 218
philosophers, ethical view of
nonhuman animals, 166-9
Pius IX, Pope, 167
Pius XII, Pope, defines death, 29
Ploch, Gabriele and Hans, 12-13
Ploch, Marion, 12-16, 20, 31, 84,
207
pneumonia, 143
Poland
Marxist-Catholic view of value
of life, 120-1; medical
paternalism, 120-1
Polster, Wilhelm, 15, 20
population
ethical limits to, 199; national
policies to increase, 198-9;
world, 98
Postma, Dr Geertruida, 144
pregnancy
abnormalities detected by
ultrasound, 92-3; maintenance
of, 84; tests, 92-3
President's Commission for the
Study of Ethical Problems in
Medicine (US), 27-8 *see also*
Harvard Brain Death Committee
pro-choice movement, 85-6 *see also*
abortion
pro-life movement, 106
attitude to new definition of
brain death, 29-30; attitude to
total-brain-death legislation,
29-30; attitude to in vitro
embryos, 94; oppose selective
non-treatment, 128
procreation
decision not to, 98; Judeo-
Christian ethic of, 198
Ptolemy, model of solar system,
187-8
Pythagoras, 167

quality of life, 106-31 *passim*
quickening of fetus, 87, 88, 103

Quinlan, Karen Ann, 10, 70-2

racism, 173-4
Re C (brain-damaged baby), 124-5
Reagan, President Ronald, 106, 131
Renaissance philosophers, 167
resources, world limits, 19
respirator, 22-3, 70-1
responsibility
    for acts challenged, 221-2; for
    consequences of decisions, 195-6
rheumatoid arthritis, 139
right, can be exercised or not, 218
right to life, can be evoked or not,
    218-19
Right to Life Association (Australia),
    41, 126-8, 130
'ring species' phenomenon, 179
Robinson, Svend, 139
Rodriguez, Sue, 138, 148, 150
Roe v. Wade (US), 90, 92, 101-2,
    106, 149
Roessler, Dietrich, 16
Roman Catholic Church, 127;
    attitude to abortion, 87, 192;
    attitude to assisted suicide
    (Netherlands), 141; attitude to
    early embryo, 94; attitude to
    fundamental value of human life,
    120-1; attitude to new definition
    of brain death, 29-30; attitude to
    value of nonhuman animals, 167;
    attitude to voluntary euthanasia
    (Netherlands), 157
Rothstein, District Judge Barbara,
    148
Royal Children's Hospital (Mel-
    bourne), 38, 126-7
Royal Dutch Medical Association,
    attitude to voluntary euthanasia,
    144-6
Ryder, Richard, 173

sanctity of human life
    distinction between species, 165;
    species boundary, 188-9;

traditional doctrine, 188;
    transition in attitude, 1-6
Sass, Hans-Martin, 103-4
Scarisbrick, Nuala, 128-9
Scheele, Dr Johannes, 13-14
Schwarzer, Alice, 13
selective non-treatment, 106-31
    passim
Shakespeare, 'life as journey' image,
    212, 216
Shann, Dr Frank, 41, 207
Silver, Judy, 44
Singer, Cora, 120
Singer, Prof. Peter
    Pediatrics article, 201; *Practical
    Ethics*, 201-2; value of human
    life, 201
Slater, Dashka, 10-11, 34-5
slavery, 85-6
Society for Voluntary Euthanasia,
    144
Sopinka, Justice, 150-1
species
    defined as interbreeding group,
    179; definition, 179; human v.
    nonhuman animals differences,
    189; no discrimination on basis
    of, 202-6; 'ring species', 179
speciesism, 173-4
    rejected, 202-6
spina bifida, 115-18
    'adverse criteria', 117-18;
    conditions associated, 117;
    description of condition, 115;
    intellectual disability, 115, 117;
    no treatment in severe cases, 118;
    operation, 116; prognosis, 116,
    127; selective treatment policy
    endorsed, 117-19; survival after
    treatment, 117; treatment, 126,
    127; treatment withheld
    (Australia), 125-8
Starzl, Dr Thomas, 163
Stein, Dr Robert, 115
Stevens, Mr Justice, 49
Stinson, Andrew, 215